MW01121488

The United Nations of the Future:

Globalization with a Human Face

Willem van Genugten
Kees Homan
Nico Schrijver
Paul de Waart

KIT – Publishers Amsterdam

Colofon:

KIT Publishers
Mauritskade 63
Postbus 95001
1090 HA Amsterdam
E-mail: publishers@kit.nl

Websites:
www.kit.nl/publishers
www.landenreeks.nl
www.hotei-publishing.com
www.samsam.net
www.leespiramide.nl

© 2006
W.J.M. van Genugten, C. Homan, N.J. Schrijver, P.J.I.M. de Waart

Ontwerp omslag: Ronald Boiten en Irene Mesu, Amersfoort
Ontwerp en opmaak binnenwerk: Henny Scholten, Amsterdam
Productie: Meester en De Jonge, Lochem

ISBN 90 6832 073 4
NUR 754

Preface and acknowledgements

Over the years, the United Nations has been criticized time and again. So, it is said that the disintegration of the Soviet Union delivered the world to the whims and caprices of the United States (US) as the only remaining world power ('*Pax Americana*'), a trend which has been strengthened considerably since the USA invasion in Iraq in 2003. Did not the USA fully bypass the UN in that specific case, making the organization as good as irrelevant? For some commentators, the Iraqi invasion by the USA led to writing necrologies for the United Nations. But what is new? Has not the organization always been subjected to severe criticisms? And is it not true too that the organization will never be able to perform at its best, given the fact that it is mainly asked to act in situations which are beyond the control of its' member states, while at the same time it is the same member states who do not allow or are not able to make the organization as effective as it (theoretically) could be?

In 2005, the United Nations had existed for sixty years. More precisely, its sixtieth birthday was on 24 October 2005, six decades after the UN Charter entered into force, although the date of the signing of the Charter (San Francisco, 26 June 1945) is also described as the anniversary. Its' – then still future – anniversary induced the 'Nederlandse Vereniging voor de Verenigde Naties' (NVVN) [Netherlands United Nations Association] to devote in September 2004 a special issue of its quarterly *VN Forum* to the future of the United Nations. The contents of the special issue were produced by the four authors of this book. In the present book the authors substantially elaborate upon their common ideas and perspectives (the number of pages having been more than doubled),

5

while their views and proposals have been updated in the light of the outcome of the UN Summit Conference of 14-16 September 2005.

The main 'message' of the book is: the United Nations has proven to be invaluable as a center for harmonizing the actions of nations in solving problems in the field of peace and security, development/poverty, environment, trade, human rights and so on. Analyzing the strengths and weaknesses of the United Nations, the authors go back to USA President Roosevelt's 1941 Four Freedoms, and the linkages between them, and to the original mandate of the United Nations, as embedded in the 1945 Charter, indicating how much such an organization is still needed at the beginning of the New Millennium. In doing so, the authors have added a series of annexes to the book, which can serve as the normative basis for as well as the conceptual filling in of the type of UN they have in mind.

The authors would like to express their gratitude to the National Commission for Sustainable Development and the NVVN for the subsidy made available for the English translation of (parts of) the book and for checking the language in the rest of the book. They would like to thank Tony Langham and Plym Peters for their skillful work in this respect. Further to that the authors are greatly indebted to Helen Tung and Marlene Havens, for going through the final version of the book (Helen) and helping the authors with all kind of assistance (Marlene).

The authors,

Tilburg, Abbekerk, Leiden, Leidschendam
December, 2005

Table of contents

Abbreviations

ACP countries	Developing countries in Africa, the Caribbean region and the Pacific Ocean
AJIL	American Journal of International Law
ASEAN	Association of Southeast Asian Nations
AU	African Union
CEDAW	Convention on the Elimination of All Forms of Discrimination against Women
CIS	Community of Independent States
CRC	Convention on the Rights of the Child
CSD	UN Commission on Sustainable Development
DKPO	Department of Peacekeeping Operations of the United Nations
ECOMOG	Economic Community of West African States Monitoring Group
ECOSOC	Economic and Social Council of the UN
EOLSS	Encyclopedia of Life Support Systems
EU	European Union
FAO	Food and Agriculture Organization of the United Nations
FMLN	Farabundo Marti National Liberation
GATT	General Agreement on Tariffs and Trade
GNP	Gross National Product
ICC	International Criminal Court
ICCPR	International Covenant on Civil and Political Rights
ICESCR	International Covenant on Economic, Social and Cultural Rights

ICJ	International Court of Justice
ICTR	International Criminal Tribunal for Rwanda
ICTY	International Criminal Tribunal for the former Yugoslavia
IFAD	International Fund and Agricultural Development
IGO	International Governmental Organization
ILA	International Law Association
ILC	International Law Commission
ILO	International Labor Organization
IMF	International Monetary Fund
INTERFET	International Force for East Timor
IO	International Organization
IOM	International Organization for Migration
ISAF	International Security Assistance Force
ITO	International Trade Organization
LJIL	Leiden Journal of International Law
LNTS	League of Nations Treaty Series
LoN	The League of Nations
MDGs	Millennium Development Goals
MONUC	UN Organization Mission in the Democratic Republic of Congo
NATO	North Atlantic Treaty Organization
NGO	Non-governmental organization
NIEO	New International Economic Orde
NILR	Netherlands International Law Review
NYIL	Netherlands Yearbook of International Law
ODA	Official Development Assistance
OECD	Organization for Economic Cooperation and Development
OHCHR	Office of the High Commissioner for Human Rights
OPEC	Organization of Petrol Exporting Countries
OSCE	Organization for Security and Co-operation in Europe
PCA	Permanent Court of Arbitration
PCIJ	Permanent Court of International Justice

PEU	Peace enforcement Unit
PMCA	Pre-Mandate Commitment Authority
RdC	Recueil des cours de l'Académie international de la Haye
SC	Security Council
SDS	Strategic Deployment Stocks
SFOR	Stabilization Forces
SHIRBIG	United Nations Stand-by Forces High Readiness Brigade
SIPRI Yearbook	Stockholm International Peace Research Institute
STABEX	Stabilization of Export Earnings
UDHR	Universal Declaration of Human Rights
UN	United Nations
UNAMIR	United Nations Assistance Mission in Rwanda
UNCED	United Nations Conference on Environment and Development
UNCIO	United Nations Conference on International Organizations
UNCTAD	United Nations Conference on Trade and Development
UNDP	United Nations Development Program
UNEF	United Nations Emergency Force
UNEP	United Nations Environment Program
UNESCO	United Nations Educational, Scientific and Cultural Organization
UNFICYP	United Nations Peacekeeping Force in Cyprus
UNGA	UN General Assembly
UNHCE	United Nations Conference on the Human Environment
UNHCR	United Nations Refugee Agency
UNICEF	United Nations Children's Fund
UNIDO	United Nations Organization for Industrial Development
UNMEE	United Nations Mission in Ethiopia and Eritrea
UNMIK	United Nations Mission in Kosovo
UNMIL	United Nations Mission in Liberia

UNOSOM	United Nations Operation in Somalia
UNPROFOR	United Nations Protection Force
UNRRA	United Nations Relief and Rehabilitation Administration
UNRWA	UN Relief and Works Agency for Palestinian Refugees
UNSAS	United Nations Stand-by Arrangement System
UNSCOB	United Nations Special Committee on the Balkans
UNSG	UN Secretary-General
UNTAET	United Nations Transitional Administration for East Timor
UNTSO	United Nations Truce Supervision Organization
U.S.C.	United States Code
USSR	Union of Soviet Socialistic Republics
WHO	World Health Organization
WW-II	World War II
WTO	World Trade Organization

CHAPTER 1

The United Nations: Some Introductory Reflections and Projections

1.1 The Purposes of the United Nations

It is said that since the disintegration of the Soviet Union the United Nations (UN) has lost significance as the center for the harmonization of the acts of states to achieve common goals, a trend which is supposed to be further strengthened after the USA invasion in Iraq in 2003, which was not authorized by the UN. But is the UN irrelevant? To our mind nothing could be further from the truth.

Let's first of all recall the original purposes of the UN:

1. *To maintain international peace and security, and to that end: to take effective collective measures for the prevention and removal of threats to peace, and for the suppression of acts of aggression or other breaches of the peace, and to bring about by peaceful means, and in conformity with the principles of justice and international law, adjustment or settlement of international disputes or situations which might lead to a breach of the peace;*

2. *To develop friendly relations among nations based on respect for the principle of equal rights and the self-determination of peoples and to take other appropriate measures to strengthen universal peace;*

3. *To achieve international co-operation in solving international problems of an economic, social, cultural or humanitarian character, and in promoting and encouraging respect for human rights and for fundamental freedoms for all without distinction as to race, sex language, or religion; and*

4. *To be a centre for harmonizing the actions of nations in the attainment of these common ends.*[1]

Over the years, these purposes have been updated in order to make the organization respond to new challenges. So for instance during the silver anniversary in 1970, the UN member states accepted the *Declaration on Principles of International Law concerning Friendly Relations and Co-operation amongst States in accordance with the Charter of the United Nations.*[2] The Declaration relates to such things as the principle of refraining from the threat or the use of force against the territorial integrity and the political independence of states, the principle of equal rights and self-determination of peoples, and the duty not to intervene in matters within the jurisdiction of separate UN member states.[3] Further to that, it states that the UN member states have the duty to co-operate with one another, irrespective of the differences in their political, economic and social systems, in the various spheres of international relations, in order to maintain international peace and security and to promote international economic stability and progress, the general welfare of nations and international co-operation free from discrimination based on such differences.

To this end:

a) *States shall co-operate with other States in the maintenance of international peace and security;*

b) *States shall co-operate in the promotion of universal respect for, and observance of, human rights and fundamental freedoms for all, and in the elimination of all forms of racial discrimination and all forms of religious intolerance;*

c) *States shall conduct their international relations in the economic, social, cultural, technical and trade fields in accordance with the principles of sovereign equality and non-intervention;*

d) *Member States of the United Nations have the duty to take joint and separate action in co-operation with the United Nations in accordance with the relevant provisions of the Charter;*

e) *States should co-operate in the economic, social and cultural fields as well as in the field of science and technology and for the promotion of international cultural and educational progress.*

States should co-operate in the promotion of economic growth throughout the world, especially that of the developing countries.[4]

The UN was again presented as a common effort, so to say, this time mainly in reaction to the then almost finalized process of decolonization and the new requirements this brought to the front for the inter-state playing rules.

In 1995, the UN celebrated the golden anniversary with a conference of government leaders and heads of state in Copenhagen – known as the Social Summit – which lead to the *Copenhagen Declaration on Social Development and Programme of Action of the World Summit for Social Development.*[5] In the document of the Summit it is stated, as a reaction to the structural character of worldwide poverty, that the participating governments "are deeply convinced that economic development, social development and environmental protection are interdependent and mutually reinforcing components of sustainable development", that "equitable social development that recognizes empowering the poor to utilize environmental resources sustainably is a necessary foundation for sustainable development", and that "broad-based and sustained economic growth in the context of sustainable development is necessary to sustain social development and social justice".[6] One of the Copenhagen commitments relates to the fulfillment of the so-called 'basics needs':

Focus our efforts and policies to address the root causes of poverty and to provide for the basic needs of all. These efforts should include the elimination of hunger and malnutrition; the provision of food security, education, employment and livelihood, primary health-care services including reproductive health care, safe drinking water and sanitation, and adequate shelter; and participation in social and cultural life. Special priority will be given to the needs and rights of women and children, who often bear the greatest burden of poverty, and to the needs of vulnerable and disadvantaged groups and persons.[7]

Further to that, the document underlines, amongst many other things, the need to better equip the UN to play its role in this sphere, together with and alongside the International Financial Institutions, the World Trade Organization, the private sector and the civil society. As to the latter it is stated that "the support and participation of [such] major groups (...) are essential to the success of the implementation of the Programme of Action", and that for that reason "they must be involved in planning, elaboration, implementation and evaluation at both the national and the international levels".[8]

In 2000, the heads of state and government leaders at the so-called Millennium Summit of the UN recognized freedom, democracy, equality, solidarity, tolerance, a respect for nature and shared responsibility as the common fundamental values. These fundamental values were translated into a number of main objectives for the 21st century – the "Millennium Development Goals" – with regard to peace, security and disarmament, development and the ending of poverty, the protection of the common environment, human rights, democracy and good governance, the protection of vulnerable groups, meeting the special needs of Africa, as well as strengthening the UN. To quote just one section from the 2000 document, which relates to the title of our book:

> We believe that the central challenge we face today is to ensure that globalization becomes a positive force for all the world's people. For while globalization offers great opportunities, at present its benefits are very unevenly shared, while its costs are unevenly distributed. We recognize that developing countries and countries with economies in transition face special difficulties in responding to this central challenge. Thus, only through broad and sustained efforts to create a shared future, based upon our common humanity in all its diversity, can globalization be made fully inclusive and equitable. These efforts must include policies and measures, at the global level, which correspond to the needs of developing countries and economies in transition and are formulated and implemented with their effective participation.[9]

The Millennium Development Goals were also extensively referred to in the Final Document of the September 2005 UN Summit.[10] The same goes for many other topics that will be dealt with in this book. In relation to the purposes of the UN, being the topic of this introductory section, it can be said that the Summit did not lead to major innovations. There is recognition of the concept of "the responsibility to protect" (see below) and such a thing as the creation of a Peacebuilding Commission – also dealt with later – which reflects the decisiveness to pay more attention to the reconstruction of societies after conflicts, while something similar can be said about some of the other elements of the document, such as the decision to spend extra money in the fight against poverty or the strong push for a comprehensive convention against terrorism. However, these lines are mainly to be seen as updates, more than new lines of thinking. In the words of the UN Secretary-General Kofi Annan the document is, despite its many shortcomings "still a remarkable expression of world unity on a wide range of issues".[11] We do agree to that. Where relevant, we will quote from the 2005 document in order to make clear where to our mind progress has been made, little as it might be.[12]

1.2 Democracy: a condition for UN membership?

The sovereign equality of states aims for equality before the law in the sense that every state has the same legal personality, irrespective of the differences in territorial size, the size of the population, military power or economic strength. However, the principle does not mean that all states are subject to rights and obligations to the same extent. For example, this applies for the right to vote in international organizations and the size of the contributions made to these. Shortly after the UN was founded, the question arose whether the conditions in the UN Charter for the admission of new members were or were not exhaustive. In fact, the USA wished to oppose the admission of communist states and only admit democratic countries. Asked for advice by the General Assembly of the UN (GA), the International Court of Justice (ICJ) stated in 1948 that the summary was exhaustive.[13] In its decision of 1986 on the dispute between Nicaragua and the United States about American support for military and paramilitary activities against the government of Nicaragua, this Court judged that there was no question of a rule which justified intervention in another state because that state embraced a particular ideology or political system.[14] Under international law, states were not obliged to be democratic. After the fall of the Berlin Wall this seemed to change. The Vienna Declaration, accepted by the World Conference on Human Rights in June 1993, clearly endorsed the support of the international community for the promotion of democracy throughout the world in relation to the development and respect for human rights.[15] In 1996 the then Secretary-General of the UN, Boutros Boutros-Ghali, presented an Agenda for Democratisation, following earlier Agendas for Peace (1992, supplemented in 1995), and Development (1995).[16]

In the UN Millennium Declaration of 2000, the heads of state and government leaders supported the promotion of democracy in all the member states.[17] The World Commission on the Social Dimension of Globalization emphasized the worldwide agreement that a democratic political system and a respect for human rights are vitally important for good governance in any constitutional state.[18] The Panel of Eminent Persons on United Nations-Civil Society Relations ('Cardoso') extended the need for democracy to the national level in its report *We the peoples: civil society, the United Nations and global governance*. It states: "The weak influence of traditional democracy in matters of global governance is one reason why citizens of the world are urging greater democratic accountability of international organizations."[19] The worldwide professional organization of international lawyers, the International Law Association (ILA), warmly supports this.[20]

The notion of the fundamental meaning of democracy – it is called a "universal value" – is also elaborated upon in the 2005 Summit document:

We reaffirm that democracy is a universal value based on the freely expressed will of people to determine their own political, economic, social and cultural systems and their full participation in all aspects of their lives. We also reaffirm that while democracies share common features, there is no single model of democracy, that it does not belong to any country or region, and reaffirm the necessity of due respect for sovereignty and the right of self-determination. We stress that democracy, development and respect for all human rights and fundamental freedoms are interdependent and mutually reinforcing.[21]

The conclusion is that old UN member states have to rethink time and again their political structures and that new states which are created as a result of the right to self-determination of peoples must seriously take into account that in their application for UN membership they will be assessed with regard to their democratic caliber. We see this as a welcome development which helps the image of the UN. After all, that image has also been damaged by the fact that the provisions in the UN Charter with regard to suspension and expulsion have not been used up to now.

1.3 Democracy from below: self-determination of peoples and the role of the civil society

The American philosopher, the late John Rawls, made democracy the cornerstone of his work, *Law of Peoples*, published in 1999.[22] In that book he extended his work, *A Theory of Justice*, dating from 1971 and devoted to national legal orders, to a just international legal order.[23] This sort of legal order extends to liberal states and authoritarian states; admittedly the latter are not liberal, but they are not totalitarian either. Totalitarian states only form part of this order to a limited extent. Rogue states fall outside it altogether. They are more or less outlaws. Rawls opted for peoples and not states as the starting point for his *Law of Peoples*. Just as the legislation, justice and government *within* states is concerned with people and not with organizations, it is peoples who matter *between* states. According to Rawls, peoples – unlike states – have moral motives and a moral nature. One problem is that there is no generally accepted definition of peoples in international law.[24] This definition is badly needed because peoples have the important right to self-determination (see Chapter 4). With regard to their relations to the authorities and the governing of the territories they live in, people as well as peoples can also claim a right to democracy in the sense of a right to a society, characterized by, *inter alia*, the right to participate in decision-making, the right to vote and the right to be elected, within states based on constitutions and governed with 'good governance'.[25]

In fact, since the fall of the Berlin Wall, states and the UN itself increasingly recognize that realization of the UN goals cannot only be dependent on them alone. The above-mentioned report, *We the peoples: civil society, the United Nations and global governance*, outlines three worldwide contemporary trends which are crucial for improving the cooperation between states, civil society and the public sector, *viz.* the shortcomings of democracy in the governance of the world, the growing capacity and influence of non-state players on the world stage, and the growing influence of public opinion.[26] In addition, there is an increasing inequality in contemporary politics as a result of the fact that the globalization of the economy, trade, communication and culture does not go hand in hand with representative representation. This is a result of the fact that essentially democracy remains limited at the national and local level, although important decision-making in this respect increasingly takes place at the international level. The panel that was responsible for the report found quite simply that the UN more than ever requires the support of the civil society, defined as the links which citizens have voluntarily made outside the family circle, friends and the business world in order to promote their interests, ideas and ideologies (see in more detail, Chapter 2, par. 2.2). The panel presents a series of proposals to transform the UN into a more outward-oriented network organization:

Moving on this goal is necessary for the survival of the United Nations. Public support will dwindle unless the United Nations can demonstrate that it can make a clear and positive difference (...) listening to peoples' concern and being answerable to them.[27]

1.4 Four Freedoms

Today's world is full of poverty, inter- and intra-state conflicts, non-sustainable development, denial of human rights, lack of transparency in decision-making, and so forth and so on. In all these fields, we see a major role for the UN. In the years – decades? – to come the UN also has the important function of maintaining consensus with regard to the common fundamental values already described above and the goals based on these in combating the international terrorism which has been unleashed all over the world following the terrible attacks on the World Trade Center in New York and the Pentagon in Washington.[28] In doing so, it can still feel inspired by the world view of the late Franklin D. Roosevelt. In 1941, this American president and spiritual father of the UN presented his vision of the future, for the world after the Second World War. His vision concerned the protection of four freedoms: the freedom of expression, the freedom of religion, the freedom from want, and the freedom from fear:

> *In the future days which we seek to make secure, we look forward to a world founded upon four essential human freedoms. The first is freedom of speech and expression – everywhere in the world. The second is freedom of every person to worship God in his own way – everywhere in the world. The third is freedom from want, which, translated into world terms, means economic understandings which will secure to every nation a healthy peacetime life for its inhabitants – everywhere in the world. The fourth is freedom from fear, which, translated into world terms, means a world-wide reduction of armaments to such a point and in such a thorough fashion that no nation will be in a position to commit an act of physical aggression against*

any neighbour – anywhere in the world. That is no vision of a distant millennium. It is a definite basis for a kind of world attainable in our own time and generation. That kind of world is the very antithesis of the so-called 'new order' of tyranny which the dictators seek to create with the crash of a bomb. To that new order we oppose the greater conception – the moral order. A good society is able to face schemes of world domination and foreign revolutions alike without fear.[29]

In fact, it was particularly the United States which subsequently repeatedly turned its back on Roosevelt's intentions. For example, it opposed the entry into effect of the 1948 Havana Charter which proposed the establishment of an International Trade Organization (ITO) with the aim of ensuring that world trade served to protect people from poverty. In the 1980s the USA also fiercely opposed the recognition of the right of people(s) to development. Even now it is still not a party to the 1966 International Covenant of Economic, Social and Cultural Rights (ICESCR), while it ratified only a remarkably small number of conventions of the International Labor Organization (ILO). This American opposition to the Roosevelt's ideals corresponds seamlessly with the vision of Adam Smith, which was that the acquisition of the wealth of states and the national and international distribution of labor as a personal source of welfare should be left to the free market. According to Smith, the government should not disturb the natural course of the tendency to engage in trade as a characteristic human quality.[30]

In the view of the UN, the freedom from fear in the current necessary fight against international terrorism should not be at the expense of the other three freedoms which the organization was established in 1945 to protect. The overwhelming concern of the UN is that combating terrorism will take place within a framework of five inextricably linked principles: the rule of law, democracy, good governance, human rights and social justice.[31] But there is even more, we would like to say. In the present book we unfold our views with regard to the UN of the Future, thereby being inspired by President Roosevelt's Four Freedoms, in a way which is adapted to the challenges of the new Millennium. We will be doing so by dealing with the following topics:

- Hegemonic power *versus* civil society
- The international protection of human rights
- Protection of national minorities and indigenous peoples
- On rights and responsibilities: the integration of vulnerable groups
- A just international economic and social order
- A sustainable human environment
- The Security Council – a world authority
- Peace-keeping and peace-enforcing operations
- Enforcement of international law
- Globalization with a human face

The titles of the chapters themselves already show the joint expectations the authors have of the United Nations of the future, as a sign of their confidence in the UN as a center for tuning globalization to the four freedoms for everyone everywhere in the world.

CHAPTER 2

Hegemonic Power *versus* Civil Society

2.1 States as subjects of international law; the role of the hegemonic powers

The world has never had a world government, although there have been world empires with hegemonic claims. In (western) Europe there was a central authority for the Christian nations in the Middle Ages in the figure of the Pope in Rome. Protestantism put an end to these foundations of the (European) world order of Christian nations at that time.[32] The Peace of Westphalia in 1648 heralded the age of the sovereign state which by definition does not allow for a world authority. In 1758, the Swiss lawyer Emery de Vattel made the principle of the sovereign equality of states the cornerstone of his natural law for states.[33] In his view, states were not artificial persons, but natural persons, just like people. He considered that, like people, states derived their existence and recognition as a legal person, not from law, but from nature. States embraced this fiction wholeheartedly precisely because they wished to prevent international entities from developing which could place themselves above them. In his *The Wealth of Nations* (1776), Adam Smith limited the responsibility of the sovereign state to the defense of the nation, the dispensation of justice and the care of public works.[34] Apart from this, both the acquisition of the wealth of states and the national and international distribution of labor as a personal source of welfare should be left to supply and demand directed by the invisible hand of the market. The absence of a world authority in the international order of sovereign states was accompanied by the absence of a world authority in the international market.[35]

International law still reserves the status of natural international legal persons for states. All other participants in international law derive their legal status and competence to act from states, *i.e.*, from national law and not from international law. This also applies for individuals. The only exception to this is the UN itself, because in the opinion of the International Court of Justice (ICJ), the founders of the UN in 1945, as the representatives of the great majority of the international community of states, "had the power, in conformity with international law, to bring into being an entity possessing objective international personality, and not merely personality recognized by them alone, together with capacity to bring international claims".[36]

The Axis powers of Nazi Germany and fascist Italy had started WW-II with their allies in order to establish a 'new order'. In 1941, USA President Roosevelt countered this with the moral order of a good society of national states. In his view, this sort of society would be able to resist foreign revolutions and plans for world domination without fear. The fact that he was not thinking of a world government is apparent particularly from the formulation of the third and fourth freedoms: the freedom from want and the freedom from fear (see Chapter 1). After all, the emphasis there lies on the responsibility of nations for the healthy and peaceful life of their inhabitants, and the prohibition of committing acts of physical aggression against any neighbor (see the wording of Roosevelt's freedom from fear, cited in Chapter 1). Furthermore, President Roosevelt was an advocate of the idea that the four great allied powers – China, Great Britain, the Soviet Union and the United States – should supervise the protection of the four freedoms like four police officers. After the WW-II, France joined as a reward for General Charles De Gaulle's opposition to the Axis powers.

The five permanent members of the UN Security Council still consider their special position in the international legal order, which is most forcibly expressed by their right of veto within the UN Security Council, as an incontrovertible fact of life, a natural and inherent acquisition of their status as great powers. The political reality is that the right of veto of the permanent members of the Security Council will not and can hardly be changed, due to the fact that changing the Charter of the UN in that sense will require the support of all of them.[37] Plans to restructure the UN, and especially the Security Council, are greatly delayed as a result or cannot be achieved because of this. (See Chapter 8 of this book.)

In the discussions on the current international power of the US, the distinction between government and governance is very important. In a formal sense the USA is not a world government. However, it does have influence/power to control developments in a certain direction. In the light of history, this situation is not unique, but the powers of veto now also sometimes are confronted with the limits of their power. For example, the USA did not succeed in controlling the International Criminal Court (ICC). The same applies with regard to the attack on Iraq, when it was not able to convince the Security Council to approve the Operation Iraqi Freedom.

Since the fall of the Berlin Wall, the USA has increasingly emerged as a hegemonic power which divides the world into friends and foes. As President Bush summarized his policy in his State of the Union address in 2002, "you are either with us or against us". The question is who determines which country is hostile. In a recent study on *United States Hegemony and the Foundations of International Law*, the French professor of international law, Michael Cosnard, defines rogue states as states which the USA labels as such ('Bush doctrine').[38] He is supported by his German colleague Nico Krisch in his contribution on sovereign equality to the same book, under the meaningful title "More equal than the rest? Hierarchy, equality and USA predominance in international law".[39] Their American colleague, Brad R. Roth, goes even further in a chapter on the use of violence entitled "Bending the law, breaking it or developing it? The United States and the humanitarian use of force in the post-Cold War era".[40] Cosnard states that the principle of the sovereign equality of states does not have any significance in terms of content. After all, the legal equality of states is a formal matter, an organizational fact, and there are different ideas about the way in which this is and should be applied. The fact that the community of states in the UN Charter is based on the principle of sovereign equality implies that this community can function only with the cooperation of the member states. In other words, the principle of sovereign equality emphasizes the external independence of states precisely to permanently obstruct the (continued) existence of supra-state authority for good. It protects the privileged position of states in relation to the other participants in international relations: international governmental organizations (IGOs), non-governmental organizations (NGOs), minorities and indigenous peoples, companies and individuals. However, it does not serve as a dam to provide protection against the hegemonic power of one or more states.

2.2 International public spirit

In their Millennium Declaration the heads of state and government leaders note that all men and women have the right to organize their lives and bring up their children "in dignity, free from hunger and from the fear of violence, oppression or injustice" and that "democratic and participatory governance based on the will of people best assures these rights".[41] The fact that this view is not superseded by the tragic events in the USA on 11 September 2001 is illustrated in, amongst many other writings, the 2002 Report *A Fair Globalization: Creating Opportunities for All*, issued by the World Commission on the Social Dimension of Globalization, chaired by Tarja Halonen, President of the Republic of Finland and Benjamin William Mkapa, President of the United Republic of Tanzania. This report actually supports a globalization with a human face, "which sustains human values and enhances the well-being of people, in terms of their freedom, prosperity and security".[42] Comparable ideas, but spread across the whole scope of action of the UN, can be found in the report *A more secure world: our shared responsibility*, written at the request of the UN Secretary-General by a High Level Panel under the leadership of the former Thai Prime Minister Anand Panyarachun,[43] and in the report *In larger freedom: towards development, security and human rights for all* of the UN Secretary-General himself.[44]

In fact, human rights and related issues have traditionally been seen, above all, as a matter of concern or active intervention respectively of states. States are the key actors. However, in recent decades it has become clear in all sorts of ways that this system no longer suffices. It is for sure that in the years 1946-1948 contributions were already made by NGOs to the discussions on the Universal Declaration of Human Rights, but also that by then the number of NGOs was still very limited. As a contrast, in his report *Strengthening of the United Nations: an agenda for further change*, the UN Secretary-General notes that at the start of the new millennium, there were more than 37,000 NGOs, of which more than 2,000 had an official consultative status in the organization.[45] They play a role in providing ideas and information, as lobbyists for their ideology, as controllers of power and sometimes, as organizations which have direct access to international (quasi) legal proceedings in which they can try to achieve their claims.[46]

In our view, the joint NGOs, as a 'countervailing power' side by side and opposite the states, deserve an increasingly important role, particularly with regard to the last point. We are aware of the fact that this multiple role sometimes places NGOs in a difficult position because they are acting at the same time as a supplier of information, as plaintiff and judge.[47] This also has as a consequence that states which could cooperate with NGOs very well in terms of the content of their views, still adopt a certain distance, for instance in order not to come into conflict with other states which are under NGO fire. In our view, however, states which are positive about the NGO world on the grounds of their content should give them the room to carry out their work to a greater extent than is now the case. The political sensitivities which would certainly result from this will in the long term not weigh up against the gains which could be made in terms of content in the field of, amongst other things, achieving human rights. Anyhow, there is still a long way to go in this field. Whatever that may be, since the fall of the Berlin Wall paved the way for the globalization of the world economy, the civil society has become increasingly aware that international law possesses special characteristics and chances in relation to issues like the banning of unlawful armed violence and the active promotion of human dignity for all people(s).[48]

The above-mentioned report, *We the peoples: civil society, the United Nations and global governance*, states that the constituency of the UN comprises three broad sectors: civil society, the private sector and the state.[49] The member states of the UN are central to the organization, collectively constituting its membership. Other actors, however, are of growing importance to the deliberative processes, operations and communications of the UN. According to the report, the private sector comprises firms, business federations, employer associations and industry lobby groups. Philanthropic foundations stemming from industrial endowments could also fit here. The media are the grey zone. Commercial media organizations are undoubtedly private firms, but free speech is an essential foundation of a strong civil society. The report defines civil society as associations of citizens (outside their families, friends and business) entered into voluntarily to advance their interests, ideas and ideologies. In doing so, the report considers of particular relevance to the UN mass organizations (such as organizations of peasants, women or retired people), trade unions, professional associations, social movements, indigenous people's organizations, religious and special organizations, academia and public benefit NGOs. The report defines NGOs as all organizations of relevance to the UN that are not central governments and were not created by intergovernmental decision, including associations of business, parliamentarians and local authorities. The report suggests that the UN view these actors as constituencies, or stakeholders, of the organization's processes. States would then not be the exclusive owners of the organization anymore, but should share that stakeholder position with the other core actors of today's international arena.

During the 2000 Millennium Summit, it was also apparent that there is an increasing awareness that maintaining peace and security, sustainable development, the protection of human rights and good governance more than ever require a UN which not only includes states, but also civil society and the private sector as their followers. As it is stated in the September 2005 Final Document, the UN member states are willing to "enhance the contribution of non-governmental organizations, civil society, the private sector and other stakeholders in national development efforts, as well as in the promotion of the global partnership for development"[50] and "they welcome the positive contributions of the private sector and civil society, including non-governmental organizations, in the promotion and implementation of development and human rights programmes and stress the importance of their continued engagement with Governments, the United Nations and other international organizations in these key areas".[51]

It sounds good, although one should keep in mind that not all UN member states are equally fond of the civil society and the private sector – for that reason the words chosen are not stronger than "welcome" etc. – and that the words should be followed by action. Embracing the civil society and the private sector requires a constant review of the organization of the international economic order and the role of world trade in this, of the distinction between sovereignty and power and of democracy as a new condition for UN membership. In addition, it requires a transformation of traditional international law as a law of and for states into a law of and for – at least *also* – peoples.

2.3 A lawless world?

The British professor Philippe Sands, the author of the standard work on environmental law *Principles of International Environmental Law,* gives his views on the increasing lawlessness in the world as a result activities of the USA in a book with the revealing title *Lawless World: America and the Making and Breaking of Global Rules.*[52] In this work, he sweeps the floor with the illegal war of USA President

George W. Bush and UK Prime Minister Tony Blair against Iraq in 2003 and the American unilateralism regarding world trade, the protection of investment, international prosecution and trials, and environmental protection, or in fact, the environmental degradation as a result of global warming. His last chapter has the challenging title "Tough Guys and Lawyers". The final sentence does not allow for any misunderstanding about the fact that the rules of international law will condemn the policy of the Bush administration: "Tough guys are not enough in international relations. In the twenty-first century you need rules and proper lawyers too."[53]

Sands clearly focuses attention on the far-reaching changes in international law in the 1990s. In those years, the state lost its monopoly with regard to the creation of international law. International law became the subject of discussion in the boardrooms of large corporations, in periodicals and Internet actions of lobbying non-governmental organizations and on the front pages of newspapers.[54] The Pinochet case and the trial against Milosević took place as a result of a growing awareness that international law serves not only for the protection of the sovereignty of states and the immunity of heads of state, but also for the protection of victims of genocide, crimes against humanity and war crimes: "Rules of international law become richer and deeper, and even more connected to daily political issues, and moral choices. As this has happened, more invasive rules have become more constraining on political choices."[55] The views of the two instigators of the action *Operation Iraqi Freedom,* President Bush and Prime Minister Blair, were diametrically opposed as to the need of such rules. According to Blair, this war showed the need for new rules, according to the American President Bush it actually showed that less rules are required.[56] During a press conference on 11 December 2003 on the American decision to exclude a large number of countries from tenders for reparation works in Iraq, President Bush answered a question about what he understood international law to be: "I do not know what you are talking about, about international law. I've got to consult my lawyer."[57] Sands opens his chapter "Terrorists and Torturers" with this quotation.[58] President Bush may have given this answer outside the context of the war against international terrorism, but he did give the key to the solution of the riddle of how the USA of his predecessor Roosevelt could slide into such a lawless world as that which now prevails in the prisons of Guantánamo Bay in Cuba and Abu Ghraib in Baghdad. Sands denounces the treatment of suspects of terrorism by American – and British – interrogators with titles which cannot be misunderstood: "Guantánamo: the Legal Black Hole" and "Kicking Ass in Iraq". He is justifiably angered by American legal advisors who supported and strengthened the President's contempt of international law and his unlimited authority as the supreme commander. A memorandum on the rules of conduct for interrogation is a striking illustration of this.[59] On 1 August 2002, the then Attorney General, Jay S. Bybee, now a federal appellate judge, sent this memo to the then advisor of President Bush, Alberto R. Gonzales, who is the new USA Attorney General as of 2005, at his request. According to the memo, American legislation defines as torture only acts in which the result of the actions concerned are comparable in intensity to serious physical pain caused by serious physical injuries, such as the amputation of limbs, the elimination of physical functions, or even death. With regard to psychological torture, the author remarks that these are only prohibited if they result in significant psychological damage, for a significant period of months or even years. The memo states that with the acceptance of the American legislation on the basis of the 1984 Convention against Torture and other Forms of Cruel, Inhuman and Degrading Treatment or Punishment, the American Congress had only aimed to follow the definition of torture in that Convention, taking into account the provisos, interpretations and declarations of the USA in its ratification. The memorandum states that every attempt of Congress to regulate the interrogation of combatants in the battlefield would undermine the constitutional authority of the President as the supreme commander. According to Bybee, there can be no doubt that "intelligence operations, such as the detention and interrogation of enemy combatants and leaders, are both necessary and proper for the effective conduct of a military campaign. Indeed, such operations may be of more importance in a war with an international terrorist organization than one with the conventional armed forces of a nation-state, due to the former's emphasis on secret operations and surprise attacks against civilians."[60]

Bybee even goes so far as to comment that in the circumstances of the current war against Al Qaeda and its allies, the application of the American legislation to interrogations "undertaken pursuant to the President's Commander-in-Chief powers may be unconstitutional".[61] No wonder that Sands qualifies this view as the most shocking legal opinion which he has ever seen.[62] However, there is a ray of light. Just as in the Netherlands, USA courts do not simply accept the view of their government that human rights in general and those of the suspects of terrorism in particular are subordinate to the protection of the security of the state and its citizens. On 28 June 2004, the American Supreme Court decided that American federal courts were competent to judge the legitimacy of unlimited detention of prisoners in Guantánamo Bay who state that they are innocent. There is nothing in the American jurisprudence to indicate that foreigners in military detention outside the USA – in this case, Guantánamo Bay – are categorically excluded from the privilege or right to submit an appeal against this to the American courts. American law gives them the right to summon the state for unlawful acts which have been carried out in conflict with written or unwritten international law. "The fact that petitioners are being held in military custody is immaterial."[63]

The advisors of President Bush may have left no stone unturned to weaken the significance of international law and the UN, but Sands' final conclusion is that the world cannot be lawless. Because, "whatever the superficial attractions of the claim that America is against international rules (or does not need them), and that Europe and others are for them (because they need them)", the approach is unsustainable, because "it does not reflect the complex realities of the modern world, and the price a country pays when it opts out".[64]

The current USA government may try to make and break international law as a hegemonic power, but in our view Sands has justifiably raised the alarm to warn against the wave of lawlessness which threatens to overwhelm the world as a result.

CHAPTER 3
The International Protection of Human Rights

3.1 The story of its development

Deeply under the impression of the large-scale violations of human rights during WW-II, states immediately placed the protection of these rights high up on the international agenda. This resulted in the acceptance of the Universal Declaration of Human Rights (UDHR) in 1948 and the International Covenants on Economic, Social and Cultural Rights (ICESCR), as well as Civil and Political Rights (ICCPR), adopted in 1966. Together they form the International Bill of Human Rights. This set of documents once again brought the individual back into the fold of international law, from which it had slowly but surely disappeared since the Peace of Westphalia in 1648.

The history of human rights has many starting points, both in documents and in the writings of philosophical authors. In history, reference is often made to the *Magna Carta Libertatum* of 1215, the document with which the British King at that time responded to complaints about the abuse of power on his part. It states that "no freemen shall be taken or imprisoned or disseised or exiled or in any way destroyed, nor will we go upon him nor send upon him, except by the lawful judgment of his peers or by the law of the land" (Article 39). In short, this was a first indication of the rule of law. Examples of philosophers include authors such as John Locke (1632-1704), Jean-Jacques Rousseau (1712-1778) and Immanuel Kant (1724-1804), who left an important mark on the ideas about human rights in the 18th and 19th centuries. Their writings, together with documents such as the French Déclaration des Droits de l'Homme et du Citoyen (1789) and the American Declaration of Independence (1776), served as a departure from the thinking up to that time, in which, to put it crudely, the people were there for those in power, rather than the other way round.

The first signs of the *international* protection of human rights date from a much later time, the late 19th century and the beginning of the 20th century. Reference can be made to the Brussels Conference of 1890, where a multilateral anti-slavery treaty was accepted and the Hague Peace Conferences of 1899 and 1907, where about fifteen conventions were drawn up in the field of the humanitarian aspects of waging war as well as international dispute settlement. At that time, the first treaties also appeared for the protection of national minorities, such as the 1878 Treaty of Berlin, in which the Balkan states such as Bulgaria, Montenegro, Serbia and Romania were required to observe freedom of religion, *inter alia*, for the Muslim minorities in Bulgaria and Montenegro and the Jewish minority in Serbia and Romania, if they were also to participate in the 'European Concert'.[65] The Covenant on the League of Nations (LoN) also contained a number of provisions relating to matters such as the achievement of human labor conditions (Article 23) and the protection of national minorities (in particular, Article 24, paragraph 1), although it did not really amount to very much. The real breakthrough in the field of the international protection of human rights is linked to the establishment of the UN, founded on the rubble of WW-II.

It was partly because of the persistency of NGOs – even then! – such as the American Jewish Committee and the Carnegie Endowment for International Peace that the UN Charter ultimately contained seven provisions on human rights.[66] One of these is Article 68, according to which the Economic and Social Council of the UN (ECOSOC) shall set up commissions for, amongst others, the protection of human rights. The Article serves as the legal basis for the Commission on Human Rights. It was this Commission, established in 1946, that was responsible, amongst other things, for the drafting of the UDHR.[67] Despite the fact that some later developments, such as the threat to human rights as a result of large-scale environmental pollution, exhausting natural resources and combating terrorism are not provided for in the UDHR, and that the notion of collective rights, such as the right to self-determination of peoples and (parts of) the right to development, are also of a later date, the UDHR can still be as seen as the worldwide core document in the field of human rights.

3.2 Standards and procedures

In the UDHR, the different human rights – civil and political ones, as well as economic, social and cultural ones – appear comfortably together, from the right not be tortured to the freedom of expression, from the right to seek asylum in other countries to the right to adequate food. The latter is, together with other 'basic needs', expressed in Article 25 of the UDHR:

> *Everyone had the right to a standard of living adequate for the health and well-being of himself and his family, including food, clothing, housing and medical care and necessary social services, and the right to security in the event of unemployment, sickness, disability, widowhood, old age or other lack of livelihood in circumstances beyond his control.*

According to Article 28 of the UDHR, everyone has a right to the existence of a social and international order in which the rights and freedoms set forth in the Declaration can be fully realized. This article clearly shows that human rights are not only concerned with the obligation of states to refrain from violations, but also with an obligation to provide support if people are not able to achieve human rights for themselves on their own strength. The Preamble to the Universal Declaration also refers to this when it speaks of the "inherent dignity and worth of the human person" and the task to fully realize this all over the world, as "a common standard of achievement for all peoples and all nations".[68]

The UN protection of human rights is primarily covered by a series of international conventions in which these human rights are worked out in more detail. On the basis of these conventions, the states which are party to these conventions undertake the obligation to report on their human rights policies and practices to supervisory committees of independent experts at regular intervals. Some of these states – *viz.* those which have become a party to the protocols concerned or which endorsed the relevant articles in the conventions – can also be challenged by individuals, NGOs and/or other states with regard to alleged violations of human rights. Sometimes all this has been described as the "quasi-legal supervision" of the observance of human rights. The term "quasi" is used because unlike for example the European Court of Human Rights, the committees which supervise the observance of human rights in the UN are not real courts and do not have real legal powers. However, this does not mean that they and their activities are less valuable as a result.

In addition to these quasi-legal procedures, there are the politically oriented instruments, particularly the instruments which are available to the UN Human Rights Commission. The Commission is currently composed of 53 UN member states and meets every year for approximately six weeks. One of the points on its agenda is the discussion of human rights situations anywhere in the world. Countries which are not party to the above-mentioned conventions may also be discussed. Moreover, the fact that a state is a party to a number of human rights conventions is not a guarantee that it will escape the Commission's scrutiny. The legal basis for tackling states with political means, *i.e.*, outside the procedures of the human rights conventions, is that these states violate rules which can be deemed to belong to customary international law, possibly even to the mandatory part of it (*ius cogens*). They cannot escape this by simply appealing to the fact that they did not become a party to the conventions concerned on a voluntary basis. The political control is also carried out on the basis of the reports of a series of Special Rapporteurs for particular countries and subjects. In addition, the job of the High Commissioner for Human Rights was created in 1993 – fulfilled consecutively by Ayala Lasso (Ecuador, 1994-1997), Mary Robinson (Ireland, 1997-2003), Sergio Vieira de Mello (Brazil, 2003-2004), and Louise Arbour (Canada, since 1 July 2004) – for the coordination of all the activities undertaken by the UN in the field of human rights.[69]

3.3 Remedying weak spots

There are a number of weak spots in the UN activities in the field of human rights. So for instance, the political proceedings will always be tainted by the use of double standards and arbitrary political acts. After all, the UN Commission on Human Rights consists of states which have their own political agenda, combined with a tendency to politicize and de-politicize debates as soon as it suits them. For this reason Turkey for instance was able to escape the serious attention of the Human Rights Commission for years in the 1980s and 1990s, while countries such as Guatemala (small) and Cuba (politically interesting) could always count on a great deal of attention. In these political skirmishes, human rights are quite often used as an instrument for achieving a political goal rather than being seen as a goal which requires attention in itself.[70]

In this section, we will deal with some of these weak spots, related to the political as well as the conventional approach to human rights violations.

3.3.1 Universality, no uniformity

The UDHR comprises the notion of the universality of human rights, for instance in its title. Nevertheless, it is important to be careful with this notion of universality, amongst other things because in 1948 the UN comprised only 58 states,[71] compared with 191 now. It was particularly during the 1950s and 1960s that many sovereign states were added, mainly as a result of the process of de-colonization, and subsequently through more incidental events such as the disintegration of states like Yugoslavia and the Soviet Union. The question of what the 133 new states would have contributed to the discussions on the UDHR in 1946-1948 and what they would have done in a vote on this is obviously hard to answer.

However, for many of them it is well known that they subsequently supported the UDHR, especially while meeting within the two World Conferences on Human Rights, in Tehran (1968) and in Vienna (1993). In the document of the latter conference, the UN member states endorse sentences in which the UDHR is characterized as a "common standard of achievement" and "source of inspiration", even though it was also determined that the "significance of national and regional particularities and various historical, cultural and religious backgrounds must be borne in mind".[72] In the September 2005 document the words of 1993 have been repeated:

> We reaffirm that all human rights are universal, indivisible, interrelated, interdependent and mutually reinforcing and that all human rights must be treated in a fair and equal manner, on the same footing and with the same emphasis. While the significance of national and regional particularities and various historical, cultural and religious backgrounds must be borne in mind, all States, regardless of their political, economic and cultural systems, have the duty to promote and protect all human rights and fundamental freedoms.[73]

Commenting upon similar words, used in successive UN documents, the Dutch Advisory Council on International Affairs stated that "universality is not uniformity".[74] This refers to the "margin of appreciation" which states have with regard to the achievement of human rights.

In our view, the starting point of the discussion on universality/non-uniformity should be that there is a series of human rights which should be observed anyhow, whether states want to do so or not. These are the rights which John Locke would have described as "natural rights", and of which Jean-Jacques Rousseau would have said that people would have included them without hesitation in their "social contract": examples are the prohibition on torture, the freedom of expression and religion, but also, for example, in the light of later developments, the right to food. Some of these rights are referred to nowadays, in line with Locke's notion of natural rights, as "non-derogable", *i.e.*, rights which may not be deviated from, even in times of emergency.[75]

Our starting point also is that in principle all internationally recognized human rights fall under the universal rights, *until* it is clear that states can argue that an exception to the rule is desirable in their situation on good grounds, the latter being judged by independent supervisory treaty bodies. A traditional case concerns the prohibition on torture and the case of the ticking bomb: is it permissible to exercise serious physical pressure on persons deemed to know about a threat of an attack? States regularly appeal to these type of cases to make exceptions to rules, sometimes even leading to the internal legal recognition that such physical pressure is permissible. For example, Israel does so. Other states practice this pressure wholly or partly in secret. In our view all these states should be prepared to have their conduct assessed by the UN Committee against Torture – *i.e.*, the Committee of independent experts that supervises the UN Convention against Torture and Other Cruel, Inhuman or Degrading Treatment or Punishment – or, if they are not a party to this convention, should apply the findings of the Committee analogously. By adopting this approach, the states which have negotiated an 'elastic relationship' to certain human rights for themselves would find themselves on the defensive, in the knowledge that in the last instance, they are not the ones who can judge the room they created for themselves. However, apart from all this there is the notion that once the norm has been endorsed, its implementation does not always have to be completely identical. As indicated above, "universality is not uniformity". The right to a fair trial is undoubtedly one of the universal human rights, but the paths to it may be very different. By way of extremes there are countries with a complete absence of an independent judiciary and countries which actually have a very sophisticated legal system developed over many years. For both, the right to a fair trial is a "common standard of achievement", but the roads leading to it are clearly different.

3.3.2 The indivisibility of human rights in relation to universality and non-uniformity

As has been underlined again in the September 2005 document, all human rights are "indivisible, interrelated, interdependent and mutually reinforcing".[76] Rightly so. The respect for civil and political rights should go hand in hand with – and cannot take place without – a respect for the economic, social and cultural human rights and *vice versa*. They come as a package, although they were elaborated in two covenants in 1966 for historical reasons. The ideas of universality and indivisibility are reflected in the extent to which states are prepared to recognize the norm and to do everything they reasonably can to achieve this. In this respect, our choice of the word "reasonably" is not arbitrary. Some states are very young and have many other concerns, in addition to strictly human rights concerns. Other states are trying to put an end to a left-wing or right-wing dictatorial past and cannot do so from one day to the next. Other states again have intrinsically political tensions which are at loggerheads with a number of fundamental ideas behind human rights. For example, in Islamic states, religion and state power are extensions of each other. Nevertheless, these states are expected to commit to freedom of religion. In this situation the question is how tolerant they are towards other religions and to what extent they try to restrain their Muslim citizens from taking action against other believers. In such a case, we believe that the slogan that universality does not imply uniformity still applies, but also reaches its limits: it is no longer a matter of actively striving to achieve the higher goal, in this case of the total recognition of freedom of religion, but of removing the sharp edges of a government policy which is aimed at privileging a particular religion. This is relevant in today's world, as it has been a matter of all times.

In daily practice the universality and indivisibility of human rights have been acquired only to a limited extent and must particularly be achieved further in everyday turbulent political contexts, where what seems to be a certainty today can be quite different tomorrow. Regimes and the related views of human rights do tend to change. Countries may be expected to use the standard of universal rights as a guideline in global or bilateral discussions, but also to be constantly aware of the obstacles which stand in the way of achieving the different human rights and be prepared to publicly acknowledge their own failures in order to prevent a polarized picture from emerging in which there is only absolute good and absolute evil.

3.3.3 Removal of reservations and understandings

Many states have become party to human rights conventions with the use of numerous reservations and understandings. As a result, the extent of ratification of the conventions at first sight seems much better than it does upon closer examination.

To our mind, states which have become party to the UN human rights conventions must make use to a much greater extent than is the case at the moment, of their possibilities of criticizing reservations of other states and declaring them to be unacceptable, rather than admitting states which might want to join for the purposes of 'window dressing' for the international community. Here, the 1994 'General Comment on issues related to reservations made upon ratification or accession to the ICCPR'[77] can serve as a guideline:

> Reservations that offend peremptory norms would not be compatible with the object and purpose of the Covenant. Although treaties that are mere exchanges of obligations between States allow them to reserve inter se application of rules of general international law, it is otherwise in human rights treaties, which are for the benefit of persons within their jurisdiction. Accordingly, provisions in the Covenant that represent customary international law (and a fortiori when they have the character of peremptory norms) may not be the subject of reservations. Accordingly, a State may not reserve the right to engage in slavery, to torture, to subject persons to cruel, inhuman or degrading treatment or punishment, to arbitrarily deprive persons of their

lives, to arbitrarily arrest and detain persons, to deny freedom of thought, conscience and religion, to presume a person guilty unless he proves his innocence, to execute pregnant women or children, to permit the advocacy of national, racial or religious hatred, to deny to persons of marriageable age the right to marry, or to deny to minorities the right to enjoy their own culture, profess their own religion, or use their own language. And while reservations to particular clauses of Article 14 may be acceptable, a general reservation to the right to a fair trial would not be.[78]

And:

Applying more generally the object and purpose test to the Covenant, the Committee notes that, for example, reservation to article 1 denying peoples the right to determine their own political status and to pursue their economic, social and cultural development, would be incompatible with the object and purpose of the Covenant. Equally, a reservation to the obligation to respect and ensure the rights, and to do so on a non-discriminatory basis (Article 2(1)) would not be acceptable. Nor may a State reserve an entitlement not to take the necessary steps at the domestic level to give effect to the rights of the Covenant (Article 2(2)). [79]

In addition the Human Rights Committee addresses those states that are making abuse of the possibility to make reservations:

States should not enter so many reservations that they are in effect accepting a limited number of human rights obligations, and not the Covenant as such. So that reservations do not lead to a perpetual non-attainment of international human rights standards, reservations should not systematically reduce the obligations undertaken only to the presently existing in less demanding standards of domestic law. Nor should interpretative declarations or reservations seek to remove an autonomous meaning to Covenant obligations, by pronouncing them to be identical, or to be accepted only insofar as they are identical, with existing provisions of domestic law. States should

not seek through reservations or interpretative declarations to deter-
mine that the meaning of a provision of the Covenant is the same as
that given by an organ of any other international treaty body.[80]

Apart from this, a significant proportion of the member states of the UN are not party to any human rights conventions at all. Furthermore, far too few states have had the courage to also become party to those parts of the conventions or additional protocols which provide for the individual right of complaint and where the conventions therefore acquire further (quasi-)legal teeth. All this requires constant and determined attention from the community of states, in the knowledge that the states which are a party to human rights conventions from that moment are, in a sense, on the defensive before the relevant supervisory bodies if they trample on human rights.

3.3.4 Strengthening the supervisory procedures

Admittedly the supervisory conventional mechanisms work, but they are not without problems: many states have fallen far behind with regard to their regularly compulsory reports, while the follow-up of the findings of the committees often leaves a great deal to be desired, both in terms of content and in terms of their international control. In addition, the number of times that the procedures for individual complaints have been used is very small. Of course, the number of cases is not indicative for the quality of the views of the Committee, but says something about the acquaintance of the procedure, etc. Whatever that may be, it will always be a matter of trying to get as many states as possible on board of the conventions and their complaint procedures, in order to serve human beings all over the world that might want to have access to (outstanding) international supervisory bodies like the UN Human Rights Committee. In addition, there is a need of constantly working on improvements of these supervisory procedures. These notions are also reflected in the September 2005 document:

We resolve to improve the effectiveness of the human rights treaty bodies, including through more timely reporting, improved and streamlined reporting procedures and technical assistance to States to enhance their reporting capacities and further enhance the implementation of their recommendations.[81]

In this respect, it is also interesting to note that the International Law Association in 2004 unanimously accepted the Committee Report on *International Human Rights Law and Practice*, including its views on the status of human rights treaty body findings.[82] It states, *inter alia*, that:

The legal norms on which the treaty bodies pronounce are binding obligations of the State parties, and therefore the pronouncements of the treaty bodies are more than mere recommendations that can be readily disregarded because a State Party disagrees with the interpretation adopted by the Committee or with its application to the facts.[83]

This conclusion has gained considerable force with for instance the advisory opinion of the International Court of Justice about the legal consequences of the construction of a wall by Israel in the occupied Palestinian territory.[84] The Court is fully clear as to the legal status and meaning of the findings of human rights treaty bodies, *in casu* in relation to the protection of human rights by Israel within the Occupied Palestinian Territory:

In 2003, in face of Israel's consistent position, to the effect that "the Covenant does not apply beyond its own territory, notably in the West Bank and Gaza (...)", the [Human Rights] Committee reached the following conclusion: "In the current circumstances, the provisions of the Covenant apply to the benefit of the population of the Occupied Territories, for all conduct by the State party's authorities or agents in those territories that affect the enjoyment of rights enshrined in the Covenant and fall within the ambit of State responsibility of Israel under the principles of public international law"

(CCPR/CO/78/ISR, par. 11). In conclusion, the Court considers that the International Covenant on Civil and Political Rights is applicable in respect of acts done by a State in the exercise of its jurisdiction outside its own territory.[85]

The same applies for the ICESCR and the Convention on the Rights of the Child:

The International Covenant on Economic, Social and Cultural Rights contains no provision on its scope of application. This may be explicable by the fact that this Covenant guarantees rights which are essentially territorial. However, it is not to be excluded that it applies both to territories over which a State party has sovereignty and to those over which that State exercises territorial jurisdiction. Thus Article 14 [concerning the implementation of primary education] makes provision for transitional measures in the case of any State which "at the time of becoming a Party, has not been able to secure in its metropolitan territory or other territories under its jurisdiction compulsory primary education, free of charge.

As regards the Convention on the Rights of the Child of 20 November 1989, that instrument contains an Article 2 according to which "States Parties shall respect and ensure the rights set forth in the Convention to each child within their jurisdiction (...)". That Convention is therefore applicable within the Occupied Palestinian Territory.[86]

All in all, strengthening the whole set of UN human rights procedures is a matter of further recognition of the importance of these instruments and supervisory mechanisms by the UN member states, and (thus) also a matter of money. The coordination and the support of the UN human rights program in terms of staff are primarily in the hands of what has been known since 1997 as the Office of the High Commissioner. This Office, however, suffers from chronic under-funding. In addition, the Office has a number of 'Field Offices', but these are not overstaffed or over-funded either.

Anyone who is prepared to acknowledge that the protection of human rights is not only an intrinsically good thing, but also that a good protection of human rights could have effects in terms of preventing social unrest and (civil) wars, should not accept that there is so little personnel and money allocated to this aspect of UN activities. In the document of the September 2005 Summit, it is therefore rightly stated that the Office of the High Commissioner needs to be strengthened, in words that do belong to the most concrete and verifiable ones of the document:

> We resolve to strengthen the Office of the United Nations High Commissioner for Human Rights, taking note of the High Commissioner's plan of action, to enable it to effectively carry out its mandate to respond to the broad range of human rights challenges facing the international community, particularly in the areas of technical assistance and capacity-building, through the doubling of its regular budget resources over the next five years with a view to progressively setting a balance between regular budget and voluntary contributions to its resources, keeping in mind other priority programmes for developing countries and the recruitment of highly competent staff on a broad geographical basis and with gender balance, under the regular budget (...).[87]

One might cynically say that doubling something which is by far not enough, will not be enough in the future either. This is all the more the case if one keeps in mind that the present Secretary-General to the United Nations – and many others with him – time and again stresses that human rights should belong to the core mission of the organization. They should not be seen as 'a separate issue', but in stead as one which is intertwined with so many other issues at the UN agenda. To take just one quote from his 2004 Report *In larger freedom*, mentioned above:

> Not only are development, security and human rights all imperative; they also reinforce each other. This relationship has only been strengthened in our era of rapid technological advances, increasing

economic interdependence, globalization and dramatic geopolitical change. While poverty and denial of human rights may not be said to "cause" civil war, terrorism or organized crime, they all greatly increase the risk of instability and violence. Similarly, war and atrocities are far from the only reasons that countries are trapped in poverty, but they undoubtedly set back development. Again, catastrophic terrorism on one side of the globe, for example an attack against a major financial centre in a rich country, could affect the development prospects of millions on the other by causing a major economic downturn and plunging millions into poverty. And countries which are well governed and respect the human rights of their citizens are better placed to avoid the horrors of conflict and to overcome obstacles to development.[88]

It is a clear and to our mind an impressive way of underlining the interrelatedness of so many issues, with the human rights as their center.

3.4 Creation of a standing Human Rights Council

It is clear that within the United Nations an extensive system of procedures has been established since the Second World War. These contribute on a daily basis to ensure that states which trample on human rights must justify their conduct. Compared to the years before WW-II, they are visibly on the defensive. At the same time, all this could be done much better and more effectively, even if we keep in mind that it is not always possible to perform at the highest desirable level, due to the political context in which the human rights machinery has to function. After all, certain rulers have an interest in violating rights, such as the freedom of expression, in order to retain power more easily. Furthermore, some states are not able to independently ensure human rights at an internationally accepted minimum level, for example because of structural poverty. Yet other states are prepared to announce a state of emergency to provide themselves with a justification for the most serious violations. As long as all these things continue to happen, the worldwide realization of human rights will remain a "common standard of achievement", as the UDHR put it. This was the case in 1948 and is not much different nearly 60 years later, although the starting point in contemporary discussions has moved: there is greater clarity about the precise norms, and more insight into the power and lack of power of supervision mechanisms.

In his report *In larger freedom*, with as part of its subtitle: *human rights for all*, the UN Secretary-General states that it is time to strengthen the human rights machinery. In that respect, he comes up with a severe critique of the Commission on Human Rights:

> *The Commission's capacity to perform its tasks has been increasingly undermined by its declining credibility and professionalism. In particular, States have sought membership of the Commission not to strengthen human rights but to protect themselves against criticism or to criticize others. As a result, a credibility deficit has developed, which casts a shadow on the reputation of the United Nations system as a whole.*[89]

It leads him to the proposal to replace the Commission on Human Rights with a smaller standing Human Rights Council, the creation of which "would accord human rights a more authoritative position, corresponding to the primacy of human rights in the Charter of the United Nations".[90]

In reaction to the Secretary-General's report, the proposal to establish a Human Rights Council has been embraced as well as criticized by many authors, NGOs and advisory bodies, such as the Dutch Advisory Council on International Affairs. The latter expressed some doubts about parts of the proposal concerning the role and purpose of the new Council. So it states, that the idea of a peer review system raises the question of whether a political body, such as the Human Rights Council, could perform this task independently. Furthermore, there is reason for concern about the fact

that scarcely any mention is made of the existing special procedures and treaty mechanisms in this area; it would be most regret-
table if the reforms were to weaken or even eliminate these monitoring systems. Moreover, according to the Advisory Council, peer
review would be voluntary, and it is not clear what information it
would be based on. Such an arrangement would make it easy for
notorious and serious violators of human rights to escape punishment, which cannot be the intention.[91]

The UN Secretary-General assumes in his report that the
Human Rights Council will be located in Geneva, as this is the
main center for UN human rights activities and also because of the
need for it to work with the Office of the High Commissioner for
Human Rights (OHCHR), which has a key part to play in mainstreaming human rights throughout the UN system. According to
him, all things considered, an upgraded Human Rights Council on
equal institutional footing with the Security Council and ECOSOC
and more capable of effective decision-making, would be more
successful in mainstreaming human rights into all UN activities in
the future than the current Commission. For that reason, the UN
Secretary-General's proposals on the subject would deserve support, while governments should also be pressed to preserve the
role of specific human rights procedures and retaining NGO
involvement as part of the structure of such a new Council.

The establishment of a Human Rights Council was also fiercely
discussed preceding and during the September summit. The
results of the debates were disappointing as well as predictable.
The good news is that the Human Rights Council as such is mentioned in the final document, while some lines have been devoted
to its core tasks:

*The Council will be responsible for promoting universal respect for
the protection of all human rights and fundamental freedoms for all,
without distinction of any kind and in a fair and equal manner. The
Council should address situations of violations of human rights,
including gross and systematic violations, and make recommenda-*

tions thereon. It should also promote effective coordination and the mainstreaming of human rights within the United Nations system.[92]

But the real message of the September 2005 document is that many core elements of the Council are still open. In the document, the states do "request the President of the General Assembly to conduct open, transparent and inclusive negotiations, to be completed as soon as possible during the sixtieth session, with the aim of establishing the mandate, modalities, functions, size, composition, membership, working methods and procedures of the Council".[93]

This leaves a situation in which it is by far not yet sure whether or not the Council will be able to avoid the weaknesses of the present Human Rights Commission.

CHAPTER 4

Protection of National Minorities and Indigenous Peoples

4.1 National minorities

As regards the rights of the nations mentioned in the Preamble of the United Charter ("We, the peoples..."), there can be no misunderstanding that despite the growing influence of the non-governmental world and of numerous (quasi-)legal international agencies, it is first and foremost the sovereign states which determine what becomes existing international law. This also relates to the position of national minorities in international law. Usually based on the argument that more rights for minorities – and indigenous peoples; see below – would lead to more problems in relation to separation and to competition between different groups in separate states, the international community has up to now only served these groups in a very small way.

One of the starting problems of the limited protection of national minorities 'as such' – apart from the protection of individual members of these minorities, which is covered by the previously discussed human rights mechanisms – is the lack of a definition. Who exactly are these national minorities who would deserve special protection as groups or collectivities? In international law, there is no such thing as an officially accepted definition of a national minority.[94] For that reason, the former High Commissioner on National Minorities of the Organization for Security and Co-operation in Europe, Max van der Stoel, always stated that he could recognize a minority when he saw one.[95] In doing so, in his view, neither the lack of a clear definition nor the (non-)preparedness by states to live up to such a definition, is decisive. A similar approach is practiced by the United Nations' Working Group on Minorities (see below).[96]

The lack of a definition is partly 'real', in the sense that it is indeed not easy to reach one which is acceptable from the different perspectives in the debate, on the other hand it is synonymous for the lack of preparedness to really protect collectivities, because of the risk of stimulating separation an the like. However, one can also argue the other way round. Protecting specific collective entitlements can also lead to diminishing tension, because of the fact that minorities are then allowed to 'mind their own business' (autonomy), at least in specific fields. In the words of the then Dutch Advisory Committee on Human Rights and Foreign Policy[97]:

> (...) The theme of self-determination, internal or external, ought not to be approached as though it entailed nothing but risk. It can sometimes serve as a solution in a conflict to which there is no other reasonable solution.[98]

In fact, over the centuries several legal instruments have been developed for the protection of minorities as a whole, especially in the religious field. In the words of Yoram Dinstein:

> From the very beginning of modern international law, treaties (especially peace treaties) have recognised the rights of selected minorities (particularly, though not exclusively, religious minorities) in territories that were ceded from one State to another or gained independence.[99]

Concentrating on presently existing legal instruments it would go too far to discuss the protection offered in the period between the Treaty of Westphalia and the Congress of Vienna (1648-1815) or during the League of Nations Period.[100] The 1945 UN Charter, however, speaks, *expressis verbis*, of "the principle of equal rights and self-determination of peoples" (and not of states) (Article 1(2)). This is clearly a provision of a real collective character, which, however, has a limited function in today's legal practice. Nevertheless, sometimes the principle is used in, for instance, cases brought before the International Court of Justice, such as in the 1975 Western-Sahara case.[101] A relatively recent case concerns East-Timor, as discussed by the UN Commission on Human Rights. In its resolution on the human rights situation on the island, the Commission states that it was guided by the principles embodied in the Charter of the United Nations (thereby not mentioning the right to self-determination explicitly), followed by welcoming "the decision of the Government of Indonesia to allow the exercise by the East Timorese of their right of self-determination (...) as well as the announcement by the Government of Indonesia (...) of its intention to honour and accept the result of the popular consultation".[102]

In other words: in the case of East-Timor, the right to self-determination as such is accepted for what *de facto* was a national minority since 1975, while the Indonesian government also accepted the material outcome of the decision-making process (secession).

Within the 1948 Universal Declaration of Human Rights, one cannot find any references to national and other minorities as such, although the general non-discrimination article mentions the duty to abstain from making any distinctions "of any kind, such as race, colour, (...) national or social origin" (Article 2). The article has been worded in the well-known terminology: "Everyone is entitled", thereby underlining the individual character of the right. It is interesting to note and often forgotten, however, that the UN General Assembly added some sort of an Annex to the Universal Declaration, in which it explained why it did not insert an article on the "complex and delicate question" of minorities with its "special aspects in each State in which it arises", and in which it underlined that it "cannot remain indifferent to the fate of minorities".[103]

Also in 1948, the UN General Assembly adopted the Convention on the Prevention and Punishment of the Crime of Genocide. As the Convention says, genocide relates to acts like "killing members of the group" or "imposing measures intended to prevent births within the group" "with the intent to destroy, in whole or in part, a national, ethnical, racial or religious group" (Article II).

The Article clearly covers national minorities. In September 1998, the International Criminal Tribunal for Rwanda was the first international tribunal ever that sentenced somebody for having committed genocide (Jean-Paul Akayesu, the former mayor of Taba).[104] His acts were clearly committed against a minority as such (the Tutsis).

One of the UN conventions in which the issue of protection of (national) minorities also occurs, is the 1965 Convention on the Elimination of All Forms of Racial Discrimination. It states in Article 1(4) special measures taken for the sole purpose of securing adequate advancement of certain racial or ethnic groups or individuals, requiring such protection as may be necessary in order to ensure such groups or individuals equal enjoyment or exercise of human rights and fundamental freedoms, shall not be deemed racial discrimination (...).

In addition, Article 2 (2) of the Convention speaks of the duty for states, "when circumstances so warrant", to take "special and concrete measures to ensure the adequate development and protection of certain racial groups or individuals belonging to them". Both articles, and the same goes for some other articles in the Convention (*inter alia*, Article 7), clearly speak in terms of collectivities (and members belonging to them) which under special circumstances deserve special treatment ('affirmative action'), although at the end the special measures required are to be seen in function of the full realization of human rights by individual members of the groups (cf. Article 1(4), quoted above) and therefore as having a temporary character.

The 1966 UN Covenant on Civil and Political Rights basically deals with individual rights, although it opens, in Article 1, with some real collective rights. Apart from the right to self-determination, it states that "peoples may (...) freely dispose of their natural wealth and resources" and that "in no way a people may be deprived of its means of subsistence". The question then is to what extent these rights do belong to colonized peoples only, or whether they also belong to national minorities, living by now on territories of sovereign states. Patrick Thornberry notes that at various stages of drafting the Covenant the tension between "people" and "minority" has been apparent, some states adopting a broad, inclusive view, others warning that "the problem of minorities should not be raised in the context of self-determination".[105] According to him, the latter approach is supported by the travaux préparatoires of the ICCPR, while "the practice of the Human Rights Committee (...) may be taken to buttress the view that minorities are not peoples".[106] The Human Rights Committee, in a General Comment having been prepared after the finalization of Thornberry's book, says literally that "in some communications submitted to the Committee (...) the right protected under Article 27 has been confused with the rights of peoples to self-determination proclaimed in article 1 of the Covenant", adding that the last one "is not a right recognisable under the Optional Protocol."[107]

Whatever the (future) possibilities for claims by minorities based on Article 1 might be, it is clear that so far a series of minority cases was based on the article in the Covenant which is especially created for the legal protection of (persons belonging to) minorities, Article 27.[108] It is relevant to note that the article does not mention national minorities, and that it does not create real collective rights: it starts from the rights belonging to individual members of the minorities, followed by the possibility to exercise these rights "in community with the other members of the group". As such, the article is an example of an "in-community-with-others-right".[109] Since the article has been invoked several times in judicial proceedings,[110] it has become clear that the emphasis is still on the rights of individuals. However, in the meantime it has also become clear, especially through the case *Lubicon Lake Band vs Canada*,[111] that the Human Rights Committee has no objection to "a group of individuals, who claim to be similarly affected, collectively to submit a communication". This, however, is not recognizing collective rights as such, but more a specific form of collective action.

The same "quasi-group" approach of Article 27, although at a more substantial level, has been recognized by the Human Rights Committee in its General Comment on Article 27, where it states that "although the rights protected under Article 27 are individual rights, they depend in turn on the ability of the minority group to maintain its culture, language or religion"; and this might sometimes lead to "positive measures by States (...) to protect the identity of a minority (...)".[112] Manfred Nowak has noted that this approach "supports the views of those authors who have interpreted Article 27 also as a group-protected provision",[113] i.e., as recognizing, at least to some extent, collective rights.

Further to this, we can refer to the 1992 Declaration on the Rights of Persons belonging to National or Ethnic, Religious and Linguistic Minorities.[114] The Declaration speaks clearly in terms of collective notions, where it says that "States shall protect the existence and the national or ethnic, cultural, religious and linguistic identity of minorities within their respective territories (...)" (Article 1). Although the article is followed by several articles in which "persons belonging to minorities" are the subjects, it is clear that the Declaration has an added value in the field of the collective approach with which it starts. In a commentary to the Declaration, Asbjørn Eide states that Article 1 relates to the protection of the existence of minorities (in a physical sense, including access to natural resources), to protection of cultural identity, and to the need to "encourage conditions for the promotion of their identity".[115] The latter element requires, inter alia, special measures intended to facilitate "the maintenance, reproduction and further development of the culture of minorities", to which the author, rightly, adds that "cultures are not static, but minorities should be given the opportunity to develop their own culture in the context of an ongoing process".[116]

In addition to all these UN instruments, it would be possible to have an additional look at a range of other instruments, adopted by the UN itself or by one of its specialized agencies, like the ILO and UNESCO.[117] For practical reasons, however, we will disregard these instruments and bodies – which is not the same as denying their possible relevance –, based on the estimated guess that they would not hand in additional insights as to the issue of protecting individual versus collective rights.

In the field of protection of national minorities on the UN level, we finally come back to the Working Group on Minorities, established in 1995. The Working Group is a forum for dialogue and sees its task as providing a greater insight into the different perspectives which minorities and governments can have with regard to minority matters and can serve as a "mechanism for hearing suggestions and making recommendations for the peaceful and constructive solution to problems involving minorities".[118] In annual meetings of only five working days and with many stops and starts, the Working Group is working on making a contribution to improving the protection of minorities from governments which are often part of their problems. In her recent doctoral dissertation, Rianne Letschert gives a detailed and thought provoking description and analysis of the mandate and the working practices of the Working Group, followed by amongst other things the conclusion that the Working Group so far has not been given a lot of space by most of the UN member states to perform its difficult tasks.[119] Although she ends on a (mixed) positive note:

If the Working Group were able to regain the attention from Government observers and representatives of other UN bodies and international and regional organizations, it provides an excellent setting where issues of mutual concern can be addressed and practical solutions sought. Moreover, the Working Group provides a forum where minority representatives have a chance to enter into personal contact with their Government observer; contacts that might be continued back home. Note that the [European] Advisory Committee on Minorities has observed in several opinions that the authorities have been reluctant to enter into dialogue with minority representatives. Maybe minorities will have more chance in Geneva [where the UN Working Group meets] to build up such contacts. Unfortunately, the Working Group may not be given the chance to regain attention, given the suggestion to cut back the annual session from 5 to 3 days. This means that the agenda has to be shortened and that less interventions and in depth discussions are possible. This might consequently lead to less attention from all participants concerned.[120]

In that situation, the circle would be closed: states that do not like too much interference in their minority affairs, try to sideline their watch dog; or better: the dog that was not even made really barking so far.

4.2 Indigenous peoples

What has been said about national minorities, in many ways resembles the legal protection of (persons belonging to) indigenous peoples, like the Saami in Scandinavia, the Inuit in Canada, the Aborigines in Australia, the Pygmies in Africa and a series of Indian tribes in the US, Mexico and Guatemala. For instance, the case *Lubicon Lake Band vs Canada*, mentioned in relation to Article 27 of the ICCPR is related to an indigenous people. The same goes for, *inter alia*, the case *Sandra Lovelace vs Canada* (the Indian woman who married a non-Indian man, and accordingly lost her right to live on Indian reserve lands).[121] We should keep in mind, however, that apart from an overlap, there are also differences: indigenous peoples are in most cases also national minorities, while national minorities are in many cases not equal to indigenous peoples. This is related to elements like "descent" in the 'definition' of indigenous peoples, as embedded in ILO Convention 169 Concerning Indigenous and Tribal Peoples in Independent Countries. This Convention applies to "peoples in independent countries who are regarded as indigenous on account of their descent from the populations which inhabited the country, or a geographical region to which the country belongs, at the time of conquest or colonisation or the establishment of present state boundaries and who, irrespective of their legal status retain some or all of their own social, economic, cultural and political institutions."[122]

Furthermore, the Convention underlines the importance of self-identification, the so-called 'subjective element' in every definition of indigenous peoples: "Self-identification as indigenous (...) shall be regarded as a fundamental criterion for determining the groups to which the provisions of this Convention apply."[123] This is similar to the (famous) definition of a national minority proposed by M. Deschênes, member of the then United Nations Sub-Commission on the Prevention of Discrimination and the Protection of Minorities:

> A group of citizens of a state, constituting a numerical minority and in a non-dominant position in that state, endowed with ethnic, religious or linguistic characteristics which differ from those of the majority of the population, having a sense of solidarity with one another, motivated, if only implicitly, by a collective will to survive and whose aim is to achieve equality with the majority in fact and in law.[124]

The definition reflects the combination of objective criteria to decide what a national minority is ("ethnic, religious or linguistic characteristics") and the subjective will by the minority itself to be recognized as such, but, as we saw, has never been adopted within a legal instrument on the protection of national minorities.

For indigenous peoples it is interesting to note that – apart from ILO Convention 169 (which is legally binding but which has been ratified by only a small number of states: as of 28 November 2005: 17 – a draft Declaration of the Rights of Indigenous Peoples is in discussion which contains a series of collective rights. See for instance Article 3: "Indigenous peoples have the right of self-determination. (...)", Article 8: "Indigenous peoples have the collective and individual right to maintain and develop their distinct identities and characteristics, (...)", or Article 26: "Indigenous peoples have the right to own, develop, control and use the lands and territories, including the total environment of the lands, air, water, coastal seas, sea-ice, flora and fauna and other resources which they have traditionally owned or otherwise occupied or used." The scope of the draft Declaration is clearly a mix of individual, 'in-community' rights, as well as real collective rights.

The discussions on the draft Declaration started in the mid-1980s, first in the Working Group on Indigenous Peoples, and since 1995 in an inter-sessional working group of the UN Human Rights Commission, therefore: in a working group composed of representatives of states. Although it was the intention that the discussion on the draft Declaration would be concluded in the first International Decade of the World's Indigenous People (1995-2004), leading to its adoption by the UN General Assembly in December 2004, it is clear that this aim has not been achieved in any way: at the end of the ten-year period, the states were only in agreement on a few of the 45 articles in the original draft. This is partly due to the content of the draft Declaration – examples of controversy are the right to self-determination, the decision-making powers with regard to natural resources, and the compensation for damages of indigenous peoples for injustice they suffered at some time in the past – and to some extent to the process of adoption.[125] On the other hand, the discussion reflects the need to do at least something, and might contribute to establishing new, be it soft law, standards, that can be used within national struggles for better protection of indigenous interests.[126]

As long as the draft Declaration is not liberated from its prefix 'draft', (individual persons belonging to) indigenous peoples will have to deal with, amongst others things the protection offered by Article 27 of the ICCPR (see above). The UN Human Rights Committee seems to support a specific indigenous life approach, when it states that "culture manifests itself in many forms, including a particular way of life associated with the use of land resources, especially in the case of indigenous peoples. That right may include such traditional activities as fishing or hunting and the rights to live in reserves protected by law."[127]

The Committee clearly speaks of the life-style of peoples as a whole, not only of its individual members, although only the latter can bring cases to it. This, however, is a matter of admissibility rather than of substantive case-law (see the *Lubicon Lake Band vs. Canada* case, quoted before).

Despite the almost non-progress in the field of the adoption of the draft Declaration on the Rights of Indigenous Peoples and in addition to the willingness to carefully deal with indigenous human rights issues in the context of the ICCPR, indigenous peoples have gained serious attention within the UN context. The final document of the Second World Conference on Human Rights (Vienna, 1993) for instance states that the General Assembly of the United Nations should consider "the establishment of a permanent forum for indigenous people in the United Nations system",[128] a request to which the General Assembly of the UN gave a follow-up, when recognizing that the establishment of such a permanent forum would be one of the important objectives of the program of activities for the International Decade of the World's Indigenous People.[129] Thus the ground was prepared for the establishment of the Permanent Forum on Indigenous Issues, consisting of eight representatives of governments and indigenous peoples, with the task of discussing all sorts of subjects related to the protection of indigenous peoples and giving them advice.[130] It choose Ole Henrik Magga from Norway as its chairperson.[131] The Permanent Forum holds annual sessions of 10 working days. Its first meetings took place in May 2002, 2003, 2004 and 2005 in New York.[132] The most important future task of the Forum might be to supervise the observance of a document which does not yet exist: the Declaration on the Rights of Indigenous Peoples.

In addition to the Forum, also the position of Special Rapporteur on the Human Rights and Fundamental Freedoms of Indigenous People has been created, by the Commission on Human Rights.[133] This was also in the light of the ongoing Decade of the World's Indigenous People and of "the growing interest of the international community in the full and effective protection of the human rights of indigenous people", as the resolution states. The Rapporteur's functions include the right "to formulate recommendations and proposals on appropriate measures and activities to prevent and remedy these violations".[134] The Rapporteur, the sociologist Rodolfo Stavenhagen from Mexico – elected despite the opposition of many indigenous NGOs and the opposing candidacy of 1992 Nobel Peace Prize Laureate Rigoberta Menchu – presented his first report at the 2002 session of the Commission, in which he identified a number of particular topics, *inter alia*, the impact of development projects on the human rights and fundamental freedoms of indigenous communities, participation of indigenous peoples in decision-making processes, and old and new forms of discrimination against indigenous people.[135] He also started making on-site country visits, to Guatemala and the Philippines (both in 2002), to Mexico and Chile (both in 2003), to Colombia and Canada (both in 2004),[136] and to South Africa in 2005.[137] These visits reflect the kind of interactive processes between international and national law that might be needed in order to effectively help indigenous peoples with solving their local problems.

4.3 The self-determination of peoples

The issue of self-determination of peoples, shortly touched upon Chapter 1, par. 1.3, and in the preceding paragraphs of the present Chapter, also deserves some special attention, in order to make clear that it is about much more than 'just another issue' only.

Peoples, including national minorities and indigenous peoples, depend in the first instance on local prosperity and natural resources and the trade in these, to combat absolute poverty. From the beginning, gaining control of these has been the impetus for the right to self-determination. The most important content of the right to self-determination is the prohibition on states to oppress peoples and the prohibition on peoples to secede. The ICCPR and the ICESCR of 1966 declare in their common first chapter/article that all peoples have a right to self-determination. On this basis, they determine their political status in complete freedom, and are free to develop their economic, cultural and social development.[138] Admittedly, the right to self-determination forms a separate section in both conventions, but nevertheless it derives its significance partly from the articles in the other sections. In the context of the ICCPR, the right to self-determination is aimed first and foremost at strengthening the civil and political rights. However, in the context of the ICESCR, it is concerned particularly with strengthening the economic, social and cultural rights. Before the acceptance of the ICCPR and ICESCR in 1966, the UN provided for the right to self-determination of peoples in the Decolonization Declaration of 1960.[139] Even before the two conventions entered into force, the General Assembly of the UN included the right to self-determination in its 1970 Declaration on Principles of International Law (cited in Chapter 1). More than twenty years later, the Second World Conference on Human Rights confirmed the status of the right to self-determination of peoples as a universal human right.[140] Since then, the right to self-determination of peoples and the prohibition on peoples to secede form a joint principle of international law and universal human rights. This means that as long as states respect the right of peoples to freely determine their political status and their economic, cultural and social development, there can be no question of their secession. In other words, the prohibition on secession of the state of which a people is part applies as long as that state conducts itself in accordance with the principle of equal rights and the self-determination of peoples as described above, and as such, has a government which represents all the people(s) in its territory without any distinction based on race, religion or color. In that case, no person, group or foreign power may encourage a people to secede. Up to now, the ICJ has only pronounced its views on self-determination in the context of more or less colonial relations such as the issue of South West Africa (Namibia), the Western Sahara, East Timor, and Palestine.[141]

The Palestinian right to self-determination is unique because the system of mandates of the League of Nations (LoN) did not contain any prohibition on secession, and actually contained a right of supervision to achieve independence as a "sacred task of civilisation".[142] In its 2004 advice on the legal consequences of the construction of the Israeli wall in occupied Palestine territory, the Court examined in detail the right to self-determination of the

Palestinian people. It states without any question that the recognition of the existence of the Palestinian people has no longer been a subject of discussion since the Oslo Agreement.[143] The Court adds that the construction of the wall impedes the Palestinian people in the exercise of its right to self-determination and that Israel is therefore violating its obligation to respect that right.[144] This places a special responsibility on the UN, because the organization has not been able to correct the errors in the LoN mandate for Palestine. This mandate has differed from other mandates in that the recognition of the historical link of the Jewish people with the Palestinian territories resulted in a serious neglect, by the LoN and the UN respectively, of the "sacred task of civilisation" vis-à-vis the non-Jewish communities, now actually expressly recognized as the Palestine people.[145]

The question now is what the status of the advice is, since it was taken over by the General Assembly of the UN. Is this a binding decision of the General Assembly of the UN or is it a recommendation 'only' which Israel and other states – in particular the USA – do not have to take into account? Whatever the answer may be, the advice certainly emphasizes the fact that the right to self-determination of peoples requires a more effective protection by the UN. This applies all the more because the right to self-determination has not been included in the civil and political rights which may not be deviated from during a state of emergency.[146] In fact, this is not in accordance with the significance of the right: to protect peoples against oppression and exploitation. The UN must provide peoples and states with a good possibility of arriving at a peaceful settlement of disputes about, for instance and as a last resort, secession.[147] The cooperation with peoples, whether they want to secede from 'their states' or not, is a large and subtle challenge for the UN of the future, particularly as to considerations which must be made with regard to the ways of achieving the colliding principles of the right to self-determination and the prohibition on secession as a principle of international law.

CHAPTER 5

On Rights and Responsibilities:
The Integration of Vulnerable Groups

5.1 The withdrawal of government in the global market

The ideological controversy between the rich(er) North, often defending the primacy of civil and political rights, and the poor(er) South, focusing its attention first and foremost on the primacy of social, economic and cultural rights is still a serious barrier to an effective human rights policy oriented at a decent society for all. This controversy reached rock bottom with the withdrawal by the USA in 1987 of its adoption of the 1969 landmark UN Declaration on Social Progress.[148] That move was inspired by the conviction that the government should withdraw in favor of the market. In the 1990s, following the collapse of states in Europe and Africa – Yugoslavia, USSR, Rwanda, Somalia – and the resulting massive exodus of refugees, the UN was confronted with the nearly impossible task of advocating the promotion of social progress as a matter of the highest priority in its international development strategy in a global society, characterized by an expanding market and a decline in the power of government. It seems a whim of history that the collapse of the command economy in the socialist countries in the 1980s belied the optimism of the then American president Ronald Reagan and the British Prime Minister Margaret Thatcher on the leading role of the free market in social progress and development. After all, since then the market has increasingly revealed itself to be an extremely efficient system for individuals and companies to reap the benefits and to burden the society with the losses.[149] This is clearly the price of a world market, which less and less holds out its 'invisible' hand to (all) consumers and more and more to producers.[150] The market economy might be just as threatening to the national and international division of wealth as the command economy was: "The writ of equality does not run the marketplace."[151]

The UN tries to make the best of things as the platform where states and NGOs draft programs of action aimed at a society for all, including vulnerable and disadvantaged groups. The previous UN Development Decades had already paved the way for this sort of truly civilized society to some extent with a gradual shift from the focus on the right of states to a New International Economic Order in the 1970s and 1980s, to a focus on the social integration of peoples and people from the 1990s, particularly as regards vulnerable and disadvantaged groups. These groups include those, who

- are vulnerable because of age, sex or handicap: children, women, elderly people, physically or mentally disabled people;
- have become vulnerable because they have committed a criminal offence: prisoners;
- are legally or actually disadvantaged because of their origin – refugees, migrant workers, stateless persons – or sexual inclination: homosexuals/lesbians.

The 2000 Millennium Declaration includes a chapter Protecting the Vulnerable, according to which the heads of state and government "will spare no effort to ensure that children and all civilian populations that suffer disproportionately the consequences of natural disasters, genocide, armed conflicts and other humanitarian emergencies are given every assistance and protection so that they can resume normal life as soon as possible. We resolve therefore:

- To expand and strengthen the protection of civilians in complex emergencies, in conformity with international humanitarian law.
- To strengthen international cooperation, including burden sharing in, and the coordination of humanitarian assistance to, countries hosting refugees and to help all refugees and displaced persons to return voluntarily to their homes, in safety and dignity and to be smoothly reintegrated into their societies.

- To encourage the ratification and full implementation of the Convention on the Rights of the Child and its optional protocols on the involvement of children in armed conflict and on the sale of children, child prostitution and child pornography."[152]

The Outcome Document of the 2005 World Summit condescendingly declared:

> We stress the right of people to live in freedom and dignity, free from poverty and despair. We recognize that all individuals, in particular vulnerable people, are entitled to freedom from fear and freedom from want, with an equal opportunity to enjoy all their rights and fully develop their human potential. To this end, we commit ourselves to discussing and defining the notion of human security in the General Assembly.[153]

A lack of social integration may lead to discrimination, fanaticism, intolerance and persecution. The harmful consequences are now widely recognized: social upheaval, separatism, micro-nationalism and ultimately civil war.[154] The 1994 UN *Agenda for Development* therefore considered the increase in productive employment as the most important remedy for poverty and social disintegration: "The laws of economics cannot be changed, but their social consequences can be eased."[155] The 1995 Social Summit committed itself to "promoting social integration by fostering societies that are stable, safe and just and that are based on the promotion of all human rights, as well as on non-discrimination, tolerance, respect for diversity, equality of opportunity, solidarity, security, and participation of all people, including disadvantaged and vulnerable groups and persons."[156]

According to the Program of Action of the Social Summit the aim of social integration is "to create 'a society for all', in which every individual, each with rights and responsibilities, has an active role to play. Such an inclusive society must be based on respect for all human rights and fundamental freedoms, cultural and religious diversity, social justice and the special needs of vulnerable and disadvantaged groups, democratic participation and the rule of law. The pluralistic nature of most societies has at times resulted in problems for the different groups to achieve and maintain harmony and cooperation, and to have equal access to all resources in society. Full recognition of each individual's rights in the context of the rule of law has not always been fully guaranteed. Since the founding of the United Nations, this quest for humane, stable, safe, tolerant and just societies has shown a mixed record at best."[157]

To summarize, it may be said that the UN Declarations of the 1990s, as well as the Millennium Declaration and the Outcome Document of the 2005 World Summit were aimed at preventing the withdrawal of governments in favor of the liberalization of the global market where it functions at the expense of the special needs of those who are disadvantaged or otherwise vulnerable.

5.2 Special needs of vulnerable groups

From its very beginning the UN has been conscious of the fact that the protection of the human rights of children, women, prisoners and refugees requires special attention. In the course of the years the UN extended this concern to children, women, elderly people, refugees and internally displaced persons, migrant workers, handicapped people and homosexuals/lesbians,[158] in addition to the national minorities and indigenous peoples that were dealt with in Chapter 4 of this book. The international arrangements for vulnerable and disadvantaged groups are aimed at preventing a situation in which legally or factually disadvantaged or otherwise vulnerable people do not enjoy the protection of universally recognized human rights because of their specific situation. The international arrangements for such groups began with refugees and migrant workers, while those supporting homosexuals are the most recent. In 1921 the League of Nations appointed the Norwegian Fridtjof Nansen as High Commissioner for Refugees to look after the Armenian, Greek and Russian refugees in Europe. He introduced the so-called Nansen passport as the travel document for refugees.[159] International attention for migrant workers dates back to 1926, when the ILO adopted the Inspection of Emigrants Convention. The ILO extended its concern to migrant workers in general in 1949.[160] The position of homosexuals came up only very recently in the cautious recognition of sexual rights as part of human rights.

5.2.1 Children, women, elderly people

At its very beginning the UN established the United Nations International Children's Emergency Fund to give aid to children who were the victims of World War II. Since 1953 UNICEF has had the broader mandate to "make the world a better place for children" by protecting children's rights and providing children with health care, nutrition, education, safe water and sanitation.[161] In 1959, the UN General Assembly adopted the Declaration on the Rights of the Child, in 1989 followed by the adoption of the Convention on the Rights of the Child (CRC).[162] For the purposes of the Convention, "a child means every human being below the age of eighteen years unless under the law applicable to the child, majority is attained earlier". State Parties "recognize that a mentally or physically disabled child should enjoy a full and decent life, in conditions which ensure dignity, promote self-reliance and facilitate the child's active participation in the community". The Committee on the Rights of the Child was established "for the purpose of examining the progress made by States Parties in achieving the realization of the obligations undertaken in the present Convention as well as the two 2000 Optional Protocols on the Involvement of Children in Armed Conflicts respectively on the Sale of Children, Child Prostitution and Child Pornography".[163] The 1993 Vienna Declaration launched the principle "First Call for Children".[164] In the Millennium Declaration the heads of state and government included in the chapter on values and principles the statement:

We recognize that, in addition to our separate responsibilities to our individual societies, we have a collective responsibility to uphold the principles of human dignity, equality and equity at the global level. As leaders we have a duty therefore to world's people, especially the most vulnerable and, in particular, the children of the world, to whom the future belongs.[165]

Moreover, they decided that from 2015, children everywhere, boys and girls alike, will be able to complete a full course of primary schooling and that girls and boys will have equal access to all levels of education. In addition, they decided to have reduced by the same date maternal mortality by three quarters, and under-five child mortality by two thirds of their current rates, as well as to provide special assistance to children orphaned with HIV/AIDS. Moreover, they pledged "to spare no effort to free all of humanity, and above all our children and grandchildren, from the threat of living on a planet irredeemably spoilt by human activities, and whose resources would no longer be sufficient for their needs".[166] The final document of the 2005 World Summit devotes special attention to the protection of children in armed conflicts and to advancing the human rights of women and children in every possible way. This includes bringing gender and child-protection perspectives into the human rights agenda.[167]

As early as 1946 the ECOSOC established the Commission on the Status of Women to prepare recommendations and reports on the rights of women in the political, social, economic and educational fields. Since then progress has been made, slowly but surely, particularly through the four World Conferences on Women, organized since 1975, most recently Beijing in 1995. In 1952 the UNGA adopted the Convention on the Political Rights of Women,[168] in 1979 followed by the Convention on the Elimination of All Forms of Discrimination against Women (CEDAW).[169] The 1993 Vienna Declaration devoted special attention to violence against women. In the same year this resulted in the adoption of the UN Declaration on the Elimination of Violence against Women.[170] In 1999 it was followed by the adoption of an Optional Protocol to the

CEDAW, providing for the recognition by a State Party of the competence of the CEDAW Committee to receive and consider communications by or on behalf of "individuals and groups, under the jurisdiction of a State Party, claiming to be victims of a violation of any rights set forth in the Convention by that State Party".[171] The Millennium Declaration emphasizes that the promotion of gender equality and the empowerment of women are effective ways to combat poverty, hunger and disease and to stimulate truly sustainable development.[172] To that end the heads of state and government, meeting at the UN Summit of September 2005, decided to actively promote the mainstreaming of a gender perspective in the design, implementation, monitoring and evaluation of policies and programs in all political, economic and social spheres, and to strengthen the capabilities of the United Nations system in the field of gender. Moreover, they stress in the Outcome Document the important role of women in the prevention and resolution of conflicts and in peacebuilding.[173]

The issue of the ageing of the population came up for discussion in the UN in 1978 for the first time. Initially there was little enthusiasm for a world conference on this subject and even less for proclaiming an international year for the elderly. Many states even went so far as to deny that there was an issue with regard to ageing at all. However, the UNGA finally approved the proposal to convene a World Assembly on the Elderly in Vienna in 1982.[174] The conference adopted a Plan of Action but did not proclaim an International Year for the Elderly. Subsequently, the implementation of the Plan of Action failed, largely because of a lack of funds. In 1990 the UNGA designated 1 October as the International Day for the Elderly.[175] In 1991 the UNGA adopted United Nations Principles for Older Person "to add life to the years that have been added to life". These principles relate to independence, participation, care, self-fulfillment and dignity.[176] On the occasion of the commemoration of the tenth anniversary of the World Assembly on the Elderly the UNGA adopted a Proclamation on Ageing and decided to observe the year 1999 as the International Year of Older Persons.[177] Thus the UN focused on the elderly for a whole year after 25 years, with the intention of creating a society for all ages on the very eve of the new millennium. Apparently this was enough for neither the Millennium Declaration nor the Outcome Document of the 2005 World Summit to breathe a word about the elderly or the sharp rise in the ageing population.

5.2.2 Refugees, internally displaced persons, stateless persons, migrant workers

As early as 1943 the allied powers, calling themselves *United Nations*, established the United Nations Relief and Rehabilitation Administration – UNRRA – to provide immediate assistance for the population in liberated territories and displaced persons. This was the start of the largest relief action in history up to that time.[178] In 1950 the UN appointed a High Commissioner for Refugees for the international protection of refugees.[179] This protection applied to victims of violations of civil and political rights – political refugees – and not to victims of violations of economic, social and cultural rights: economic refugees. This was due to the fact that the international protection of refugees originated in Europe, where it was not so much poverty as the fear of persecution and the threat to life that made people flee their country. The regulations for refugees of 1926, 1928, 1933 and 1938 related to refugees in Europe only. This also initially applied to the 1951 Convention relating to the Status of Refugees. The European states were, *inter alia*, eager to prevent the roughly 900.000 Palestinians fleeing from Israel in the years 1947-1949 from being able to claim the status of refugee by virtue of the 1951 Convention. Israel and the Arab states also shared this view, but for different reasons.[180] Israel argued that the Palestinians had left the territory voluntarily and were therefore not refugees but emigrants. For that reason they blocked their right to return, recognized by the UNGA in 1949.[181] Be this as it may, the 1951 Convention excludes from the definition of refugee "persons who are at present receiving from organs or agencies of the United Nations other than the United Nations High Commissioner for Refugees protection or assistance".[182] For the Palestinian refugees this agency was the UN Relief and Works Agency for Palestinian Refugees (UNRWA), established by UNGA in 1949.[183] The 1952 session of UNGA decided to postpone the discussion on the Palestinian Question indefinitely, leaving the matter to the parties themselves or the superpowers. After that, the role of the UNRWA prevailed in the debates of the General Assembly for quite some time, *i.e.*, until 1970, when the General Assembly condemned the denial of the right to self-determination, especially to South-Africa and Palestine. From 1967 onwards the term "refugee" also became applicable to persons who fled their country as a result of events which occurred after 1 January of that year.[184]

The increasing poverty in the third world made the rich first world afraid of extending the right to asylum to so-called economic refugees. The UDHR had recognized that right, but (western) states opposed its insertion in the ICCPR. Including it in the ICESCR was also out of the question. By way of compromise the UN then adopted the 1967 Declaration on Territorial Asylum, but did not succeed in adopting a treaty on this particular topic.[185]

Another historical debacle resulting in massive streams of refugees in Europe, *i.e.*, the civil war in several parts of Yugoslavia, again led the European states to focus on their asylum policy in the 1990s to the detriment of persons coming from developing countries.[186] The consequence was that they were less willing than ever to accept victims of serious violations of economic, social and cultural rights as asylum seekers. At the same time, the clear boundaries between political and economic refugees faded away:

Governments are urged to address the root causes of movements of refugees and displaced persons by taking appropriate measures, particularly with respect to conflict resolution; the promotion of peace and reconciliation; respect for human rights, including those of persons belonging to minorities; respect for independence, territorial integrity and sovereignty of States. Moreover, factors that contribute to forced displacements need to be addressed through initiatives related to the alleviation of poverty, democratization, good governance and the prevention of environmental degradation. Govern-

79

ments and all other entities should respect and safeguard the right of people to remain in safety in their homes and should refrain from policies or practices that force people to flee.[187]

According to the UNHCR the number of people at risk at the start of 2005 was 19.2 million. They included 9.2 million refugees (48%), 839,200 asylum seekers (4%), 1.5 million returned refugees (8%), 5.6 million internally displaced persons (29%) and 2 million others of concern (11%).[188] However, those people who left their own country to escape from political terror, armed conflict and human rights abuses constitute only a proportion of the global migrant population. While the available statistics are rather inconsistent, the number of people living outside their country of birth or citizenship appears to have increased from around 75 million in 1965 to a figure of about 190 million today. Nearly half are female.

Statelessness is a separate issue about which the international community appears to know little, though at the same time it is seriously concerned about the plight of the stateless.[189] Many groups that consist of both *de jure* and *de facto* stateless persons attract attention because of the problem of their rights as a minority or as refugees – think of the stateless Russian *minority* in Latvia or the stateless Bhutanese *refugees* in Nepal. Yet we must not forget that these individuals lack a(n) (effective) nationality: they are *stateless*. The total figure of people who are stateless worldwide – and it is a truly global concern, turning up sporadically or 'en masse' in all four corners of the world – is estimated at 11 million.[190] An issue of this magnitude, which is seen as a cause of both mass population displacement and violent conflict,[191] has not escaped the eye of the international community entirely. The 1954 Convention relating to the Status of Stateless Persons and the 1961 Convention on the Reduction of Statelessness provide the basic tools for addressing the matter. However, these instruments suffer from a very poor level of ratification, lack an effective supervisory mechanism and have even been described as "orphan conventions".[192] There is therefore much work still to be done in this field.

Migrants represent only 2.9% of the global population, but the socio-economic and political visibility of migrants, especially in highly industrialized countries, is much greater than this percentage would suggest.[193] A worldwide approach to involuntary migration requires a careful analysis of its causes. The rich(er) states are not highly enthusiastic about this as they are afraid that they will have to foot the bill. This explains that as yet no rich state has become a party to the 1990 International Convention on the Protection of the Rights of All Migrant Workers and Members of their Families.[194] The content of the Convention does not explain this reluctance, for it does not do much more then guarantee foreign workers the protection of their universally recognized human rights. Moreover, the extra provisions do not extend beyond assigning migrant workers the privilege of transferring their earnings to support their families, to participate in local elections in their state of origin and to enjoy equal treatment to the nationals of the state of employment with regard to access to education, housing, social security and cultural life. In addition, the Convention establishes a Committee on the Protection of the Rights of All Migrant Workers and Members of Their Families.[195]

In the Millennium Declaration the heads of state and government only decided to take measures to ensure a respect for and protection of the human rights of migrants, migrant workers and their families, to eliminate the increasing acts of racism and xenophobia in many societies, and to promote greater harmony and tolerance in all societies.[196] The 2005 Summit Outcome Document, however, clearly recognizes the important connection between international migration and development and the need to deal with the challenges and opportunities that migration presents to countries of origin, destination and transit. In 2006 the UNGA will hold a high level dialogue on international migration, "which will offer an opportunity to discuss the multidimensional aspects of international migration and development in order to identify appropriate ways and means to maximize their development benefits and minimize their negative impacts".[197]

5.2.3 Prisoners

In 1957 and 1977 the ECOSOC approved Standard Minimum Rules for the Treatment of Prisoners in respect of accommodation, personal hygiene, housing and bedding, food, exercise and sport, medical services, discipline and punishment, instruments of restraint, information and complaints, and so on.[198] In 1979 the UNGA adopted a Code of Conduct for Law Enforcement officers, followed in 1985 by the United Nations Standard Minimum Rules for the Administration of Juvenile Justice: "The Beijing Rules."[199] At that time, it also endorsed the Basic Principles on the Independence of the Judiciary and Human Rights in the Administration of Justice.[200] The 1984 UN Convention against Torture and Other Cruel, Inhuman or Degrading Treatment or Punishment is also of great importance for prisoners.[201] The same applies to the Principles of Medical Ethics relevant to the Role of Health Personnel in the Protection of Persons against Torture and other Cruel, Inhuman or Degrading Treatment or Punishment.[202] The Millennium Declaration and the Outcome Document of the 2005 World Summit do not 'waste' words on the treatment of prisoners. This might be understandable in the context of the Millennium Development Goals, but it is nevertheless rather alarming in the context of the fight against terrorism (see Chapter 2, par. 2.3). It should certainly not remain empty words that international cooperation to fight terrorism must be conducted in conformity with international law, including the Charter and relevant international conventions and protocols (see Chapter 8, par. 8.5.3).

5.2.4 Disabled persons

An estimated ten percent of the world population has some sort of mental or physical disability.[203] The majority – about 400 million people – live in poorer parts of the world. The UN justifiably considers that as far as possible the disabled should have the same rights as other people. Obviously this applies for the universally recognized human rights.[204] For that reason the central theme of the 1981 International Year of the Disabled was the equality and full participation of the disabled in society.[205] Since then many states have increasingly provided facilities to improve access for the disabled in streets and buildings. The 1993 Vienna Declaration clearly stated that the universality of all human rights extends to mentally or physically disabled persons without exception:

> *The place of disabled persons is everywhere. Persons with disabilities should be guaranteed equal opportunity through the elimination of all socially determined barriers, be they physical, financial, social or psychological, which exclude or restrict full participation in society.*[206]

In doing so, the Declaration called upon the UNGA and the ECOSOC to adopt standard rules for giving equal treatment of disabled persons and other people. These rules were actually adopted in 1993 as the result of the experience gained during the UN Decade for Disabled Persons 1983-1992. The Standard Rules on the Equalization of Opportunities for Persons with Disabilities are not compulsory. However, they can become international customary rules when they are applied by a great number of states with the intention of respecting a rule in international law (*opinio iuris*). They certainly provide an instrument for policy-making and action to persons with disabilities and their organizations. In addition, they provide the basis for technical and economic cooperation among states, the UN and other international organizations.[207] The 2005 World Summit Document recognizes the need for persons with disabilities to be guaranteed full enjoyment of their rights without discrimination and also affirms the need to draft a comprehensive convention on the rights of persons with disabilities.[208]

5.2.5 Homosexuals/lesbians

The 1994 Cairo Declaration, resulting from the United Nations International Conference on Population and Development, only discussed sexuality in relation to reproduction and health. It referred to universally recognized human rights in order to exclude sexual rights. However, the 1995 World Conference on Women (Beijing) referred to all human rights in order to include sexual rights. In doing so, it stated that women's rights are human rights. Moreover, the Beijing Conference inserted a broader definition, in which sexuality is linked to human rights:

The human rights of women include their right to have control over and decide freely and responsibly on matters related to their sexuality, including sexual and reproductive health, free of coercion, discrimination and violence. Equal relationships between women and men in matters of sexual relations and reproduction, including full respect for the integrity of the person, require mutual respect, consent and shared responsibility for sexual behaviour and its consequences.[209]

Some delegations rejected this compromise text and stated that they are against the recognition of homosexuality and that sexual rights only concern heterosexual relations.[210] The present disagreement regarding homosexuality prevented the adoption of the concept of sexual orientation in the 1995 Beijing Declaration for the very reason that this concept had not been used before because it provoked so much opposition.[211] The comments on the recognition "that women face barriers to full equality and advancement because of such factors as their race, age, language, ethnicity, culture, religion or disability, because they are indigenous women or because of *other status*" were also very significant.[212] The interpretative explanation of a number of western countries left no room for doubt that these states had preferred the expression "sexual orientation" to "status".[213] The discussion on the "right to be otherwise inclined" is a good illustration of the significance and limits of the UN as a center for the harmonization of actions of nations, in which, according to the Vienna Declaration, the significance of national and regional particularities and various historical, cultural and religious backgrounds must be borne in mind (see Chapter 3, par. 3.3.1). From that point of view, the many reservations and explanations with regard to the vote might be considered as positive as long-term developments in defining positions, instead of negative as a short-term undermining of the present impact of the Beijing Declaration. Be that as it may, it is not surprising that neither the Millennium Declaration nor the 2005 World Summit Outcome Document pursues the question of sexual orientation.

5.3 Human rights and responsibilities

The pursuit of a decent society for all and the fulfillment of the special needs of vulnerable groups in the global market lead to the question whether these aims can be achieved as long as the Universal Declaration of Human Rights is not complemented with a Universal Declaration of Human Responsibilities/Duties. The 1948 UDHR stated not only that everyone is entitled to a social and international order in which the rights and freedoms set forth in this Declaration can be fully realized, but also that everyone has duties to the community, the only way in which alone the free and full development of his personality is possible.[214] However, in the Cold War era western states opposed the idea of codifying human duties because they were afraid that totalitarian regimes might not protect universally recognized human rights under the pretext that citizens would evade their responsibilities. Moreover the West still identifies human rights first and foremost with civil and political rights. It is significant that the ICCPR not only established a treaty body to study reports of states parties on their measures to implement the recognized civil and political rights, but actually named it the Human Rights Committee.[215]

It is significant that in 2000 the UN Commission on Human Rights was able to adopt a resolution on human rights and human responsibilities/duties with only the smallest minority of 22 votes to 21, with 10 abstentions, and that its Sub-Commission on the Promotion and Protection of Human Rights was not yet able to meet the request for the interim study, let alone the complete study on the topic, as requested in the resolution.[216] The resolution recalled that human responsibilities were an integral part of the negotiating process leading to the UDHR and is an integral part of the Declaration itself, "but have since been ignored". It therefore stressed the urgent need to describe the specific responsibilities defined in all human rights instruments. Private initiatives to draft declarations on human duties did not fall on fertile ground either.[217] The Millennium Declaration and the Outcome Document of the 2005 World Summit refer only to the responsibilities of states. According to the Millennium Declaration:

> *Responsibility for managing worldwide economic and social development, as well as threats to international peace and security, must be shared among the nations of the world and should be exercised multilaterally. As the most universal and most representative organization in the world, the United Nations must play the central role.*[218]

In the Outcome Document of the 2005 Summit, the heads of state and government reaffirm that their common fundamental values, including freedom, equality, solidarity, tolerance, respect for all human rights, respect for nature and shared responsibility, are essential to international relations.[219]

It should be clear that the failure of the responsibility to respect life and not incite or legitimize hatred, fanaticism or religious wars can justify limitations to be determined by law to meet the just demands of morality, public order and general welfare in a democratic society, but can never violate non-derogable civil and political rights. This violation would really be a serious threat to democratic values and achievements in the field of human rights.[220]

The pretext that national security, which is in many ways so closely linked to the issue of the non-protection of vulnerable groups, as discussed in this chapter, prevails over and above even non-derogable human rights ignores the tried and tested structure of civil and political rights. On the one hand, this structure recognizes that in times of public emergency which threatens the life of the nation and the existence of which is officially proclaimed, states parties to the ICCPR may take measures derogating from the obligations under the ICCPR, but on the other hand, that some human rights may not be derogated from even then, such as the prohibition of torture or cruel, inhumane or degrading treatment or punishment. The 'war on terrorism' has regenerated the debate on the question of the absolute or relative character of human rights. (Also see Chapter 2, par. 2.3). In his book, *Warrior Politics: Why Leadership Demands a Pagan Ethos,* Robert D. Kaplan warns that in the future one should not expect wartime justice to depend on international law. For, as in ancient times, this justice will depend upon the moral fiber of military commanders themselves, whose roles will often be indistinguishable from those of civilian leaders.[221] He stresses the asymmetry between terrorism and international law in that terrorists "operate beyond accepted international norms and value systems on a plane where atrocity is a legitimate form of war".[222] In his book, *The Lessons of Terror: a History of Warfare against Civilians,* Caleb Carr argues in respect of humanitarian law that nearly every country unilaterally rewrites or rejects any provision of any agreement that stands in the way of its private pursuit of supposed or actual national security.[223] Carr rejects the idea that one cannot defeat the practices of terror without practicing such tactics oneself as a "fig leaf behind which naturally malicious, vengeful, and bloodthirsty characters attempt to hide their own barbarity".[224] His lesson from terror is that terrorism is "simply the contemporary name given to, and modern permutation of, warfare deliberately waged against civilians with the purpose of destroying their will to support either leaders or policies that the agents of such violence find objectionable".[225] Carr believes that the successful answer to the terrorist threat lies in the formulation of a comprehensive, progressive strategy of pre-emptive military offensives.[226] It is up "to military thinkers – historians, theorists *and* officers – to devise methods of uniting the acceptance of progressive war (and the attendant abandonment of total war) with the vigorous pursuit of American national security".[227] In other words, there should be no intervention by international lawyers, let alone international law. However, in its report on terrorism and human rights the Inter-American Commission on Human Rights emphasizes in no uncertain terms that ensuring human rights in all the above situations does not contradict the obligation of states to protect their populations from terrorist violence.[228] Ensuring that anti-terrorism initiatives comply fully with fundamental human rights and freedoms is "one of the crucial components for a successful campaign against terrorist violence".[229] It is rightly said that the "inflated language of war whether used by States or by Islamic militants should be deprecated".[230] Moreover, the ICJ left no room for doubt in its 2004 landmark advisory opinion on the legal consequences of the construction of the wall in the occupied Palestinian territory that "the protection offered by the human rights conventions does not cease in case of armed conflict, save through the effect of provisions of derogation of the kind to be found in Article 4 of the International Convention on Civil and Political Rights".[231]

The acceptance of a universal declaration of human responsibilities will leave no doubt that in a democratic society at the national and international level, the law subjects everyone everywhere in the world to limitations in times of peace and to derogations in times of public emergency, with the exception of the peremptory norms concerning some of the basic rights of the human person. These basic rights include for everyone everywhere in the world the right not to be arbitrarily deprived of their life, the right not to be subjected to slavery in all its forms or to torture or cruel, inhumane or degrading treatment or punishment, the right to be free from racial discrimination, and, for example, the right to freedom of thought, conscience and religion, even though that right can be subject to limitations.[232] We consider that an elaboration of human responsibilities will be in the interests of the protection of universally recognized human rights against violations in the name of an effective fight against terrorism, amongst other things, and will serve sustainable justice in the long run.

CHAPTER 6

A Just International Economic and Social Order

6.1 The promotion of economic and social progress

The aims of the UN, as formulated in Article 1 of the UN Charter, promote the economic and social progress of all countries. In addition, Chapter IX of the UN Charter deals with international economic and social cooperation. In 1945 this was viewed as an important condition for achieving stability and international peace and security. The promotion of full employment, development and respect for human rights are also part of the aims of this cooperation.[233] However, this is actually the only time that the word 'development' appears in the UN Charter. Therefore it does not deal in much detail with development cooperation. This can be explained by the fact that in 1945 the developing countries still hardly participated in international politics. After all, in 1945, 45% of the world population still lived under colonial government, including that of the Netherlands, *viz.* Indonesia, Surinam and the Netherlands Antilles. This changed rapidly in the years following the establishment of the UN, and as a result the number of members increased in the period 1945-1960 from 51 to 100 states. The right to political self-determination played a very important role in this process of de-colonization.[234]

In addition to de-colonization, the development of the countries and people in the South of the world soon emerged as an important new objective. The Third World (*Tiers Monde*) and developing countries – first described as 'underdeveloped' and subsequently as 'less developed countries' – became the customary terms for describing that part of the world.[235] In the late 1940s the UN was already establishing the first programs for technical aid and programs of grants. The World Bank, which initially focused

89

almost exclusively on the reconstruction of countries destroyed by WW-II in Europe and Asia, also hesitantly began to provide more aid to developing countries for the construction of infrastructure such as roads, airports and ports. In addition, the General Agreement on Tariffs and Trade (GATT, 1947) and the International Monetary Fund (IMF, 1944) gradually started to take into account the special problems of developing countries. However, the big changes only really started to take place in the 1960s, when developing countries started to organize themselves as a group and presented common wishes, if not demands.

6.2 The wealth of nations

The de-colonization of the 1960s and the discussion on a New International Economic Order (NIEO) following this in the 1970s took place more in the context of the balance of power between the Soviet Union and the USA on the role of the state in the production and distribution of welfare, than in a context of solidarity between rich and poor countries.[236] The American vision of the role of the state was governed from the start by a belief in the free market as put forward in the eighteenth century by Adam Smith in his standard work referred to above, *The Wealth of Nations*. In his view, states with the greatest degree of free trade were most enriched by foreign trade. After all, both states and individuals consider that they would be crazy to make something themselves if they can buy it more cheaply elsewhere.[237]

The USA took advantage of the victory in the First World War to restrict the colonial system with the introduction of the system of mandates in the LoN Covenant.[238] The victory in the Second World War led to international economic and social cooperation between states being founded from then on in the UN Charter on a respect for the principle of equal rights and the self-determination of peoples. Before the establishment of the UN, the USA had already taken the initiative during WW-II to regulate the post-war economic, financial and monetary relations by establishing international organizations which were intended to prevent depressions such as that which had occurred between the wars. After all, the crisis in the 1930s had helped to sow the seed for WW-II. Initially, the spirit of Roosevelt's New Deal determined the organization of world trade for the whole world. The 1944 Bretton Woods agreements formed the basis for the IMF and the World Bank, while the 1948 Havana Charter provided for the establishment of the International Trade Organization (ITO). The ITO aimed to link world trade to promoting employment and good working conditions. This proved to be too ambitious, particularly for the US, which therefore blocked the establishment of the ITO. The GATT, which was established provisionally, determined world trade from then on without devoting attention to employment or social development. The foundation of the new World Trade Organization (WTO) in 1995 did not change this, at least not so far (see below, par. 6.5).

6.3 Trade and development

The very first large UN Conference on development issues was organized in 1964 on the initiative of the developing countries, supported by the Soviet bloc at that time, and very much against the wishes of the western countries: this was the UN Conference on Trade and Development (UNCTAD). Before this, 77 developing countries – 75 plus two who joined subsequently – had met to prepare in 1963. It was also on the basis of their own studies, mainly from Latin America, that this Group of 77 demanded more economic independence for developing countries in international economic relations, higher (and more just) prices for raw materials, regulations for foreign companies, debt cancellation and sovereignty over their own natural resources ('control over their own land').[239] The Conference resulted in an interesting Declaration, with general and special development principles and the establishment of UNCTAD as a permanent UN organ which started to deal specifically with development issues along with the World

Bank, the IMF and the GATT.[240] Other conferences followed, often also accompanied by the establishment of further new specialized development agencies. Important examples of these include the UN Development Program (UNDP, 1965), the UN Organization for Industrial Development (UNIDO, 1966), and the International Fund for Agricultural Development (IFAD, 1976).

In the 1970s, the Group of 77, initially supported by the Organization of Petroleum Exporting Countries (OPEC), tried to impose much further-reaching changes. Making use of the rather unstable economic and financial situation in the West as a result of increasing inflation, growing unemployment and the unaffordable Vietnam War and strengthened by the high increase in the prices of oil and raw materials, the developing countries drew up a list of demands for an NIEO. Amongst other things, they demanded the establishment of more OPEC-like associations for raw materials, an increase in the participation of developing countries in international economic decision making, positive discrimination for developing countries in international trade, the compulsory transfer of technology and the exploitation of the deep seabed on the basis of the principle of the common heritage of mankind. Even though the NIEO was not established along these lines, a great deal changed in the policy of the 'established' international economic organizations.[241] The funds of the World Bank were extended, particularly also to the advantage of the poorest countries; on the proposal of the UNCTAD, the GATT introduced a Generalized System of Trade Preferences; in the IMF a number of additional facilities were established to restore a balance of payments in the developing countries, including 'Oil Facility Funds' for the control of sudden problems in the balance of payments as a result of high oil bills and extra credit facilities in the medium term (the so-called 'Witteveen facility'). The Lomé Convention, which the European Community concluded in 1975 with 46 developing countries in Africa, the Caribbean region and the Pacific Ocean (ACP countries), could also be seen in many respects as an NIEO treaty, as revealed by the unique contractual obligation to provide a specific sum of development aid, a guarantee for the stabilization of export revenue of certain agricultural raw materials (STABEX) and extra preferences for certain groups of problem countries in the ACP group.[242]

To some extent the UN Convention on the Law of the Sea concluded in 1982 can also be seen as a product of the NIEO age. The sovereign economic rights of coastal states were considerably extended across adjacent maritime regions with the recognition of a 200-mile Exclusive Economic Zone and an extended continental shelf. The new principle of the common heritage of humankind was applied to the deep sea bed and its natural resources (manganese nodules). In addition, the Convention contains various regulations on financial aid and transfer of technology to developing countries.[243] By now, several of these North-South instruments have undergone or have had to undergo thorough changes. Many of the regulations have been adapted to the demands of a market economy, particularly after the establishment of the WTO with its liberal orientation. As a result special regulations favoring developing countries have become increasingly difficult and have been subject to erosion. Secondly, a significant number of developing countries, especially many Asian and Latin American countries, have made significant advances. There is less and less point in formulating the same package of demands for them as for poorer countries, particularly those in Africa. In the third place, the extent to which many western countries are prepared to provide development cooperation is relatively small. Many of them suffer from 'donor fatigue', sometimes because of the absence of any direct visible results. The problems related to the environment formed an important new stimulus for development cooperation. In this the North and South have a shared interest in combating serious pollution, maintaining biological diversity and creating a healthy environment, even though the way in which this problem is experienced differs greatly from country to country. Not only are there big differences between developing countries and industrialized countries, but also between the industrialized countries themselves, for example, between Europe and the US.

6.4 Millennium Development Goals

In 2000, the Millennium Assembly of the UN General Assembly has accepted eight ambitious objectives for a policy on development at the national and international level, the Millennium Development Goals (MDGs).[244] For example, the number of people living in extreme poverty is to be halved by 2015. By then all children in every country should be able to follow primary education and the mortality rate of children under the age of five in developing countries was to be reduced by two thirds. Guarantees for a sustainable environment for 2015 must be created by integrating sustainable development in national policy, by reversing the loss of natural resources and by halving the number of people without access to safe drinking water. In this context the Millennium Assembly called for the conclusion of a "global partnership for sustainable development", a global cooperative venture with agreements on good governance, the development of an open and fair, predictable, rule-based and non-discriminatory trading and financial system, a solution for the problems of debt and the transfer of new technologies.

This Millennium Declaration is a document with target goals which cannot be assigned any binding significance as such. Nevertheless, for many states and organizations, the goals have clearly touched a sensitive spot. Politically they continue to receive a great deal of attention. For example, apart from the UN itself, even the club of the most important industrialized countries, known as the Group of Eight, repeatedly refer to them. Many western donor countries including France, the United Kingdom and the Netherlands, have also adopted the MDGs as the starting point for their policy on bilateral development cooperation. Clearly the idea has taken root that they should be less free of obligation than they might appear to be at first sight. It is also worth noting that a UN Summit on Development Financing in Monterrey in March 2002 reconfirmed the joint responsibility for aiming for sustainable development, as well as the 0.7% GNP ODA norm as part of this. Both the EU and the USA committed themselves to increasing their aid budget; surprisingly this also subsequently happened to some extent.[245]

According to the Director of the UN Millennium Project, Jeffrey D. Sachs, this is the age of investing in development. His *Practical Plan to Achieve the Millennium Goals* includes ten recommendations of ten taskforces dealing with a wide range of topics, the implementation of which is essential for giving globalization a human face with larger freedom for all. The reports of the taskforces focus on hunger, education and gender equality, child health and maternal health, HIV/AIDS, malaria, TB and access to essential medicines, environmental sustainability, water and sanitation, improving the lives of slum dwellers, trade, and, finally, science, technology and innovation. Sachs presents the results as "the triumph of the human spirit", which "gives hope and confidence that extreme poverty can be cut by half by the year 2015, and indeed altogether within the coming years".[246]

According to the report, the MDGs matter because they promote basic human rights – the rights of each person on the planet to health, education, shelter and security as pledged in the Universal Declaration of Human Rights and the Millennium Declaration.[247] In this connection investing in core infrastructure, human capital and good governance are essential because it accomplishes several things:

- *It converts subsistence farming to market-oriented farming.*
- *It establishes the basis for private sector-led diversified exports and economic growth.*
- *It enables a country to join the global division of labour in a productive way.*
- *It sets the stage for technological advance and eventually for an innovation-based economy.*[248]

Public investments and policies to empower poor people should be designed around seven broad clusters:

1. *Promoting vibrant rural communities, by increasing food productivity of smallholder farmers, raising rural incomes, and expanding rural access to essential public services and infrastructure.*
2. *Promoting vibrant rural areas, by encouraging job creation in internationally competitive manufactures and services, upgrading slums, and providing alternatives to slum development.*
3. *Ensuring universal access to essential health services in a well-functioning health system.*
4. *Ensuring universal enrolment and completion of primary education and greatly expanding access to post-primary and higher education.*
5. *Overcoming pervasive gender bias.*
6. *Improving environmental management.*
7. *Building national capacities in science, technology, and innovation.*[249]

The Sachs report also underlines that the successful scale-up of investment strategies to achieve the MDGs requires a commitment to good governance. The latter can be improved "by investing in other factors (such as education and health) that support overall economic growth and human capital accumulation. This two-way causation is highly important from the vantage point of the Millennium Development Goals".[250]

In addition, in the Sachs report the positive role companies can plan in relation to the realization of the Millennium Development Goals is strongly underlined, whereby the report singles out several angles:

> *Private enterprises can contribute directly to the Goals through core pursuits such as increasing productivity and job creation or seeking opportunities for service delivery through public-private partnerships. In all these activities, companies need to adhere to high standards of responsible corporate governance and citizenship. However, companies and their leaders can also take action to support the Goals more broadly, by contributing to MDG-based policy design, by advocating publicly for the Goals, and by pursuing various models of corporate philanthropy. In these ways, businesses can 'engage as reliable and consistent partners in the development process', as called for in the Monterrey Consensus.*[251]

As to multinational corporations, the Millennium Project report observes in the same positive sphere, that "when major multinational corporations decide to invest in developing countries, either to enter local markets or to build production platforms for global markets, they often foster local 'business ecosystems' with vertical supply chains and horizontal industry clusters. Such networking is invaluable for diffusing technologies and skills, bringing local firms into the formal economy, and increasing market opportunities for local suppliers (…). Some foreign investors, when provided appropriate incentives and adequate labor standards, can also place a special emphasis on labor-intensive production technologies that create dignified employment opportunities as an instrument to poverty reduction."[252]

The 2005 World Summit Outcome Document clearly endorses the Millennium Development Goals. Apart from this, the (large) Part on *Development* is largely repetitive of the earlier Millennium Declaration and the equally seemingly endless and largely non-committal Programme of Implementation adopted by the World Summit on Sustainable Development in Johannesburg in 2002. It also repeats the results of the G-8 Gleneagles Summit in the Scottish place Perthshire (July 2005), especially with respect to debt cancellation and meeting the needs of Africa.[253] In a way, it is useful to have the current UN development ideology formulated and somewhat updated but what counts now is especially implementation.

6.5 The role of the World Trade Organization and the International Labor Organization

In the initial years after the start of the WTO in January 1995, an intense debate took place on the issue whether or not the organization should give space to products made under bad labor conditions (like forced and child labor, and the denial of such rights as the right to organize trade unions and the right to strike). The debate is known as "the social clause" discussion. At the first WTO

Ministerial Meeting, in Singapore December 1996, it was already accepted that the issue is highly controversial, given the completely different views industrialized and developing states as well as employers and trade unions have on the topic, sometimes bringing employers' organizations in the developing states' camp and trade unions alongside states like the USA. Keywords of the discussion: protectionism, Western domination, cultural relativism, peremptory norms of international law. During the Singapore meeting, the WTO member states, adopted a document stating that they are committed to respect for core labor standards, but also that it is not up to the WTO to supervise their implementation. That should be done by the International Labor Organization (ILO). As the final document of the Singapore meeting says:

> We [the WTO Member States] renew our commitment to the observance of internationally recognized core labour standards. The International Labour Organization (ILO) is the competent body to set and deal with these standards, and we affirm our support for its work in promoting them. We believe that economic growth and development fostered by increased trade and further trade liberalization contribute to the promotion of these standards. We reject the use of labour standards for protectionist purposes, and agree that the comparative advantage of countries, particularly low-wage developing countries, must in no way be put into question. In this regard, we note that the WTO and ILO Secretariats will continue their existing collaboration.[254]

The quote can be seen as reflecting the type of 'solution' for the lack of consensus the WTO member states were prepared to think of. In the years to follow, the WTO and the ILO strengthened their co-operation, without, however, making substantial progress in the discussion on inserting human rights abuses in trade issues. As a matter of fact, until today the issue is still too tense, as successive debates after 1996 have shown. In the 2001 Doha Ministerial Declaration, the last one adopted so far,[255] the WTO member states "reaffirm [their] declaration made at the Singapore Ministerial

Conference regarding internationally recognized core labour standards", while they "take note of work under way in the International Labour Organization (ILO) on the social dimension of globalization".[256]

Despite this situation at the political/diplomatic level, the work of the WTO is in many ways relevant from a core labor standards' as well as a more general human rights perspective. So in the Preamble of the 1994 Marrakech Treaty establishing the WTO, it is stated that the WTO member states recognize "that their relations in the field of trade and economic endeavour should be conducted with a view to raising standards of living, ensuring full employment (...)". Obviously, there is a close link between these lines and, for instance, Article 11 of the 1966 International Covenant on Economic, Social and Cultural Rights (ICESCR), which states that everyone has "the right (...) to an adequate standard of living for himself and his family (...) and to the continuous improvement of living conditions". In addition, it is added in the same article that states shall take measures "to improve methods of production, conservation and distribution of food by making full use of technical and scientific knowledge, by disseminating knowledge of the principles of nutrition and by developing or reforming agrarian systems in such a way as to achieve the most efficient development and utilization of natural resources", thereby taking into account "the problems of both food-importing and food-exporting countries, to ensure an equitable distribution of world food supplies in relation to need". The similarities between the WTO treaty and this specific human rights treaty are striking.[257]

Apart from that, the WTO is simply bound to live up to international human rights law because core labor standards, like the ones related to the abolition of forced labor and (the worst forms) of child labor,[258] belong to the peremptory standards of international law (ius cogens), and because the WTO as belonging to the "UN family" – although in a somewhat distant manner, not having the inclination to establish a treaty-based relation to the UN, like for instance the ILO – has to live up to its standards. In addition, international law is increasingly 'horizontalizing', which means that organizations like the WTO cannot set themselves apart and neglect peremptory standards of international law anyhow, irrespective of being related to the UN or not.[259]

Apart from all this, states – WTO member states included – are urged in many international legal and quasi-legal instruments to directly work on such core issues as poverty alleviation and poverty related human rights violations, and to take structural measures needed in order to really make an end to it, or to reduce it at least to a substantial degree. See for instance Millennium Development Goal 1, target 1, which states that before 2015 the number of people whose income is less than $1 a day should be halved. The addressees are, no doubt, basically and first of all the UN member states, but there is also a role to be played by the WTO (and the ILO).

As far as the WTO is concerned one can primarily think of the Doha Development agenda, formulated at the 2001 Ministerial WTO Conference in Doha, Qatar. In the Doha Declaration it is stated that the WTO member states do "recognize the need for all our peoples to benefit from the increased opportunities and welfare gains that the multilateral trading system generates", that "the majority of WTO members are developing countries" and that "we [the WTO member states] seek to place their needs and interests at the heart of the Work Programme adopted in this Declaration".[260]

In the previously mentioned report *A more secure world: our shared responsibility*, at several places attention is given to the importance of an equitable international trading system, including the promises made by the Western world at the Doha meeting:

> *In Monterrey and Johannesburg, leaders agreed that poverty alleviation is undermined by continuing inequities in the global trading system. Seventy percent of the world's poor live in rural areas and earn their income from agriculture. They pay a devastating cost when developed countries impose trade barriers on agricultural imports and subsidize agricultural exports. In 2001, the World Trade Organization (WTO) Doha Declaration explicitly committed signatories to put the needs and interests of developing countries at the heart of*

negotiations over a new trade round. WTO members should strive to conclude the Doha development round at the latest in 2006.[261]

And:

In 2002, world leaders agreed at Monterrey that aid donors and aid recipients both have obligations to achieve development. The primary responsibility for economic and social development lies with Governments, which must create a conducive environment for vigorous private-sector-led growth and aid effectiveness by pursuing sound economic policies, building effective and responsible institutions and investing in public and social services that will reach all of their people. In return for substantive improvements in the policies and institutions of developing countries, donor nations agreed to renew their efforts to reduce poverty, including by reducing trade barriers, increasing development assistance and providing debt relief for highly indebted poor countries.[262]

As to be expected, in the Millennium Project report, also mentioned above, the issue of further developing the WTO system in order to make it contribute as much as possible to the alleviation of the needs of the developing countries is given a central place. The report discusses amongst other things the original mission of the multilateral trading system ("achieving more open and fair markets for the promotion of development")[263], and states that:

Throughout most of its existence, however, the trading system has mainly served the interests of developed countries. Developing countries, sometimes by their own decision and other times by explicit exclusion dictated by richer countries, have not been influential in the system's design. Moreover, most of today's multilateral rules have emulated to a great extent the policies, the practices, and most important, the laws and regulations of only a few developed countries.[264]

Furthermore, according to the Millennium Project report "the system is thus unbalanced against the interests of developing countries", while it "will give developing countries greater economic growth potential, a major stake in developing multilateral trade rules and disciplines and in pursuing trade liberalization, and more effective capacity to expand trade and defeat poverty".[265] That goal was, as the Report mentions, also "the motivation underpinning the Doha Development Agenda Round of trade negotiations launched in November 2001, at least according to the rhetoric".[266] The latter six words are, euphemistically said, a bit cynical, and rightly so. Did not the 2001 Doha Declaration say that the WTO member states will put the needs and interests of the developing countries "at the heart of the Work Programme adopted in this Declaration"?[267] In the words of the Millennium Project report the situation is, that the key deadlines are missed and that progress is practically nil on every issue contained in the Doha Development Agenda.[268]

Having said so, the report goes through all kinds of issues that so far blocked the progress that is so much needed from a developing world perspective: agriculture ("the biggest and costliest aberration"), the liberalization of non-agricultural markets, services ("a major sources of gains for developing countries"), preferences ("to be replaced with equivalent development assistance"), free trade agreements, trade facilitation for developing countries, trade related intellectual property rights, promotion of the export supply side in low-income countries, and special and differential treatment.[269]

In his reaction to both reports, it is not surprising to read that the Secretary-General to the UN shares the frustrations as to the (non-)progress made in the Doha Round: All of what has been promised has not been delivered, and "that failure is measured in the rolls of the dead – and on it are written millions of new names each year".[270]

In the document of the September 2005 Summit, the issue is, apart from several other indirect references to it all over the document, covered as follows:

- A universal, rule-based, open, non-discriminatory and equitable multilateral trading system, as well as meaningful trade liberalization, can substantially stimulate development worldwide, benefiting countries at all stages of development. In that regard, we reaffirm our commitment to trade liberalization and to ensure that trade plays its full part in promoting economic growth, employment and development for all.
- We are committed to efforts designed to ensure that developing countries, especially the least-developed countries, participate fully in the world trading system in order to meet their economic development needs, and reaffirm our commitment to enhanced and predictable market access for the exports of developing countries.
- We will work towards the objective (...) of duty-free and quota-free access for all products of the least developed countries to the markets of developed countries, as well as to the markets of developing countries in a position to provide such access, and support their efforts to overcome their supply-side constraints.
- We are committed to supporting and promoting increased aid to build productive and trade capacities of developing countries and take further steps in that regard, while welcoming the substantial support already provided.
- We will work to accelerate and facilitate the accession of developing countries and countries with economies in transition to the World Trade Organization consistent with its criteria, recognizing the importance of universal integration in the rules-based global trading system.
- We will work expeditiously towards implementing the development dimensions of the Doha work programme.[271]

The issue was again on the agenda of the WTO, at the Ministerial Conference in Hong Kong of December 2005, i.e., shortly before the finalization of this book. Hong Kong's Commerce, Industry and Technology Secretary John Tsang, who chaired the conference, outlined the achievements in the Hong Kong Ministerial WTO Declaration as follows:

- We have secured an end date for all export subsidies in agriculture, even if it is not in a form to everybody's liking.
- We have an agreement on cotton.
- We have a very solid duty-free, quota-free access for the 32 least-developed country members.
- In agriculture and NAMA (non-agricultural market access), we have fleshed out a significant framework for full modalities.
- And in services, we now have an agreed text that points positively to the way forward.[272]

This sounds like an impressive list, especially in the light of the failure of the Cancún Ministerial Conference of 2003. But chairs often see more positive news than the outside world. Future will have to judge. Anyhow, making progress here, be it in terms of small steps only, would mean that one is at least working along structural lines, in stead of, what's happening so often so far, mopping up the water, while the tap is open (as a Dutch saying goes).

6.6 International financial institutions

In his final report dating from 1992, the Special UN Rapporteur on the Realization of Economic, Cultural and Social Rights, Danilo Türk, wrote that despite the more recent visions of adjustment by the IMF and World Bank, these programs still appear far too often to be inspired by economic theory, rather than practical experience of the human, political, social and economic impact adjustment has had upon the more than 70 countries which have applied what is often referred to as a "bitter medicine".[273] In response, Joe Oloka-Onyango and Deepika Udagama wrote in their 1999 report about *Human rights as the primary objective of international trade, investment and finance policy and practice*, published for the Sub-Commission for Human Rights, that "although these institutions [the IMF and the World Bank] have come some way from outright rejection (characteristic of their position in the 1960s and 1970s) of the applicability of human rights standards to their operations, they still adopt a rather ambivalent approach to the notion of human rights. Thus, they selectively apply certain aspects and leave out others."[274]

And, they add, the IMF "is even more adamant that its operations have nothing to do with human rights, and its methods of work amply demonstrate this".[275] Admittedly, both authors also refer to some positive points, such as the emphasis of the World Bank on "social safety nets, enhancing the ability of countries to provide basic education and health care and the notion of 'good governance'", and the IMF discussion on "the distributional aspects of its policies with a view to the protection of the well-being of vulnerable groups",[276] but essentially they remain very critical about the human rights content of the activities of these two financial organizations.

The views formulated by Türk and Onyango/Udagama could certainly still be seen as being characteristic of the subject 'World Bank/IMF and human rights' in the 1990s. However, there appear to be some changes. For example, both organizations have now made the subject of combating poverty one of the spearheads of their policy, each in its own way, which is generally considered to be a serious contribution to a series of human rights for the most deprived people on earth. At the same time, the idea that combating poverty is good for human rights per se gives rise to many questions. For example: who exactly benefits from the programs for combating poverty: the macro level of society as a whole or the micro level of individual families? To what extent does the current approach of the World Bank and the IMF recognize that it is not only a matter of economic, social and cultural *needs*, but also of economic, social and cultural *rights*? With regard to this last point: is it conceivable that organizations such as the World Bank and the IMF, both as (special) specialized agencies, members of the 'UN family' should *not* be bound by internationally recognized human rights in the execution of their activities?[277]

In that respect, there are various different conflicting views. For example, the view of the present Secretary-General of the

United Nations, Kofi Annan, who clearly states that "the promotion of human rights must not be treated as something separate from the Organization's other activities. Rather it is the common thread running through all of them (...)".[278] Others consider that the special character of the World Bank and the IMF should be taken into account and that they should not be saddled with human rights obligations. However, the consequence of "Honoring the Charter" in the words of the above-mentioned Joe Oloka-Onyango and Deepika Udagama is that the World Bank – and *mutatis mutandis* the IMF – are in this way placed above any international obligations which the Bank may have by virtue of membership in the United Nations family. Such an approach could imply that any action permitted by the Bank's charter may appropriately be pursued regardless of the adverse human rights or other consequences that may result or the fact that it may offend the Charter of the United Nations or the Universal Declaration of Human Rights.[279]

We support the line taken by the Secretary-General that many human rights norms have a mandatory character and that these two (and other) financial institutions cannot withdraw from them; the World Bank and the IMF are specialized agencies which are linked to the work of the UN via 'Relationship Agreements' and on that basis are obliged to conduct themselves in accordance with the law and the principles of the organization of the United Nations. Quite apart from this, the two organizations are the 'property' of states, and these cannot morally or legally permit themselves to act in conflict with internationally recognized human rights either.[280]

6.7 The business community

In the last few decades a large number of businesses all over the world have stipulated in internal codes of conduct that they will observe human rights. In addition to the internal codes, there are also a number of international codes. The *Guidelines for Multinational Enterprises* of the Organization for Economic Cooperation and Development (OECD) dating from 1976, and in later years having been revised and supplemented several times, is one of these. Another important international code is the *Tripartite Declaration of Principles Concerning Multinational Enterprises and Social Policy* adopted by the ILO in 1977. With regard to the protection of human rights, this code states, amongst other things, that the parties concerned by this Declaration, including enterprises, should, in the light of the tripartite structure of the ILO respect the Universal Declaration of Human Rights and the corresponding International Covenants adopted by the General Assembly of the United Nations, as well as the Constitution of the International Labor Organization and its principles according to which freedom of expression and association are essential to sustained progress.[281]

It is often said that these codes are not legally binding and are therefore free of legal obligations. Quite apart from the question of whether this is correct, it can be said with regard to current legal developments that because of the mandatory character of many human rights norms, in combination with the concept of the horizontal operation of human rights, enterprises are also directly obliged to comply with human rights norms.[282] Examples include the prohibition on child labor, as well as the obligation to respect the freedom of religion of employees and to refrain from harsh treatment of employees who advocate the freedom of trade unions.[283] There are, however, hardly any international legal procedures for directly addressing enterprises with regard to their responsibilities. As a rule, it is the states which are addressed with regard to the observance of human rights and which pass any judgments on, in this case, to the companies under their jurisdiction. For the *direct* liability of enterprises, it is currently still necessary to think mainly in terms of national legal proceedings.[284]

In the context of the UN, a working group of the UN Sub-Commission on Human Rights examined the development of 'Universal Human Rights Guidelines for Companies' in recent years. The

'Guidelines' were presented to the UN Human Rights Commission, and thus also to the community of states. In 2005, the Commission decided to ask the UN Secretary-General to appoint a Special Representative on the issue of human rights and transnational corporations and other business enterprises with a fivefold mandate:

- *To identify and clarify standards of corporate responsibility and accountability for transnational corporations and other business enterprises with regard to human rights;*
- *To elaborate on the role of States in effectively regulating and adjudicating the role of transnational corporations and other business enterprises with regard to human rights, including through international cooperation;*
- *To research and clarify the implications for transnational corporations and other business enterprises of concepts such as "complicity" and "sphere of influence";*
- *To develop materials and methodologies for undertaking human rights impact assessments of the activities of transnational corporations and other business enterprises;*
- *To compile a compendium of best practices of States and transnational corporations and other business enterprises.*[285]

The Special Representative is expected, in carrying out the above mandate, to liaise closely with the Special Adviser to the UN Secretary-General for the Global Compact and to consult on an ongoing basis with all stakeholders, including states, the Global Compact, international and regional organizations such as the International Labor Organization, the United Nations Conference on Trade and Development, the United Nations Environment Programme and the Organization for Economic Co-operation and Development, transnational corporations and other business enterprises, and civil society, including employers' organizations, workers' organizations, indigenous and other affected communities and non-governmental organizations.[286]

For the time being, the Special Representative is given two years to do this.

Apart from this, the private sector also plays a prominent role in contemporary thinking on the UN and the way in which it can achieve its many different tasks. By way of illustration we refer to *In larger freedom,* which once again emphasizes that "States (...) cannot do the job alone", that "we need an active civil society and a dynamic private sector", while it is clear, according to the report "that the [UN] goals (...) will not be achieved without their full engagement".[287] It is the Secretary-General's partnership approach. As formulated in his recent report on this issue:

> *Partnerships are defined as voluntary and collaborative relationships between various parties, both State and non-State, in which all participants agree to work together to achieve a common purpose or undertake a specific task and to share risks and responsibilities, resources and benefits.*[288]

According to the same report partnerships can be loosely grouped under the following four functions:

a) *Advocacy: taking into account national ownership and leadership of the development process, the United Nations partners with business and civil society in order to advance a cause or to place an issue on the global agenda. Such partnerships leverage the reputation and networks of the United Nations and key stakeholders to promote vital development issues, including the Millennium Development Goals;*

b) *Developing norms and standards: the United Nations engages with stakeholders in order to develop common standards, norms, shared values and ethical behaviour that help facilitate market transactions and promote United Nations goals;*

c) *Sharing and coordinating resources and expertise: the United Nations partners with business in order to benefit from complementary resources and to coordinate contributions to key development issues, including humanitarian relief efforts. Especially important is the dissemination and sharing of existing know-how, knowledge and technology that often contributes to capacity-building;*

d) *Harnessing markets for development: the United Nations partners with business to support the development and expansion of sustainable markets locally, regionally and globally. There are two types of partnerships: partnerships that provide access to markets (producer networks); and partnerships that bridge or deepen markets (providing incentives for business to invest).*[289]

This passage is followed by, amongst other things, the observation that the private sector "brings resources to the table, including its networks, experience and skills, all of which have tremendous value not only for the partnership itself, but in many cases also for the United Nations, which benefits from a transfer of knowledge and skills".[290] In addition, however, the private sector can contribute to advocacy partnerships with the United Nations "not only through financial support, but also through its expertise (*e.g.*, in marketing) and its extensive contacts with consumers".[291]

The report *Investing in development; a practical plan to achieve the Millennium Development Goals*, written by the UN Millennium Project,[292] also underlines what positive role companies can play, more specifically in relation to the realization of the Millennium Development Goals. They can do so through many different channels, such as creating jobs, producing essential goods and services, and providing a larger source of tax revenues to the government, which then can be used for public investments.[293] The latter are, as the report says, "crucial for a 'private-based' market economy":

> *Every successful economy relies heavily on public spending in critical areas including health, education, infrastructure (electricity grid, roads, seaports), environmental management (national parks and protected reserves, water and sanitation), information and communications, scientific research, and land for affordable housing.*[294]

These observations fit into the UN Secretary-General's partnership approach.

6.8 About development and human security for all

According to the 1986 Declaration on the Right to Development, development is "an inalienable human right by virtue of which every human person and all peoples are entitled to participate in, contribute to, and enjoy economic, social, cultural and political development, in which all human rights and fundamental freedoms can be fully realized".[296] Although the Declaration is 'only a Declaration', and thus as such not legally binding, and although eight important states abstained from voting – amongst them (West-)Germany, France and Japan – and although one economically and politically even more important state – the USA – voted against, the Declaration is generally considered to belong to the UN human rights codex, as part of the broader concept of the 'third generation of human rights' or 'solidarity rights'. Even states who are more equal than others, cannot back out of these (political/moral/legal) obligations, unless they stick to a legalistic mindset. This by the way, is after 1986 often recognized, also by the states that voted against or abstained when the Declaration on the Right to Development was adopted,[297] although a state like the USA in later years kept resisting to the adoption of the right to development related resolutions.[298] Despite all this, the right to development still serves as the normative underpinning of the notion of 'a just international economic and social order'.

What has been said so far – *i.e.*, in the Chapters 3 to 5 – in relation to the standards related to an existence worthy of human beings all over the world, is in today's international arena often labeled as 'human security for all'. According to the United Nations Commission on Human Security, chaired by Sadako Ogata, former United Nations High Commissioner for Refugees, and Amartya Sen, Master at the Trinity College of Cambridge University, human security means protecting a mix of vital freedoms by empowerment: "to protect the vital core of all human lives in ways that enhance human freedoms and human fulfilment. Human security means protecting fundamental freedoms – freedoms that are the essence of life. It means protecting people from critical (severe) and pervasive (widespread) threats and situations. It means using processes that build on people's strengths and aspirations. It means creating political, social, environmental, economic, military and cultural systems that together give people the building blocks of survival, livelihood and dignity".[299]

Presenting its views, the Commission discusses such things as protecting people in violent conflict; protecting people from the proliferation of arms; supporting the security of people on the move; establishing human security transition funds for post-conflict situations; encouraging fair trade and markets to benefit the extreme poor; working to provide minimum living standards everywhere; according higher priority to ensuring universal access to basic health care; developing an efficient and equitable global system for patent rights; empowering all people with universal basic education; clarifying the need for a global human identity while respecting the freedom of individuals to have diverse identities and affiliations.

CHAPTER 7
A Sustainable Human Environment

7.1 Sustainable development

In a relatively short time, the term 'sustainable development' has gained a prominent place as an objective of the international community. It is interesting that the term also has a legal basis in a large range of legal instruments, including many environmental treaties, EU law and the treaty establishing the WTO. Sustainable development has also played a role several times in international legal proceedings, including in a dispute between Hungary and Slovakia before the ICJ about a dam in the Danube and before the International Tribunal for the Law of the Sea in Hamburg in disputes between Australia and New Zealand with Japan about unsustainable tuna fishing and between Malaysia and Singapore about the effects of land reclamation. Gradually, 'sustainable development' has become the collective term for the key objectives in the field of environmental protection, combating poverty/development and certain aspects of human rights.[300]

The great challenge now is how the policy in these three fields can be better coordinated and form a coherent whole. This sort of comprehensive approach has up to now been most clearly reflected, at least on paper, in the international law of the sea, and in EU law, and in relative terms, has done worst in international economic law. In its 'New Delhi Declaration on Sustainable Development' in 2002, the above-mentioned ILA tried to present seven key principles of international law in the field of sustainable development. These are:

1. the obligation on the sustainable use of natural resources;
2. the principle of fairness and combating poverty;

3. the principle of shared but differentiated responsibilities;
4. the precautionary principle and environmental impact reports;
5. public participation;
6. the principle of good governance; and
7. the principle of integration and mutual coordination.[301]

It is to be hoped that these principles will form a useful source of inspiration in the further development of law between states and transcending states in the field of sustainable development.

The above does not mean that environmental problems have not appeared on the UN agenda for many years. Even in 1957 there were concerns about the pollution of the atmosphere and climate change in the context of the International Geophysical Year. During the first UN Conference on the Law of the Sea in 1958, the problem of over-fishing already played a major role, while the term "maximum sustainable yield" was also introduced. In the 1960s there were constantly reports about the harmful affects of the use of DDT, population pressure and pollution, which prompted Sweden to propose convening a UN Conference on the Human Environment. This finally took place in 1972 in Stockholm just after the publication of the alarming report of the Club of Rome, *Limits to Growth* (1971).

7.2 The Stockholm Conference

The Stockholm Conference resulted in an important declaration with 26 principles for the good management of the Human Environment, usually known as the 'Stockholm Declaration'. In addition to formulating important principles of environmental law, the Declaration stated that economic and social development are essential for a healthy human environment. In that context, good returns for raw materials from developing countries and those countries' own processing possibilities were considered very important, amongst other things, for the good management of the environment. In addition, the Stockholm Conference led to the establishment of a special UN environmental organization, the United Nations Environment Program (UNEP) which was the first UN agency to have its headquarters in a developing country, *viz.* in Nairobi, Kenya.[302] Although the criticism of UNEP has often been stringent, the organization – like UNCTAD – managed to play an important role as a catalyst and coordinator in the field of environmental policy during the first twenty years of its existence in the UN. In addition, with its modest budget and relatively small staff, UNEP has undertaken quite a number of operational activities. These include the Regional Seas Program, now involving about 120 countries, and integrated environmental and development programs for the river basins of large rivers such as the Zambezi and the Mekong. UNEP also paved the way for various multilateral and regional environmental conventions including those concerning the ozone layer (1985), dangerous waste materials (1989) and biological diversity (1992). Despite all these activities, international attention for environmental problems, like those for development problems, appeared to ebb away slightly in the 1980s.

7.3 The Rio Conference

In 1983, the General Assembly of the United Nations established the World Commission on Environment and Development which soon became known by the name of its chairman as the 'Brundtland Commission'. The main task of the Commission was to develop long-term strategies in order to ensure a stronger position for the environment, as well as development in the year 2000 and subsequently, and how to achieve greater cooperation between developing countries themselves and between developing and developed countries for that purpose. In 1987, the Commission published its final report under the promising title, *Our Common Future*.[303] In this report the Commission explores the various environmental problems such as desertification, deforestation, pollution and global warming, indicating in each case the connection with the problem of underdevelopment and the conditions for development, also for future generations. It is well known that in that context, the Brundtland Commission used the term "sustainable development", defining it as development which satisfies the needs of the present generations of people without jeopardizing the possibility of future generations to meet their needs.[304]

On the basis of the Brundtland report, the General Assembly of the United Nations decided to convene a new UN Conference on Environment and Development. This United Nations Conference on Environment and Development (UNCED) took place in Rio de Janeiro, Brazil, in 1992, and is therefore usually simply abbreviated as the 'Rio Conference'. 176 UN member states participated in this, as well as more than 50 intergovernmental organizations, while thousands of environmental, development and human rights NGOs came together in the Flamingo Park, near Rio. The Conference also led to important results in various fields, though many still considered that it was too little. In the first place, a new Declaration on Environment and Development was adopted twenty years after the Stockholm Declaration. This 'Rio Declaration', which consists of 27 principles, formulates the right to a healthy environment and the right to development for present and future generations of mankind, sovereignty over natural resources with liability for cross-border environmental damage, the need to change unsustainable patterns of production and consumption, particularly in the industrialized countries, and a number of principles of international law such as precaution, early notification, consultation and cooperation. The coordination between development and environmental protection and the need for a comprehensive approach were constantly emphasized.[305]

In the wake of the Rio Conference there was a great deal of international and national activity. Many new environmental treaties were concluded. These include the Anti-Desertification Convention – a fervent wish of the African countries –, the Treaty of Århus regarding the access of citizens and NGOs to information and appeal procedures and the public participation in decision making on environmental matters, as well as protocols with more concrete obligations to the Climate Treaty – the Kyoto Protocol, 1997 – and the biodiversity treaty: the Cartagena Protocol, 2000. Despite all these activities in the environmental field, it soon became clear that the changes to which the international community had committed itself in Rio in 1992 were not really taking place. Despite all the treaties and protocols, CO_2 emissions only increased rather than being drastically reduced and there was no halt on deforestation, climate change and the loss of biological diversity. Furthermore, no (or very few) new agreements, let alone treaties, were being concluded in the field of development cooperation. In the context of the World Trade Organization, plans were developed to start a 'Development Round' on the basis of the so-called Doha Agenda (2001; see Chapter VI). This was to discuss the regulation of investments, trade in agricultural products, special and differentiated treatment for developing countries and the position of the least developed countries, amongst other things. However, up to now the negotiations on this have become bogged down every time. States guarded against – and still guard against – accepting concrete obligations.

7.4 Sustainable development summit: Johannesburg 2002

In 2000, ten years after Rio de Janeiro, the General Assembly of the United Nations decided to draw up a balance of the execution of the Rio package of measures in the field of environment and development. This was done in the light of the many new treaties and national legislation which had been established since the summit in 1992, the UN Millennium Goals, the Doha Development Agenda of the WTO and the Monterrey consensus on development financing, obviously as well as the many development and environmental problems which still appeared to exist in the light of the analysis. During the World Summit on Sustainable Development, Johannesburg 2002, held for the evaluation of the Rio objectives, it was therefore not so much a matter of introducing new norms, but rather a matter of observing those which had already been agreed and a better integration between environmental, economic and social development policy. On the proposal of the UN Secretary-General, Kofi Annan, the summit focused on five concrete subjects abbreviated in the acronym WEHAB: water and sanitary provisions; energy; healthcare; agriculture; and biological diversity. This time participation again took many forms, and it was noticeable that in addition to the colorful procession of NGOs, industry was now also prominently represented. It was strongly encouraged to conclude partnership agreements with several states (developing countries, donor countries), relevant international organizations (e.g., the World Bank) and NGOs concerned (e.g., the World Conservation Union), in order to achieve particular projects jointly, for example, in the field of access to water or the sustainable management of a piece of tropical rainforest.[306]

The so-called 'Partnership II Agreements', several hundred of which have by now been concluded, are an interesting result of the summit in Johannesburg and clear the way for new forms of sustainable development financing and the role of non-state entities. As such, they are more interesting than the political results of the World Summit: a short political Johannesburg Declaration on Sustainable Development and an extremely detailed Johannesburg Plan of Execution which formulates the main points of the international and national policy to be implemented. This Johannesburg Plan deals (consecutively) with combating poverty and sustainable food strategies, unsustainable patterns of consumption and production which are to be changed, a better protection and management of natural resources (including sustainable fish management) as the basis of economic and social development, the effects of globalization, health, small island economies, the special situation of Africa and an institutional framework for sustainable development. In fact, the Plan of Execution is not a real plan, but a long shopping list of policy intentions. As such, it does provide a good summary of prevailing views on how to combat environmental degradation, poverty and underdevelopment. However, the Johannesburg documents also conceal many differences of opinion. For example, the EU would have liked to make quantitative agreements with time limits on many subjects. This only succeeded for a few subjects: access to drinking water, the use of chemicals, the restoration of fish stocks and sustainable fishing. For others, such as the use of sustainable energy (where the powerful 'Texas lobby' and the Arab countries conspired), this was not successful.

The 2005 World Summit Outcome Document reaffirms the Johannesburg Plan of Implementation. It is interesting to note that the world leaders state that their efforts in this respect will include promoting:

> *The integration of the three components of sustainable development – economic development, social development and environmental protection – as interdependent and mutually reinforcing pillars. Poverty eradication, changing unsustainable patterns of production and consumption and protecting and managing the natural resource base of economic and social development are overarching objectives of and essential requirements for sustainable development.[307]*

The question of integration is possibly the greatest challenge in the entire project of sustainable development policies. How should the various and quite different lines of standard-setting and policies in the three relevant areas (development, environment and human rights) be linked to each other, adjusted to each other and formed into a coherent and not fragmented whole in the pursuit of sustainable development? To a certain extent the UN Convention on the Law of the Sea pursues such an approach of all questions concerning the management and uses of the seas and oceans, but also in this case there is still no supervisory authoritative body. How to improve the international architecture for sustainable development?

7.5 The international architecture in the field of sustainable development

The international institutional structure for the implementation of agreements in the field of sustainable development has been greatly fragmented. There is the United Nations Environment Program (UNEP), there are various treaty secretariats (climate, biological diversity, anti-desertification and various others, although they are all accommodated in different cities), there are many specialized agencies active with different parts of the problems of sustainable development, including the World Bank, the World Food and Agriculture Organization (FAO) and the World Health Organization (WHO). The coordination and cooperation between all these institutions, however, is weak.

There are regular discussions about the advantages and disadvantages of establishing a new World Environment Organization, or a World Organization for Sustainable Development, as proposed by the Brundtland Commission. Obviously there are many arguments against this, because there are already so many international organizations. Furthermore, it could be said that establishing a 'specialized organization' would be in conflict with other aims. After all, the problem of sustainable development should actually be an integral part of a general financial trade and development policy. From that point of view, the position of UNEP as a subsidiary organ of the UN General Assembly is not that bad in a formal sense. However, this does require a powerful policy organ which will make efforts in this respect and supervise the implementation. At the moment, this is missing. In practice, UNEP does not succeed in fulfilling this role.

The UN Commission on Sustainable Development (CSD), established after the Rio Conference with many expectations, has proved to be disappointing in many respects and has simply become yet another UN Commission. However, considering that the mission of sustainable development requires an organization of stature, this very inadequate international structure is, in our view, still the best one to endeavor to establish a new World Organization for Sustainable Development as advocated by the Brundt-land Commission. This would be able to place the problem of sustainable development more forcefully on the international agenda and could also form an effective center for the coordination of international environmental and development policy and operational activities. The UN Conference on Trade and Development (UNCTAD) and UNEP are too weak to take on these tasks themselves. They should be incorporated in this sort of new organization.

CHAPTER 8

The Security Council – A World Authority

8.1 The Council mandate

A number of important changes occurred after 1945 in the practice of the Security Council. Some of these are dealt with below, including the mandate and the composition of the Security Council, decision making in the Security Council and the term "threat to the peace", as well as the big challenges confronting the Security Council at the beginning of the new millennium.

The Security Council was established in 1945 as one of the principal organs of the UN. It was charged with the primary responsibility of maintaining or restoring international peace and security.[308] Unlike the General Assembly of the UN, the Security Council has always had a limited composition, on the basis of the view that in the case of a breakdown or threat to peace, the Council would have to be able to act quickly and impose its decisions on all the member states. Therefore unlike the LoN Council, the Security Council was assigned important competences. Apart from its role in the peaceful settlement of disputes, amongst other things, by negotiations and mediation, based on Chapter VI of the UN Charter, the Security Council was authorized to use enforcement measures if necessary (Chapter VII). These could consist of non-military measures such as trade measures, an arms or air embargo or diplomatic sanctions, or measures such as blockades or other operations by the air, sea or land forces of the members of the UN.[309] The other unique aspect, compared to the LoN Council, was that the Security Council could decide on measures with a majority of votes, although non-procedural decisions also require the agreement – or at least no vote against – of all the permanent members (see par. 8.2).

Since 1945, permanent Security Council members adopted the right to intervene with military force in member states which do not observe the binding decisions of the Council. These developments expose a serious shortcoming of the current UN Charter, viz. it does not provide for the peaceful settlement of disputes between (member) states and UN agencies, or between UN agencies themselves, about the interpretation and application of the UN Charter. This failure is all the more serious as there is an increasing tendency to ignore the broad interpretation of the UN Charter by the great powers, which can themselves prevent an amendment of the UN Charter from entering into effect with their veto.[310] The broad interpretation is justified by appealing to the constitutional character of the UN Charter. Unlike ordinary multilateral treaties, which can in general be interpreted restrictively, they argue that the explanation and application of treaties change, depending on the demands of the time, without an official amendment. This doctrine of so-called implied powers has also been embraced by the International Court of Justice.[311] This can benefit the development of the law, provided states and other interested parties – for example, nations which wish to exercise their right to self-determination – are able to protect themselves against the use of a doctrine of implied powers that is too broad and/or arbitrary.

In 1945, it was first of all a matter of maintaining the 'negative peace', i.e., maintaining the status quo and preventing the use of force in international relations.[312] When a state intended to change the status quo with the use of violence or was actually doing so, the Security Council would have to qualify this as a "threat to the peace", or "breach of the peace" and under Chapter VII of the Charter would have to recommend a ceasefire or certain enforcement measures, such as sanctions. However, because of the legal developments in the field of the right of peoples to self-determination and in the field of human rights, the General Assembly of the UN, closely followed by the Security Council, also reluctantly started to recognize that peace can also be threatened by the refusal of a state to put an end to a status quo which is considered intolerable, such as colonial domination, apartheid or the suppression of the people within the context of a state. This changing attitude arose from the notion that the 'negative peace' could not be maintained in the long run in the case of permanent and flagrant violation of human rights and therefore of 'positive peace'. For that reason the Security Council identified, amongst other things, the Apartheid regime in South Africa, the dictatorship in Haiti and the treatment of certain population groups in Rwanda and Sudan as threats to the peace, and ordered certain measures. The fact that the Security Council therefore assumed the right to characterize flagrant violations of human rights as threats to the peace, thereby opening the door to measures under chapter VII of the Charter, is one of the most fundamental changes in the direction of the UN after 1945.

8.2 Decision-making

The UN Charter provides that votes on important matters require a majority of 9 out of 15 votes, including those of the five permanent members.[313] At the time of the Cold War this all too often meant that the Security Council was not able to take decisions because of a lack of agreement between the permanent members. For that reason a practice developed by which a permanent member could also abstain from voting. In a number of matters, for example, the introduction of peacekeeping operations or the Middle East, the permanent members were admittedly unable to arrive at any agreement, but none of them wished to block decision-making totally by using the right to veto. In the first case, the Soviet Union was obstructive, and in the second case the USA is all too often obstructive. In those cases abstention is a method by which a decision can be taken while the abstaining permanent member does not bind itself politically to this decision. This practice of abstention was sanctioned by the International Court of Justice in its *Namibia* advisory opinion (1971) as a practice which developed in customary law and which changed the written rule of Article 27, paragraph 3 of the Charter on this point.[314]

In practice also another fundamental change took place: the adoption of the so-called *Uniting for Peace* procedure.[315] In 1950 the Security Council was only able to arrive at decisions in the case of Korea as a result of the temporary absence – the policy of the 'empty chair' – of the Soviet Union. This meant that the Council could identify North Korea as the aggressor in the conflict and undertake collective military action. The USA realized that upon the return of the Soviet Union, the Council would again become paralyzed as a result of the East-West conflicts and therefore took the initiative to give the UN General Assembly the right in those cases to order collective measures. In the case of a breach of the peace established by the Assembly, this could even be the right to order armed military action. The Soviet Union fiercely opposed this violation of the privilege of the Security Council (and its' veto right in the Council), but was voted down in the UN General Assembly by the then still pro-western majority. This *Uniting for Peace* procedure actually fails to correspond with the Charter and the primary role of the Security Council in matters of war and peace.[316] Nevertheless, the procedure has been applied a number of times: in fact, the first time was actually on the initiative of the Soviet Union itself. This was in the Suez crisis (1956), when France and Great Britain were in conflict with Egypt about the nationalization of the Canal Company and blocked the decision making in the Security Council. In 2003 the General Assembly of the UN applied the *Uniting for Peace* procedure for obtaining the above-mentioned advice of the ICJ with regard to the wall in occupied Palestine territory. This was in response to a veto by the United States regarding a draft resolution of the Security Council which judged the construction of the wall to be unlawful.

The right of veto is in itself an anachronistic and undemocratic right. However, it will also have to be seen whether abolishing it would be very wise. After all, abolishing the right could strengthen the temptation (even further) particularly of the US, to act outside the UN and the rules of the UN Charter, as in the case of the Iraq war in 2003. If the increasing unilateralism is the result of more democracy in the Security Council, this is a matter of putting the horse behind the cart. In principle, the current system of voting with the right of veto encourages intensive negotiations between the great powers, and at least the consultation of the non-permanent members in order to obtain a majority.

8.3 Composition

The Security Council was established in 1945 with eleven members: five permanent and six non-permanent members. The five permanent members are the same as they are now: Great Britain, France, Russia, China and the United States, though China was represented up to 1971 by Nationalist China and Russia was preceded up to 1992 by the Soviet Union. At the time that it was established, the UN was composed of 51 member states. As a result of the process of de-colonization, there was an enormous increase in the number of members: on the 15th anniversary of the UN in 1960 it had 100 members, at its 25th anniversary in 1970 it had 144, and on its 60th anniversary in 2005 it had 191. Proposals are put forward fairly regularly to reconsider the composition of the Security Council in light of the changing overall membership of the United Nations, to improve the decision-making in the Security Council and to restrain the use of the veto.

Although the Security Council has been able to function better during the period after the Cold War, despite its present composition one might add, the issue *representativeness,* and therefore also the *legitimacy* of the Security Council, is a major problem. It is clear that the Permanent Five are no longer representative of the modern community of states, let alone the international community. After all, they owe their seats to the balance of power at the end of WW-II and probably also to the possession of nuclear weapons. However, by now this balance has changed to an enormous degree. The Soviet Union no longer exists and in the eyes of many developing countries the Russian Federation is a fourth (!) western member amongst the five permanent members. France and the United Kingdom have surrendered a great deal of their former glory as world powers, and from an international point of view have now become primarily EU countries. At the same time, Latin America, particularly after the wave of democratization there, and Asia, because of its huge population and rapid economic development, have become more important. Proposals to greatly increase the size of the Security Council obviously lead to many questions, amongst other things, its' efficiency. After all, a larger number of members makes it even more difficult and time consuming to achieve a consensus. Nevertheless, for the more profound challenge of the representativeness of the Council and therefore for the legitimacy of the decisions of this world organization, it is inevitable that changes will have to be made. The Security Council must be seen and experienced to be acting on behalf of the international community.

On the initiative of the already independent Asian, African and Latin- American countries, a discussion started in the 1960s on expanding the number of non-permanent seats in the Security Council. On 17 December 1963, the General Assembly of the UN adopted an amendment to the UN Charter in order to extend the Security Council with four non-permanent seats, bringing it up to a total of fifteen.[317] There were no discussions at that time about extending the number of permanent seats. It is striking that this resolution was adopted, though France and the communist countries voted against it and the United Kingdom, the US, Portugal and South Africa abstained. This meant that (nationalist) China was the only permanent member to vote for the extension. Nevertheless, all the permanent members subsequently proved to be prepared to ratify this proposed amendment of the UN Charter in accordance with the requirement of Article 108 that two thirds of the members of the UN, including all the permanent members of the Security Council, must ratify an amendment. Thus on 31 August 1965 this amendment entered into effect and from 1 January 1966 the Council had fifteen members.[318]

The resolution provided that the ten non-permanent seats should be divided across the regions as follows: five for Africa and Asian states, two for Latin American states, two for the West European and other states (Canada, Australia and New Zealand), and one for the East European states. This has been the distribution key up to today. It is also worth noting that the 1963 resolution of the General Assembly of the UN stated that the "current composition of the Security Council is unjust and unbalanced".[319] It was recognized that extending the number of members of the UN required the extension of the Security Council, so that in this way, the Council would provide "a more balanced geographical representation of non-permanent members" and enable it to carry out its' functions under the UN Charter more effectively.[320] Thus the criteria of democracy, representativeness, legitimacy and effectiveness were linked from an early stage.

Since that time the composition of the Security Council has remained an almost permanent subject of discussion, but up to now this has not led to any new changes in the Charter.[321] In recent years there has been a great deal of speculation about the possible inclusion of Germany and Japan as permanent members of the Security Council, in view of their important economic power and high financial contributions to the UN. Because this means that the European domination of the Security Council would increase even further, it is fairly generally held that their inclusion would be acceptable only if another large Asian country (India?), a large African country (Nigeria or South Africa?) and a large Latin American country (Brazil?) also become permanent members at the same time, and a number of new non-permanent seats were created as well. This means that the Council would have five new permanent members and, for example, an additional four non-permanent members increasing the number of members to 24. It is quite clear that the choice, particularly of the new permanent members, would be far from easy, and up to now there has been no agreement on this. The most fervent opponents are the medium-sized countries such as Pakistan, Turkey, Italy, Argentina and Mexico. After all, as regards the permanent seats, they would fall outside the group. They have joined together on this matter regarding the Security Council in the so-called 'coffee table club'.

Another important and constantly recurring proposal is to replace the seats of France and Great Britain by one of the EU. In view of the reduced role of these two countries since 1945, and the greatly increased importance of the European Union, there is a great deal to be said for this. Furthermore, this would make a seat for Germany superfluous, while Japan could take the seat that became available as a result. However, not surprisingly, the British and French are fiercely opposed to this and with their right of veto – in this case also see Article 108 of the UN Charter – they can stop this sort of change for a long time. Therefore for the time being the composition of the Security Council will probably stay as it is now: the Permanent Five and ten non-permanent members who are elected on the basis of their contribution to maintaining international peace and security and on the basis of a fair geographical distribution.[322]

8.4 Reform of the Council as a Millennium Goal

In its' December 2004 report *A more secure world: our shared responsibility*,[323] the previously mentioned High Level Panel chaired by Anand Panyarachun made recommendations to change the composition of the Security Council with the aim of improving its' representativeness and effectiveness. In addition to a better geographical distribution, the Panel considered that seats should be allocated to the countries which contribute most to the UN financially, diplomatically and militarily. The Panel presented two alternative models for this purpose. Both models lead to a Council of 24 (rather than the current 15) members, with a distinction between four main regions in the world: Africa, Asia and the Pacific, Europe and the Americas. Model A argues for six new permanent seats (in addition to the current five), but without the right of veto, as well as three new non-permanent seats. Model B does not allow for any new permanent seats, but does introduce a new category of eight seats with a four-year mandate which is renewable, as well as one extra non-permanent seat. The Panel also argues for restricting the right of veto by introducing a system of advance indication of voting and agreeing that permanent members will never use a veto in the case of genocide or large-scale violations of human rights. Furthermore, the Panel suggests that the right of veto is not allocated to new permanent members, whether it is model A or model B that is adopted. The Panel did not allow for the possibility of proposing that the right of veto was taken away from the 'old' permanent members, but did state:

> (...) As a whole the institution of the veto has an anachronistic character that is unsuitable for the institution in an increasingly democratic age and we would urge that its use be limited to matters where vital interests are genuinely at stake. We also ask the permanent members, in their individual capacities, to pledge themselves to refrain from the use of the veto in cases of genocide and large-scale human rights abuses.[324]

As to the present composition of the Security Council, the Panel once again underlines that the 53 African states have no permanent seats at all, that the 56 Asian and Pacific states occupy only one permanent seat, while the 47 European states have three of them.[325]

In his *In larger freedom* the UN Secretary-General reminds the UN member states of the Millennium Declaration, where it states that all states are resolved to intensify their efforts "to achieve a comprehensive reform of the Security Council in all its' aspects".[326] Having said that he refers to the two models presented by his advisory High Level Panel and some of the core arguments behind it, asking the UN member states to use the 2005 Summit for a breakthrough on this issue, while adding that "if they are unable to reach consensus this must not become an excuse for postponing action".[327] The Summit, however, has not been able to make progress on this issue. The Outcome Document only states that the UN member states "support early reform of the Security Council as an essential element of our overall effort to reform the United

Nations in order to make it more broadly representative, efficient and transparent" and "thus to further enhance its effectiveness and the legitimacy and implementation of its' decisions", followed by the intention "to continuing our efforts to achieve a decision to this end".[328] For what is worth.

To our mind, the Security Council of the future should include important regional organizations such as the European Union and African Union as permanent members, in addition to a few large powers such as the US, the Russian Federation, China and Japan. In addition, elected non-permanent members should continue to exist in order to achieve the values of democracy, representativeness and legitimacy. The Council should not comprise more than 15 to 20 members. The right of veto cannot be abolished, but the current practice of self-limitation should be maintained. Ideally, vetoes should be pronounced by at least two permanent members for a majority decision of the Security Council to be opposed. Similarly, vetoes should only concern cases falling under Chapter VII. The Security Council should also have access to many more funds to be able to act both with 'positive measures' (comprehensive 'new style' peace operations), and to act with weapons inspections and sanction mechanisms. For an effective policy for the prevention of conflicts, and for post-conflict peace reconstruction, much more streamlined cooperation is required with the development organizations of the UN, such as the UN Children's Funds (UNICEF), the United Nations Development Program (UNDP) and the specialist organizations, such as the World Bank, IMF and FAO. This requires the strengthening of the hierarchical position of the Security Council as a world agency which not only stands above the states.

8.5 Big challenges for the future collective security

8.5.1 Pre-emptive self-defense?

Preventing the use of force in international relations is one of the basic principles of the UN Charter. The UN was established above all as an organization for peace. However, in the post-9/11 world there has been an increasing re-evaluation of the use of force as a means of international politics. It is often stated that 'blue helmets' alone are no longer sufficient, and that it should be possible to go on the offensive against certain regimes or groups of rebels, using military force. The right to self-defense is also considered applicable in combating terrorist groups which operate internationally, such as Al Qaeda. In the National Security Strategy of September 2002, USA President Bush demanded the right to pre-emptive military action, *i.e.*, an action of self-defense as a first step at an early stage. The question is what this re-evaluation of the use of violence means for the prohibition of violence in the UN Charter and for the acts of the Security Council.[329]

Article 51 of the UN Charter refers to the "inherent right to individual and collective self-defense in the case of an armed attack on a member of the United Nations". International law accepts that an attack such as that of 11 September 2001 falls under these terms, even though the wording in 1945 referred more to aggression between states themselves than to attacks by groups such as Al Qaeda. However, the question whether pre-emptive or preventive action against an expected new terrorist attack on one or more Western states would constitute sufficient justification to appeal to the article on self-defense (where "pre-emptive" refers to an immediate threat, when there is no time to be lost and a military response is the only option, while "preventive" refers to actions against threats which could occur somewhere in the future). With regard to pre-emptive action, international law provides the necessary space, but this does not apply for permitting preventive action. Obviously there is a grey area between pre-emption and prevention: when is something an immediate threat and when is it not? Do the airplanes actually have to be underway? We would think not, but good intelligence work must determine that something concrete is going to happen for pre-emptive action to be legally permitted.

In this respect, there is a difference in the approach of the USA and (what) other states (should do). The USA adopts the fixed starting point that attacks are being prepared, while other states should make sure that they prove that this is the case and when it is demonstrably proved, what is the best method of combating it. These states can choose between joining the "Bush doctrine" and continuing to develop an independent approach based on a respect for existing international law and acting in accordance with the situation on the basis of thorough intelligence work (possibly resulting in a pre-emptive approach). This "respect for existing international law" is not an argument for a strict legal positivism, because it is by far not clear that existing international law has been adapted to the challenges of the present age. However, it is an argument not to simply push aside international law – as it had developed both in good times and bad times – and casually reject it because it is obstructive. It is much more a matter of carefully considering what is permissible in pursuance of the law which applies now and determining equally carefully what other legal developments are necessary, given the current challenges.

In the words of Richard N. Gardner, Professor at Colombia University, following the American attack in Iraq, this concerns "neither Bush nor the 'Jurisprudes'", and he calls upon the USA to present concrete proposals for adapting international law, as well as makes the statement that the USA "needs to claim no more from international law", and that the rest of the world "should concede no less".[330] In this context, the above-mentioned High Level Panel report *A more secure world* is also interesting. It states that a policy based on permitting unilateral action against the many "perceived potential threats" from this world is full of risks, and as we conclude, will eventually erode the international legal order rather than advance it. For this reason too, the High Level

Panel also considers that the article in the Charter on self-defense should not be extended and that it is up to the Security Council to take a decision in matters such as these on the basis of Chapter VII of the Charter.[331] In his *In Larger Freedom*, the UN Secretary-General follows the same line: after subtly stating that there has recently been a significant difference of opinion regarding the question whether states may defend themselves preventively against latent or non-imminent threats, he states that there is no reason to look for a new authority outside the UN Security Council for the use of violence outside the framework of traditional self-defense. The views of the Secretary-General can be summarized by saying that the Council should first define the limits of current international law.[332] We agree wholeheartedly with this view.

8.5.2 Mediation and diplomacy

Quite apart from this, it seems self-evident that the UN itself should make every effort with regard to the peaceful resolution of conflicts and the prevention of conflicts. It is above all the mediation for peace in the form of diplomacy, the peacekeeping role and the 'new style' peace operations with regard to demobilization, the organization of elections, police protection, humanitarian aid, arms inspections and the supervision of human rights where the UN holds its relatively strongest cards. A military offensive 'peace enforcement' under the UN flag which must explicitly choose for one of the parties in the conflict is much less appropriate for the United Nations, particularly also in view of the large question marks which arise with regard to the strength and effectiveness of this sort of military UN action. (See the next chapter.) It would do better to limit itself to its own (diplomatic and related) activities and mandate the use of force in exceptional cases, if it is quite inevitable, to regional organizations such as the African Union or NATO or ad hoc coalitions of countries able and willing to take action.

8.5.3 Combating terrorism

Combating international terrorism also presents the Security Council with enormous challenges. Until recently, the Security Council virtually always addressed *states* to urge them to change their conduct in order to maintain or restore peace and security. Even when the Security Council did address non-state entities, this always concerned identifiable opposition movements within a state, such as the FMLN in El Salvador in the early 1990s or the rebel movement in Haiti. Even before 11 September 2001, the Security Council was involved in combating international terrorism, but at that time this always concerned acts which were – either justifiably or unjustifiably – attributed to a particular state, such as Libya, following the attack on the discotheque in Berlin and the bomb in the airplane above Lockerbie, Sudan because of its' involvement in the assassination attempt on the Egyptian President Mubarak, or Afghanistan and Sudan because of their involvement in the attacks of Osama bin Laden and his followers on the American embassies in Nairobi and Dar Es Salaam.

Since the terrorist attacks on the United States the world has been more emphatically confronted with terrorist threats by criminal groups or stateless individuals operating worldwide. The international law doctrine of accountability and state liability no longer apply to this.[333] This also applies for warlords operating internationally, who have established the unbridled plundering of raw materials in southern and western Africa. Therefore it is important to develop the international criminal responsibility of individuals for terrorist activities, and to ensure that the Security Council can also address companies and banks with regard to their international social responsibility, for example, to oppose the money laundering of black money or the certification of 'blood diamonds'.

In the review of the 1998 ICC Statute in 2009, international terrorism should be explicitly included as an international crime, in addition to genocide, war crimes and crimes against humanity. However, there is still no general, clear definition of terrorism, and this alone is an obstacle to the creation of a comprehensive multilateral treaty against terrorism. The matter of 'state terrorism' and the separation between terrorism on the one hand, and violence in the context of a legitimate struggle of nations for self-determination on the other hand, are important obstacles. In this context, the UN Secretary-General's clear position that no matter how noble the motives, any act can be qualified as terrorism when it concerns the considered and deliberate killing of innocent civilians with the aim of inspiring fear in the population or forcing a government to do something or to not to do something, was very brave.[334] In addition, there are great differences of opinion about the method of combating terrorism (a comprehensive or collective approach). The current negotiations have become totally bogged down and none of the parties appears to be prepared to make room for concessions.

Nevertheless, the UN member states are nearing agreement about a definition. The specific anti-terrorism treaties contain useful definitions of terrorism, focusing on terrorist activities within their particular scope.[335] One general definition can be found in recent Security Council resolution. This described terrorism as:

> (...) *Criminal acts, including against civilians, committed with the intent to cause death or serious bodily injury, or taking of hostages, with the purpose to provoke a state of terror in the general public or in a group of persons or particular persons, intimidate a population or compel a government or an international organization to do or to abstain from doing any act, which constitute offences within the scope of and as defined in the international conventions and protocols relating to terrorism, are under no circumstances justifiable by considerations of a political, philosophical, ideological, racial, ethnic, religious or other similar nature, and calls upon all States to prevent such acts and, if not prevented, to ensure that such acts are punished by penalties consistent with their grave nature.*[336]

If there is sufficient political will, it should be possible to use this as a good working definition. A great deal can be achieved by interpreting and applying the principles and rules of international law as 'living instruments', with the aim of responding appropriately to new challenges, as described above, in accordance with recently agreed interpretations of Charter terms, such as armed attacks or threats or violations of the peace. In addition, a more progressive development of international law and international cooperation is necessary in the field of combating terrorism, international criminal responsibility and international cooperation for development. If it is applied in a committed and comprehensive way, the current system of collective security and international economic and social cooperation, as contained in the UN Charter and in general international law, can be very important for combating international terrorism and be very useful in reining in and ultimately preventing it by tackling the source.

In the document of the September 2005 meeting, the UN member states strongly condemn terrorism "in all its forms and manifestations, committed by whomever, wherever and for whatever purposes", "welcome the Secretary-General's identification of elements of a counter-terrorism strategy", and stress "the need to make every effort to reach an agreement on and conclude a comprehensive convention on international terrorism during the sixtieth session of the General Assembly", i.e., before September 2006.[337] In addition, it is underlined that "international cooperation to fight terrorism must be conducted in conformity with international law, including the Charter and relevant international conventions and protocols. States must ensure that any measures taken to combat terrorism comply with their obligations under international law, in particular human rights law, refugee law and international humanitarian law".[338]

This relates mainly to the sensitive issue of keeping up (a high level of) human rights protection in times of the fight against terrorist attacks.

CHAPTER 9
Peace-Keeping and Peace-Enforcing operations

9.1 Categorization

News items and discussions in the media about peacekeeping operations are currently a daily occurrence. After all, modern peacekeeping operations mainly take place in the context of conflicts within states which are characterized by a great deal of violence and violations of human rights, in which it is mainly citizens who are the victims. At the moment – *i.e.*, Mid November 2005 – the UN itself is directly undertaking sixteen peacekeeping operations, *viz.*, seven in Africa, two in Asia, three in Europe, three in the Middle East and one in South America. Altogether almost 70.000 military and civil police officers from 107 member states are taking part in these operations, as well as more than 4.500 international and approximately 8.300 local civilian employees recruited by the UN.[339] In addition, many military personnel and civilians have been used in peacekeeping operations which are not led by the UN, but may or may not have been mandated by the Security Council.[340]

In the recent past the instrument of 'UN peacekeeping operations' has been the subject of a great deal of criticism. It was above all the UN peacekeeping operations United Nations Protection Force (UNPROFOR) in Bosnia, the United Nations Assistance Mission in Rwanda (UNAMIR) and the United Nations Operation in Somalia II (UNOSOM II) that have seriously undermined the authority and credibility of the UN. Therefore the UN often subcontracts out the new complex peacekeeping operations to regional organizations or coalitions of member states which are better equipped for them. This is above all because of the contemporary dominant conflicts within states for which the traditional 'peacekeeper' concept is not suitable.[341] The UN peacekeeping operations can be divided into traditional peace forces: peacekeeping (first generation), peacekeeping with additional humanitarian tasks (second generation) – which must be distinguished from humanitarian intervention – and peacekeeping forces in an environment with violence (third generation). The so-called Brahimi report in the field of UN peacekeeping operations – in detail discussed below – identifies the shortcomings in this. The problem of units that can be deployed rapidly and the trend of tackling peacekeeping operations on a regional basis are given special attention. With regard to the later, the report also refers to the recent developments in this field in Africa and Asia.

9.2 Traditional peacekeeping

In the last fifty years the UN has carried out no fewer than 60 peacekeeping operations, involving more than 770.000 personnel. The first, though little known peacekeeping mission, was the United Nations Special Committee on the Balkans (UNSCOB). This concerned a mission of 18 people which was established on 21 October 1947 by the General Assembly of the UN,[342] with the mandate to ensure that Albania, Bulgaria, Greece and Yugoslavia resolved their differences of opinion peacefully by means of normal diplomatic relations and good neighborliness. The United Nations Truce Supervision Organization (UNTSO), which is still active, is better known. This mission of observers has supervised the lines of the truce in the Middle East since 1948.

The more substantial traditional 'peacekeeping' concept dates from 5 November 1956, when the General Assembly of the UN provided a mandate for the United Nations Emergency Force (UNEF).[343] This peacekeeping force, which was meant to separate Egypt and Israel in the Sinai as a buffer, was based on principles which subsequently applied to most of the traditional first generation UN peacekeeping operations. UN peacekeeping operations must:

- be instituted with the agreement of the parties concerned;
- use violence only in the case of self-defence;
- be composed of troops who have joined voluntarily;
- be impartial; and
- operate under the leadership of the Secretary-General of the UN.[344]

These traditional peacekeeping operations are aimed primarily at controlling buffer zones with lightly armed blue helmets and using unarmed observers to observe violations of a peace agreement or ceasefire. The creation of buffer zones is meant to prevent parties previously engaged in hostilities from starting to fight again. This means that the buffer zone must be demilitarized and that the peacekeepers contribute to the cooling down of the conflict with their visible presence, and if possible allow for a solution of the conflict. The creation of buffer zones is based on the assumption that the parties will cooperate and will observe the agreed truce. The peacekeepers carry out their tasks without using heavy arms because they are not there to enforce the peace or to wage war. "They represented more authority rather than the force of arms", in the words of Shashi Tharoor, the special assistant of the Under Secretary-General for Peace Operations.[345] During the Cold War, traditional peacekeeping was usually the maximum that could be achieved. In general it was relatively successful, because the risk of escalation in that period was slight. There was a peace to be maintained and in the eyes of the parties to the conflict, the action was impartial because, unlike in cases of self-defense, no violence was used. The other side to this situation was that the dynamics were sometimes removed from the conflict, mainly in cases where buffer zones were created so that there was no reconciliation and no permanent solution could be achieved in the long term. The result is that traditional operations sometimes have to be maintained for decades. For example, the United Nations Peacekeeping Force in Cyprus (UNFICYP) has been active since 1964.

9.3 The extension of mandates

The traditional concept was gradually extended with important additional mandates which led to the term 'second generation peace operations'. For example, humanitarian tasks, such as the supervision of refugees when they return home, controlling the observance of human rights, disarming militias, the preparation and organization of elections, the administration of a country, the creation of a police force, clearing minefields, etc. form part of peace operations.[346] This is particularly the result of the emergence of conflicts within states which had not been foreseen when the UN Charter was drawn up. Initially the prospects for second generation peacekeeping operations appeared to be favorable because they were operations defined in time with a clear exit strategy, such as the end of successfully organized elections. However, subsequently the UN became involved in situations in which the conflict within a state had not yet been resolved and where the UN peacekeeping force was asked to create a situation which could lead to a solution. It was found that this concerned parties which had announced a ceasefire and signed peace agreements for reasons which had little to do with peace. Thus these groups caused a number of peacekeeping operations based on the principle of the agreement of the parties to fail. Angola and Sierra Leone are examples of states where peacekeeping processes were bogged down for years because certain people enjoyed a source of income from the illegal trade in diamonds, drugs or other valuable goods and were therefore able to mobilize opposition to the peacekeeping process.

In some second generation UN peacekeeping operations, the military component becomes less relevant and the civilian specialists on human rights, humanitarian law, constitutional law and elections have a predominant presence. The peacekeeping forces must primarily ensure a stable and safe environment which should enable civilian actors to do their work. In fact, the question which arises is to what extent these can still be considered peacekeeping operations. Operations such as the United Nations Mission in Kosovo (UNMIK) and the United Nations Transitional Administration for East Timor (UNTAET) are operating *sui generis*. In this case, the UN becomes the *de facto* authority and exercises the related powers. A great increase in the need for armed civilian police, which does more than merely monitoring the situation, but also has extensive executive powers, is one of the consequences.

9.4 Peacekeeping in surroundings with violence

At the start of UNPROFOR in Croatia and Bosnia Herzegovina in 1992 there were third generation peacekeeping operations. In fact, from the very beginning UNPROFOR was cautiously assigned the right to use any means to secure its mandate. As the *peacekeepers* were used in a twilight zone between interstate and intrastate conflicts, where they were attacked and the execution of their humanitarian tasks was obstructed, there were references to the possibility of allowing the peacekeeping force to enforce the peace and the peace agreements. On the basis of Chapter VII of the UN Charter, peace enforcement was put forward as a new mandate in peacekeeping. The tasks of UNPOFOR, the United Nations Operation in Somalia (UNOSOM I and II) and of UNAMIR, were carried out in an environment of active civil war between parties which did not consider themselves to be bound by any rules. This led to situations in which the traditional concept of peacekeeping no longer has any point. The Security Council then made the great mistake of giving the peacekeeping forces the possibility of using arms without making the necessary means available. However, carrying out enforcement with no more than the means of peacekeepers is an impossible mission.[347]

9.5 The Brahimi report and the follow-up to it

The failure of the UN in Bosnia, Somalia and Rwanda led to a review of peacekeeping operations in the UN. At the end of 1999 UN Secretary-General Kofi Annan published a report on the fall of Srebrenica, in which he was also penitent about the part he had played. In addition, he agreed to the findings of an external report on Rwanda. Both these reports clearly revealed the shortcomings of the UN. Following the 2000 Millennium Report, the Secretary-General established the *Panel on United Nations Peace Operations* under the chairmanship of the Algerian former minister of foreign affairs, Lakhdar Brahimi.[348]

The mandate of this panel consisted not only of evaluating the shortcomings of the existing system, but also of providing specific and realistic recommendations. The Brahimi report, named after the chairman, was presented to the Secretary-General of the UN on 17 August 2000, and contains a thorough analysis of the UN peace operations.[349] Without beating about the bush, the report acknowledges that the UN repeatedly failed to tackle the existing problems adequately, and that this will in fact not be possible without some drastic measures. Amongst other things, the panel criticizes the often vague mandates of the Security Council, sending out poorly armed and trained soldiers, the inadequate financing and numbers of personnel, the inadequate planning, and the mismanagement in the field. Although the report aims to maintain the principle of impartiality, it interprets this principle now as being a respect for the principles of the UN Charter and for the objectives of the mandate of the operation. In this way, it rejects strict neutrality, because it soon becomes a matter of a policy of concessions (appeasement) with regard to actors who do not observe the rules that have been agreed. In those cases, the report considers that violence is justified not only operationally, but also from a moral point of view.[350]

The main aim of the reforms which the UN carry out on the basis of the Brahimi report and of subsequent reports is to improve the peace operations as an instrument, particularly by increasing the role of the Secretariat in the analysis, design, organization and leadership of the operations and with a better preparation of the military and civilian means provided by the member states. Most of the reforms in the management and structure concern the Department of Peacekeeping Operations (DPKO). The staff of DPKO was extended by almost 50%, and the departments of the military advisor, the civilian police and training particularly benefited from this. The management and structural reforms have now been virtually completed. The implementation of the recommendations of the Brahimi report has now entered a new stage, in which attention is focused on concrete measures: the development of worldwide strategies for complex operations, improving the training of personnel, improving the use of earlier experiences when new operations are carried out, and strengthening regional means for peace operations, particularly in Africa. As expected, the report devotes a great deal of attention to the problem that personnel and equipment are not deployed rapidly and are not sufficiently available.[351] In fact, these problems are not new, because since its establishment, one of the most important shortcomings in UN activities has been the lack of military units that can be deployed when they are called upon. In fact, every UN operation has to be built up from the ground, which means that a great deal of valuable time is lost.

9.6 Rapidly employable forces

Peace enforcement using military means is increasingly delegated to an ad hoc coalition of countries which are prepared and capable of this as a 'coalition of the able and willing'. Examples include the International Security Assistance Force (ISAF) in Afghanistan and "the International Force for East Timor (INTERFET) led by Australia". Article 43 of the Charter had already provided that the member states would conclude agreements with the Security Council in which forces would be made available to the UN on a permanent basis. In fact, these agreements were never concluded as a result of the East-West confrontation. The Military Staff Committee provided for in the UN Charter which was to prepare and lead actions of the UN forces, was also condemned to become inactive as a result of the Cold War. The end of the East/West confrontation did not change this situation. Over the course of the years, the lack of an independent UN military force led to a series of proposals to resolve this gap (although on a more modest basis). The first United Nations Secretary-General, Trygve Lie, launched his idea for a police force as long ago as 1948 and suggested the establishment of a so-called UN legion in 1952. His successor, Dag Hammerskjøld, made several different suggestions for a UN military force in emergency situations. Following the establishment of the UN peacekeeping force for the Middle East (UNEF) in 1956, and the intervention in the Belgian Congo, the ideas about a permanent UN military force were rather forgotten. Up to 1989 the most that could be achieved were the operations of blue helmets in which the permanent members of the Security Council did not participate themselves.

The achievement of Article 43 of the UN Charter as envisaged by the founders of the UN did not seem to be very realistic. After all, no country would be prepared to write out a blank cheque in advance, entailing the risk that its' troops would risk their lives in a controversial UN operation. In order to speed up the deployment of units, several initiatives have been put forward since the establishment of the UN. One of these was the United Nations Stand-by Arrangement System (UNSAS), which was developed from January 1993. The system is based on national promises of units which can be deployed within a short period of time for peacekeeping operations in a UN context. Within a year and a half approximately 50 countries had made promises, so that in principle more than 70.000 troops were available to the UN. However, the system came up against a number of problems, such as the moderate level of preparation for specific military tasks, the lack of interoperability and the fact that the deployment of these units was always subject to national decision making. Thus in May 1994, the Security Council decided to extend UNAMIR but none of the nineteen countries which had appointed UNSAS units at that time was prepared to make a contribution.

In November 1994, the Dutch Minister of Foreign Affairs, Hans van Mierlo, and his Canadian colleague, André Ouellet, once again emphasized the importance of rapidly deployable forces in the 49th General Assembly of the United Nations. Van Mierlo presented the idea of a UN brigade which would be available to the Security Council. This would have to be a "full-time professional, at all times available and rapidly deployable UN Brigade to enable the UN to save lives in situations such as Rwanda".[352] Soon afterwards the Secretary-General of the UN came up with the idea of a rapidly employable military force in his *Supplement to an Agenda for Peace* in January 1995.[353] This would have to be composed of units from the member states which would be trained and equipped in accordance with equal standards, amongst other things. On the whole the response of the international community was rather lukewarm. For many people, making a military force subject to permanent international authority was still a bridge too far. However, in 1996, the UN Stand-By Forces High Readiness Brigade (SHIRBRIG) was established on a Danish initiative. This is a multinational non-standing brigade with a response time of fifteen to thirty days, whose deployment was limited to *peacekeeping* under chapter VI of the Charter, including humanitarian operations. By putting together units provided for UNSAS by a large number of countries, the response time of the UN was increased. Elements of SHIRBRIG were deployed for the first time in the United Nations Mission in Ethiopia and Eritrea (UNMEE) in 2000.

A recent development which is relevant for the UN was the initiative of the European Union with regard to the establishment of European rapidly deployable military forces (Battle Groups).[354] These will make it possible to fulfill the UN needs with regard to the rapid deployment of troops more quickly in the future, under Chapter VII of the Charter. A unit comprises about 1.500 military troops with the necessary support, and can be deployed after between five and twenty days for crisis management operations.

After a maximum of 120 days they are replaced by a regular peace-keeping force. With the creation of the EU Battle Groups initiative, the response times of units can be significantly reduced and the crisis management capacity of the EU and the UN can be significantly increased. Operation Artemis in the Congo in 2003 served as a model for this initiative, in which an EU peacekeeping force served to pave the way for a UN operation. Blue helmets had been stationed in the Democratic Republic of the Congo as part of a UN mission since 1999. Following a serious deterioration in the security and humanitarian situation in the region of Ituri, the Security Council authorized the UN to deploy an interim military force as an emergency measure. This military operation on the African continent made it possible to stabilize the situation in the Bunia region and provided support for the UN observers mission United Nations Organization Mission in the Democratic Republic of the Congo (MONUC). The mandate that had been given under Resolution 1484 (2003) of the Security Council to an EU response force consisting of 1.500 troops under French command came to an end on 1 September 2003. A strengthened MONUC then took over the peacekeeping operation.

The concept of the EU Battle Groups is reminiscent of the idea of 'peace enforcement units' (PEUs) which Boutros Boutros-Ghali put forward in his *Agenda for Peace* in 1992.[355] The PEUs would be deployed for restoring and maintaining a ceasefire. Under pressure from the Security Council, which considered that these units went too far, Boutros-Ghali subsequently abandoned this idea. On the basis of the recommendations of the Brahimi report, in the field of traditional peacekeeping, the UN now aims to develop a traditional 'peacekeeping force' within 30 days after the acceptance of the resolution concerned by the Security Council, and a more complex operation within 90 days. Two reforms were approved for this purpose at the end of 2002:

- *The stationing of 'strategic deployment stocks' (SDS) at the logistic base of the UN in Brindisi (Italy). This increases the reserves in the field of logistics, as well as the availability so that there are fewer delays. In the past, supply contracts still had to be concluded for every operation. The base in Brindisi now has sufficient stocks for a small-scale operation, while work is being carried out on further expansion.*

- *Strengthening the UNSAS arrangements, by improving the availability of personnel and reducing the warning times (the introduction of a new category of 'rapidly employable units', and on-call lists and the expansion of the system with teams of civilian experts as well as the civilian police).*[356]

Some of the new UN missions in Africa have already benefited from these measures. For example, the United Nations Mission in Liberia (UNMIL) for which the mandate was given on 1 October 2003, was already operational at the end of March 2004. Although this operation still did not meet the aimed for period of 90 days, it is an important improvement in comparison with earlier missions. This was made possible by using the SDS and a 'rapid deployment team roster'. The mission also benefited from the so-called *pre-mandate commitment authority* (PMCA), *i.e.*, the possibility of making funds available for preparatory activities anticipating a definitive mandate.

Nevertheless, the scope and complexity of current peacekeeping operations has arguably overtaken the Brahimi process. The Brahimi report was intended to equip the Department of Peace-keeping Operations to launch one large mission a year: in 2004 alone it was tasked to establish four. It also has to keep in mind that UN peacekeeping operations also include tasks in broad areas such as support to public order, protection of civilians, and public administration.[357]

9.7 Regionalization

9.7.1 Africa

At the regional level, the UN has particularly been active in Africa in recent years.[358] Currently the United Nations manages eight peacekeeping missions with more than 60.000 people. One problem with the peace operations in Africa is that 'the willing are not able' and the 'able are not willing'. In other words, it is mainly military units from developing countries which contribute to the UN operations in Africa.[359] The troops from Europe are involved mainly in the more robust operations, such as those in the Balkans, Afghanistan and Iraq. The peace operations in Africa are all complex, with a great deal of attention to disarmament, demobilization and reintegration. There is a clear need to train the military forces of African countries better and equip them for peace operations in their own continent. The UN recognizes that more coordination is also needed between different peace missions in Africa. This is not only in order to improve efficiency and reduce costs, but also because it is recognized that even internal armed conflicts often comprise a regional element and therefore require a regional solution.

In Africa, the UN has particularly depended to a large extent on regional organizations, but up to now these have not fulfilled the expectations as regards maintaining the peace. In recent years regional action has been particularly disappointing because of the lack of unity between the African states and the lack of inter-operable military means.[360] However, the European countries and the United States are putting pressure on the African countries to take responsibility themselves for resolving armed conflicts on their continent, where possible with regional organizations in coordination with the UN. In the spring of 2004, the African Union (AU) decided to establish its own peacekeeping force as well as establishing a security council. The size of the peacekeeping force will be moderate for the time being: 15.000 troops divided over five regional brigades. At the same time, the EU Committed 250 million euros to peacekeeping operations to be undertaken by the AU. At the G8 summit in June 2004, President Bush proposed that western countries should train 75.000 extra African peacekeepers who would have to be deployed by 2010, mainly in Africa. Bush asked Congress for 660 million dollars from Fiscal Year 2005 through Fiscal Year 2009 for the G8 *Action Plan for Expanding Global Capability for Peace Support Operations*. The 108th Congress appropriated just over 100 million dollars in Fiscal Year 2005 funding the action plan. The action plan focuses on sub-regional and regional organizations, particularly the AU. The G8 also suggest devoting particular attention to 'carabinieri or gendarme-type' units, which could close the gap between military and policing tasks. In addition, the African means should be expanded in the field of peacekeeping by coordinating existing training programs and concluding agreements for the support of transport and logistics. Between 1996 and 2002, the Americans trained 8.600 military personnel from eight countries under the 'Africa Crisis Response Initiative'.[361] In addition, the British, French, Canadian and Scandinavian countries also trained thousands of African peacekeepers. Nevertheless, the number of African militaries that are ready to engage in peacekeeping operations immediately has barely increased. In 1992 there were 10.300, in 2002 11.560.[362] Hopefully the AU and G8 plans will change this.

9.7.2 Asia: a role for ASEAN?

In Asia, initiatives have also been taken to introduce regional cooperation in the field of peacekeeping. Indonesia proposed the creation of a regional peacekeeping force in the Association of Southeast Asian Nations (ASEAN).[363] This proposal is part of an action plan to establish an ASEAN Security Community by 2020. Together with an ASEAN Economic Community and an ASEAN Social and Cultural Community, this Security Community should form an integrated ASEAN Community. The ASEAN Peacekeeping Force would operate on the basis of a *stand-by* arrangement. The institutions for carrying out peace missions should be operational by 2012. The peacekeeping operations of the ASEAN would focus particularly on the comprehensive and peaceful solution of the internal conflicts of member states. For this purpose, the peace-keeping force of the ASEAN would have to deploy neutral troops where appropriate in places such as Aceh in Indonesia or in the Southern Philippines, where the violence of the separatists continues. In addition, civilian organizations will focus their activities particularly on the stage of 'post-conflict peacebuilding'. However, not all the members of the ASEAN are positive about the Indonesian proposal for a regional peace force.[364] For example, the Minister of Foreign Affairs of Singapore, S. Jayakumar, declared that ASEAN is the wrong organization to fulfill a peacekeeping role. He emphasized that ASEAN is not a security or defense organization. His colleagues from Vietnam, Thailand, the Philippines and Malaysia also expressed their doubts about an ASEAN peacekeeping force. For example, there is a fear that this could lead to intervention in the national matters of a country. As the country in which the peacekeeping force operates must give its consent to this, this fear seems unfounded. However, the non-intervention principle on which the solidarity between the ASEAN countries is based has become an obstacle and often also a justification for a lack of action.

9.8 Peacekeeping of the future

9.8.1 Decisive factors for success of peacekeeping operations

The Under-Secretary-General of the UN Peace Operations, Jean-Marie Guéhenno, developed a sort of non-official evaluation framework on the basis of years of experience of peace operations with the UN, which can be used in the decision making on sending out a UN mission. In fact, there are ten critical factors which can make the difference between the success and failure of an operation. These factors are:

- The international community must make sure that it has correctly diagnosed the problem before prescribing peacekeeping treatment. Peacekeeping is not the same as war-fighting or enforcement. If the latter is required, then the UN is not the right organisation to run such operations. Before initiating a peacekeeping operation, the international community must be sure that it has made a correct diagnosis of the problem. After all, peacekeeping is not the same as waging war or peace enforcement. The UN is the appropriate organization to lead these last operations.
- The majority – if not all key parties to the conflict – must have reached the conclusion that they cannot achieve their objectives through military means, and thus are willing to stop fighting. The majority, if not all the parties involved in the conflict, must have come to the insight that they cannot achieve their aims with military means. Therefore they must be prepared to stop fighting.
- All the key parties to the conflict must consent to the UN's role in helping them resolve their dispute. All the important parties to the conflict must agree to the role of the UN to help to resolve their dispute.
- Members of the UNSC – its' permanent members in particular – have to agree on the desired outcome of the operation, and ensure it's a clear mandate. Members of the Security Council – in particular, the permanent members – must be agreement about the desired outcome of the operation and provide a clear mandate.
- Members of the UNSC have to ensure that the mandate is achievable. Achievable means that you cannot say the operation will protect thousands of civilians from slaughter, with only a lightly armed battalion on the ground. Achievable also means that you cannot authorise a mission with tens of thousands of troops, if you know that member states will not then come forward with sufficiently trained and equipped troops (or will not agree to pay for them).Members of the Security Council must be sure that the mandate is achievable. Achievable means that a lightly armed battalion is completely inadequate for an operation to prevent a bloodbath involving tens of thousands of citizens. Achievable also means that no mission may be authorised with tens of thousands of military troops, if it is known that the mem-

ber states will not make sufficient trained and equipped troops available (or are not prepared to pay for this).

- Speed of deployment is often critical. The credibility of an operation can be lost at the outset, if the troops, police, civilian personnel and/or money required trickles in a piecemeal fashion. The speed of development is often critical. The credibility of an operation may be lost from the start if the military units, police, civilian personnel and/or the required money arrive in dribs and drabs.

- The peacekeeping operation must be treated as part of an overall strategy aimed at resolving a conflict. This requires a myriad of political, economic, developmental, human rights and humanitarian efforts to be conducted in parallel. The peacekeeping operation must be seen and approached as a part of an overall strategy focusing on resolving the conflict.

- Many of today's conflicts must be seen from a regional perspective. What happens in Liberia impacts upon the prospects of peace in Sierra Leone. Similarly, the Congo is greatly affected by developments within the entire Great Lakes Region. Consequently, political and economic attention must be stepped up within the region or sub-region concerned, in order to ensure that the progress made in the country to which the operation has deployed does not get undermined by problems across its borders. Many of the contemporary conflicts should be seen from a regional perspective. What happens in Liberia has an influence on the prospects for peace in Sierra Leone. At the same time, the situation in the Congo is influenced to a great extent by the developments in the whole of the Great Lakes area. As a result, attention must be devoted both politically and economically to the whole region or sub-region concerned. This is to ensure that the progress which is made in the country where the operation takes place is not undermined by problems across the borders.

- The international community has to be prepared to stay the course. The wounds of war rarely heal overnight, particularly when so much blood has been shed. It takes time for former warring factions to regain each other's trust. The international community must be prepared for a long-term process. It takes a long time for the war wounds to heal after the end of the conflict, particularly when a great

deal of blood has been shed. It takes a lot of time before former com-
bating parties trust each other again.

- *International civil servants who work for the UN – whether in the*
  field or at headquarters – have to perform the tasks entrusted to
  them with professionalism, competence and integrity. International
  civil servants working for the UN – whether in the field or at head-
  quarters – must carry out tasks entrusted to them in good faith in a
  professional and competent way.[365]

It is partly as a result of the recommendations of the Brahimi
report that the UN has been better able to lead peace operations in
recent years. These are concerned primarily with first and second
generation peace operations. In many cases, the operations which
are undertaken by the UN will have access to more robust military
units and have greater authority to use violence than was the case
in the past. In addition, there is still a need for traditional peace
operations such as those in Cyprus, Kashmir and the Middle East.
The UN peace operation UNMEE, between Ethiopia and Eritrea,
underlines this once again. For the time being, the UN will not be
able to lead any peace enforcement operations. Since the mid-
1990s it has become established practice that these are contracted
out to regional organizations or 'coalitions of the willing' under
the leadership of a state, the 'lead nation'. Finally, the sovereignty
of the UN member states and the related lack of willingness to
accept the authority of a state above them will continue to be the
main obstacles or time being to the establishment of a UN Stand-
by Force.

9.8.2 Peacekeeping operations in the 2005 Summit Document

It is interesting, although maybe not surprisingly, to see that
almost all of the above mentioned elements of the broader concept of peacekeeping do come back in the 2005 September Summit document. This speaks of "improvements made in recent
years in United Nations peacekeeping, including the deployment

of integrated missions in complex situations, and stressing the need to mount operations with adequate capacity to counter hostilities and fulfill effectively their mandates", but also of urging "further development of proposals for enhanced rapidly deployable capacities to reinforce peacekeeping operations in crises".[366] In addition, the states do endorse "the creation of an initial operating capability for a standing police capacity to provide coherent, effective and responsive start-up capability for the policing component of the United Nations peacekeeping missions and to assist existing missions through the provision of advice and expertise".[367] Further to that the UN member states once again recognize the importance of contributions to peace and security by regional organizations and of forging predictable partnerships and arrangements between the United Nations and regional organizations, thereby "noting in particular, given the special needs of Africa, the importance of a strong African Union":

a) *We support the efforts of the European Union and other regional entities to develop capacities such as for rapid deployment, standby and bridging arrangements;*

b) *We support the development and implementation of a ten-year plan for capacity-building with the African Union.*[368]

In addition, issues such as the illicit trade in small arms and light weapons, the ban of anti-personnel mines, and sexual exploitation and abuse by United Nations peacekeeping personnel are touched upon.[369]

The core of the 2005 document, however, relates to the establishment of a Peacebuilding Commission:

Emphasizing the need for a coordinated, coherent and integrated approach to post-conflict peacebuilding and reconciliation with a view to achieving sustainable peace, recognizing the need for a dedicated institutional mechanism to address the special needs of countries emerging from conflict towards recovery, reintegration and reconstruction and to assist them in laying the foundation for sus-

tainable development, and recognizing the vital role of the United
Nations in that regard, we decide to establish a Peacebuilding Com-
mission as an intergovernmental advisory body.[370]

According to the document the main purpose of the Peacebuilding Commission is "to bring together all relevant actors to marshal resources and to advise on and propose integrated strategies for post-conflict peacebuilding and recovery", thereby focusing "attention on the reconstruction and institution-building efforts necessary for recovery from conflict and support the development of integrated strategies in order to lay the foundation for sustainable development".[371] In addition, it should "provide recommendations and information to improve the coordination of all relevant actors within and outside the United Nations, develop best practices, help to ensure predictable financing for early recovery activities and extend the period of attention by the international community to post-conflict recovery".[372]

Further to that, the Peacebuilding Commission should meet in various configurations. For that reason the so-called "country-specific meetings of the Commission" should representatives from:

a) *The country under consideration;*
b) *Countries in the region engaged in the post-conflict process and other countries that are involved in relief efforts and/or political dialogue, as well as relevant regional and subregional organizations;*
c) *The major financial, troop and civilian police contributors involved in the recovery effort;*
d) *The senior United Nations representative in the field and other relevant United Nations representatives;*
e) *Such regional and international financial institutions as may be relevant.*[373]

Acting so, the Commission can operate as tailor-made as possible. And in order to gain full support, including by those who are responsible for the financial parts of the reconstruction of countries after conflict, among them "top providers of assessed contributions to the United Nations budgets and voluntary contributions to the United Nations funds, programs and agencies, including the standing Peacebuilding Fund", and "top providers of military personnel and civilian police to United Nations missions (...)", and "representatives from the World Bank, the International Monetary Fund and other institutional donors".[374] In addition, the UN Secretary-General is requested " to establish a multi-year standing Peacebuilding Fund for post-conflict peacebuilding, funded by voluntary contributions (...)", which can be used for the "immediate release of resources needed to launch peacebuilding activities and the availability of appropriate financing for recovery".[375] Having been formulated that way, the Commission and Fund can be seen addressing need of today's world: recovery after disasters like longstanding inter- as well as intra-state (civil) wars. Apart from situations linked to underdevelopment, which by the way often overlap the ones identified under the label of 'peacebuilding', these situations are the worst from the perspective of innocent civilians and the impossibility of reconstructing their lives into lives worthy of human beings.

CHAPTER 10

Enforcement of International Law

10.1 Humanitarian interventions and the responsibility to protect

10.1.1 The principle of necessity

The phenomenon of humanitarian interventions – *i.e.*, the use of military violence in order to do something about gross violations of human rights, whether or not authorized by the Security Council – deserves to be discussed separately. After all, this concerns a collision between two fundamental and extremely important UN principles: a respect for the sovereignty of states and the obligation to protect human rights. In the last few decades, numerous articles, reports and books have been written on this subject, also by the authors of this contribution, in particular with regard to the importance ascribed to these two starting points, both in an abstract sense and in specific situations.[376] In his doctoral dissertation, Gelijn Molier discusses the underlying questions of international law and examines in detail some of the practical examples from the period both before and during the period of the UN, with a great deal of attention for the classic examples such as the intervention of India in East Pakistan in 1971, of Tanzania in Uganda in 1979, of a number of Western states in North Iraq in 1991, and of NATO in Kosovo in 1999. On this basis he concludes that there is no question of a rule of customary international law which can justify an intervention outside the UN Charter, and that it seems sensible to appeal to the necessity principle in these cases.[377] The 'necessity principle' relates to gross violations of human rights, basically at the level of a (risk of) genocide or systematic crimes against humanity, and the need as well as the right to do something when the official UN system does not react. Obviously the question is when the need is so great that the law – in this case, the UN Charter – should be ignored. The law dictates that the

Security Council is the competent organ to intervene in the case of a threat to the peace, breach of the peace or act of aggression, that it must decide with a majority of nine of the fifteen votes, including the five members with a veto which may certainly not vote against (see par. 8.2), and that an intervention is not possible if the Council is not able to make this sort of decision.[378]

10.1.2 A legal basis for unauthorized humanitarian intervention?

In their 2000 Advisory report on *Humanitarian Intervention*[379] the Dutch Advisory Council on International Affairs and the Advisory Committee on Issues of Public International Law state that current international law provides no legal basis for an intervention for humanitarian purposes outside the United Nations framework, and that such a legal basis is not (yet) emerging either. Nevertheless, both advisory bodies believe that that is no reason to stop thinking. How about situations in which the UN Security Council is paralyzed, while a genocide takes place or is about to start? Can one then accept to be a 'silent bystander'?

In their report both advisory bodies, amongst other things, address the question whether or not the concept of humanitarian intervention can be more clearly formulated in terms of international law. In doing so, they refer to customary international law, which "acknowledges that there are circumstances in which the wrongfulness of certain actions by states is precluded or in which states cannot be held legally responsible for such actions – a principle summed up in the saying 'necessity knows no law'. The 'justificatory-grounds' are set out in a number of draft articles drawn up by the UN's International Law Commission (ILC) as part of its debate on state responsibility. [The Advisory Council on International Affairs and Advisory Committee on Issues of Public International Law] consider it desirable – given the growing significance of the international duty to protect and promote human rights – that a separate justification for humanitarian intervention should be worked out as part of the doctrine of state responsibility."[380]

Whatever the concrete solutions proposed, the issue implies according to both advisory bodies that, if the Security Council is not able to come to an agreement, "the maximum degree of legitimacy must be obtained by other means", which means that if the attempt to obtain Security Council authorization fails, the next logical step would be "to submit the matter to the General Assembly, taking the procedure laid down in the Uniting for Peace resolution as a basis".[381] According to the advisory bodies "the involvement of the General Assembly helps to generate maximum legitimacy for humanitarian intervention without Security Council authorization", but that procedure will not always successful. And then the advisors to the Dutch government come up with the notion that non-authorized humanitarian interventions might be admissible in extreme cases and as an "emergency exit".[382]

For these emergency situations, however, at least an assessment framework should be available. According to both advisory bodies such a framework would have to clarify the minimum conditions to be satisfied by states, and could help to structure deliberations within the UN on specific instances of intervention. At the same time, it can provide the UN community of nations with a basis for assessing cases of unauthorized humanitarian intervention that have already taken place and for tolerating them provided that sufficient account has been taken of "legitimacy considerations".[383]

10.1.3 Obligations "owed to the international community as a whole"

Notions like the ones discussed in the preceding paragraphs can also be found in the rules on the Responsibility of States for Internationally Wrongful Acts, drawn up by the International Law Commission and which were presented to the UN member states by the General Assembly of the UN, "without prejudice to the question of their future adoption or other appropriate action".[384] Article 48 refers, amongst other things, to invoking the liability of a state by states other than the indirectly injured party in the case that the violated obligation is "owed to the international community as a whole". The resolution of the General Assembly of the UN dating from 2001 was followed in 2004 by a new resolution in which the Secretary-General was asked "to invite Governments to submit their written comments on any future action regarding the articles" and to prepare a report himself with "an initial compilation of decisions of international courts, tribunals and other bodies referring to the articles and to invite Governments to submit information on their practice in this regard (...)".[385] This should take place before the 62nd meeting of the General Assembly of the UN in 2007. We are particularly curious about the responses of states with regard to the obligations they have to the "international community as a whole". How broadly or narrowly will states wish to define their obligations, and to what extent will they want to join the existing developments or actually put the brakes on these?

The jurisprudence of the ICJ fairly regularly shows that there are certain norms of international law which have a special status. The judgment in the *Barcelona Traction* Case, dating from 1970, is a famous example in which the Court states that certain obligations have an *erga omnes* character – they raise obligations for everyone, in relation to everyone –, and that states must support the achievement of these obligations, even if they are not directly affected by them.[386] By way of illustration: if no Dutch nationals are involved in a genocide such as that in Rwanda, does the Netherlands still have an interest, as a member of the international community of states, in being permitted to intervene? Neither the ICJ, nor the rules on state responsibility of the ILC give an answer to the question whether this intervention may also take place in the form of a military operation.

10.1.4 Ius cogens standards and erga omnes obligations

For some, the question of humanitarian intervention is a moral or political/philosophical issue: on the basis of what moral principles may a state or group of states decide to impose order on another state? For others it is a legal question of positive law: are there legal grounds for military actions outside the system of the UN Charter? However, the two perspectives are interdependent: ideally, applicable law has a strong moral foundation in which varying views on what is permissible and what is not can influence what is defined as applicable law or as developing law. In the UN Charter the principle of the sovereignty of states exists next to the obligation to promote human rights as an international community, while the Charter has not yet dealt with the question of what to do in the case of a collision between the two starting points. This is the issue at stake when discussing the living up to obligations with a peremptory (*ius cogens* and *erga omnes*) character.

The development of the law of the last sixty years shows that human rights no longer fall under the exclusive internal jurisdiction of states: when states go too far they are confronted with the legitimate right of interference or even intervention on the part of other states. Their sovereignty is not unlimited, but rather perforated. Article 2, par. 7 of the UN Charter limits the protection of national sovereignty to matters which "*essentially* fall within the domestic jurisdiction of States" (emphasis added), which allows for the possibility of interpreting the article in the light of applicable views about what does and what does not exclusively fall under the domain of national jurisdiction.[387] The question then arises whether in a situation in which the whole of the Security Council with the exception of one or two members (at least one of which has the right of veto) is for military intervention and in which the blocking state does not put forward any substantive grounds against the intervention, but is demonstrably acting on the basis of related grounds, such as ethnic links, etc., it is necessary to accept the fact that the legal system is as it is. On that point, there are two possibilities: working on the 'royal route' of a change in the UN Charter, or leaving the door open, after all, for interventions outside the official system. If the latter route is chosen, there is obviously a possibility of a slippery slope, and all the risks entailed. It would be foolish to ignore this. However, accepting that positive law is by definition the final answer would not be correct either. There is no denying that there are situations in which it would almost be a case of civil disobedience or of (moral) necessity breaking the law, if (groups of) states do not take their responsibility. To this it can be added immediately that these sorts of interventions would have to comply with a number of very strict criteria, such as weighing up the seriousness of the violations of human rights to be opposed, the extent to which non-military means have been exhausted, the demonstrable necessity of (acute) military intervention, the relationship between means and ends (proportionality), etc. Furthermore, it is difficult to indicate *in abstracto* when the critical limits of 'serious violations of human rights' have been exceeded, quite apart from the more operational and often equally difficult question of whether a military intervention is the right way of tackling these violations. Cases in which this is clear (genocide, etc.) are actually relatively easy, because they are so clear. Things become more difficult in the grey areas. In those cases the substantive criteria prove to be much more difficult to formulate and it would seem sensible to rely on a formal principle, for example, that twelve of the fifteen members of the Security Council, or forty of the fifty-three members of the Commission of Human Rights or 150 of the 191 members of the UN General Assembly describe the situation as serious and in principle ready for intervention. Such an approach looks for a legal basis by including precisely those actors who are competent to create new international law – whether or not they are stimulated, urged and controlled by their international counterparts, the NGO world – *i.e.*, the joint sovereign states. Obviously a formal criterion is without prejudice to the fact that the intervening states have a heavy burden of proof, both in advance and retrospectively. They will have to justify their actions with convincing arguments with regard to matters such as motives, having exhausted all other means, timeliness, proportionality and reflecting on the situation which arises after withdrawal.

The key question of all this is how great a chance there is that the international legal order will display imperialist tendencies and start to follow the dangerous path of inappropriate interventions of the sovereignty of states in particular cases, and ultimately forget that that very sovereignty is actually also a *conditio sine qua non* for upholding human rights. In the paraphrased words of Michael Ignatieff: in the course of the years, western states have increasingly proclaimed that protecting human rights is one of the key elements of their foreign policy, with the result that they become embroiled in conflicts of interests fairly regularly.[388] When states in the west start to criticize states such as Indonesia, Turkey or Iran because of their human rights violations, they cannot justify providing those very same states with arms which can be used in the struggle against internal civilian opposition. According to Ignatieff, many states are skating on the thin ice of the above-mentioned conflicts in policy (human rights *versus* (short-term) stability). They are often pragmatic in their considerations – Kabila as the leader in the Congo, rather than no leader at all – often opt for the instrument of tacit diplomacy in order to avoid obvious violations of the sovereignty of states and regularly and inevitably adopt a practice of double standards. Ignatieff then describes ten cases of armed interventions with or without a mandate of the Security Council, to conclude that the results of all these interventions must be considered very ambiguous, not least because the interventions often lack an exit strategy. In fact, it was Ignatieff who was one of the advocates of the war against Saddam Hussein's Iraq in 2003:

> The fact that states are both late and hypocritical in their adoption of human rights does not deprive them of the right to use force to defend them. The disagreeable reality for those who believe in human rights is that there are some occasions – and Iraq may be one of them – when war is the only real remedy for regimes that live by terror.[389]

Here, Ignatieff's approach turns to the importance of human rights and the need to, sometimes, neglect the sovereignty of states, *in casu* Iraq. Taken the two arguments together, Ignatieff's central proposition in itself seems extraordinarily valid: despite the perforation of state sovereignty, it should not be seen as an outdated principle.[390] It should be seen as the cornerstone of both international peace and security and as the protection of human rights. Nevertheless, it is a matter of constantly defining in which cases and to what extent states can be sovereign, and where they are justifiably confronted with external intervention. Even sovereignty is not a static phenomenon; on the contrary, it is a concept that is subject to change. By their nature, states are inclined to interpret this to their own advantage, but other forces, briefly summarized as the 'civil society' and (groups of) citizens who stand up for their rights, permit them to do so less and less. Whether all this should result in ignoring the sovereignty of states in the case of gross human rights violations and using military force, is a question to which there is no easy answer. Because while human rights organizations and public opinion sometimes demand, and what might be permissible in special circumstances from a theoretical legal point of view does not always amount to a practical and useful response. The reality of the interventions of recent years has provided plenty of negative examples. However, there can and will always be examples in which a military intervention could be the most appropriate response. In addition to weighing up the seriousness of the human rights violations to be prevented, the extent to which non-military means have been exhausted, the need for (acute) military intervention and the probability that this will resolve something, the relationship between means and ends (proportionality), etc., this will always concern situations in which sovereign power is abused in a way which cannot be left unopposed on moral grounds.

10.1.5 The responsibility to protect innocent populations

The issue of humanitarian interventions is often also labeled as the duty/obligation/responsibility to protect innocent people from genocide, crimes against humanity and war crimes. The issue has also been addressed in the September 2005 Summit Outcome Document. It states that "each individual state has the responsibility to protect its populations from genocide, war crimes, ethnic cleansing and crimes against humanity. This responsibility entails the prevention of such crimes, including their incitement, through appropriate and necessary means. We accept that responsibility and will act in accordance with it. The international community should, as appropriate, encourage and help states to exercise this responsibility and support the United Nations in establishing an early warning capability".[391]

In addition, it is said that "the international community, through the United Nations, also has the responsibility to use appropriate diplomatic, humanitarian and other peaceful means", "to help protect populations from genocide, war crimes, ethnic cleansing and crimes against humanity", and that in that context the UN member states are prepared "to take collective action, in a timely and decisive manner, through the Security Council, in accordance with the Charter, including Chapter VII, on a case-by-case basis and in cooperation with relevant regional organizations as appropriate, should peaceful means be inadequate and national authorities manifestly fail to protect their populations from genocide, war crimes, ethnic cleansing and crimes against humanity. We stress the need for the General Assembly to continue consideration of the responsibility to protect populations from genocide, war crimes, ethnic cleansing and crimes against humanity and its implications, bearing in mind the principles of the Charter and international law. We also intend to commit ourselves, as necessary and appropriate, to helping states build capacity to protect their populations from genocide, war crimes, ethnic cleansing and crimes against humanity and to assisting those which are under stress before crises and conflicts break out."[392]

It is a step forward on the long road towards better protection – or to protection at all – of innocent populations all-over the world against leaders who are abusing their powers, who never heard of something like the separation of powers, or who are simply too long in their comfortable seats.

10.2 Upholding the law

10.2.1. The League of Nations

The High Contracting Parties to the Covenant of the League of Nations (LoN) intended to achieve international peace and security "by the firm establishment of international law as the actual rule of conduct among governments". To that end they agreed to submit their disputes either to arbitration or to the Council (see Chapter 8, par. 8.1). Moreover, the members anticipated establishing a Permanent Court of International Justice (PCIJ), competent to hear and decide on disputes with an international character and to give advisory opinions about any dispute or question referred to the Court by the Council or the Assembly.[393] On 13 December 1929, the Assembly of the LoN approved the Statute of the PCIJ. It entered into force on 25 September 1921, when 27 LoN Members had ratified the Protocol in which the Statute was recorded.[394] The members also had the opportunity to sign an optional Protocol, in which they declared that they recognize "as compulsory ipso facto and without special agreement, in relation to any other Member or State accepting the same obligation, the jurisdiction of the Court in all or any of the classes of legal disputes".[395] The corresponding Article 36 (2) of the ICJ Statute is still known as the "optional clause", although this Statute now is an integral part of the UN Charter, and all the UN members are *ipso facto* parties to it.[396] According to its Statute, the PCIJ was established "in addition to the Court of Arbitration organized by the Conventions of The Hague of 1899 and 1907, and to the special Tribunals of Arbitration to which States are always at liberty to submit their disputes for settlement".[397] The Permanent Court of Arbitration (PCA) was in fact only organized by the Hague Conventions as a procedure, and not established as an institution. After all, the PCA is neither permanent nor a court but a bureau, which draws up a list of arbitrators and facilitates arbitration procedures. Each state party – "Contracting Power" – selects at most four persons "of the highest moral reputation and disposed to accept the duties of Arbitrator" for inclusion on the list. Parties to a dispute can select their arbitrator(s) from that list.[398] This system prevented the PCA arbitration from expanding substantially. The outbreak of World War I wrecked plans to set up a Court of Arbitral Justice,[399] but the LoN "opened new opportunities for determining the selection of Judges, which had posed an insurmountable problem to the projected Court of Arbitral Justice".[400] The greatest obstacles had been:

> *The irreconcilable views of the greater and smaller powers. By 1920, however, a similar difficulty had been surmounted by the League of Nations. Availing itself of this analogy, the Committee of Jurists, by entrusting the election to the League Assembly and the Council, was able to break the deadlock. One may argue, therefore that it was the creation of the League of Nations which was the prerequisite for the successful launching of the Court.*[401]

The Court began its work on 15 December 1922 in the Peace Palace in The Hague, built in 1910 for the PCA. It was concluded on the day of inauguration of the ICJ: 18 April 1946.[402] It is a tribute to the PCIJ that its judgments and advisory opinions were incorporated in the jurisprudence of the ICJ.[403] Thus the PCIJ was not dragged down in the political bankruptcy of the LoN itself. Moreover, the ICJ Statute is based upon the Statute of the PCIJ. It would be difficult to conceive of a greater compliment to the 1920 Committee of Jurists, which prepared plans for the PCIJ. These included the plan submitted by the Scandinavian countries, the Netherlands and Switzerland, which had not participated in World War I.[404]

10.2.2 The United Nations

Unlike the LoN Covenant, the UN Charter does not firmly establish international law as the actual rule of conduct among governments but is determined "to establish conditions under which justice and respect for obligations arising from treaties and other sources of international law can be maintained".[405] In so doing, the UN and its members act in accordance with seven principles,[406] the very first of which is that the organization is based on the principle of the sovereign equality of its' members. This principle is closely connected with the sovereignty of states as "one of the oldest concepts of international law".[407] The third principle states that members shall settle their international disputes by peaceful means, in such a manner that international peace and security and justice are not endangered. In the context of the first principle and the fourth principle, prohibiting members to use force against the territorial integrity or the political independence of any state, as well as the seventh principle, prohibiting the UN from intervening in matters which are essentially within the jurisdiction of any state, "the principle of the peaceful settlement occupies a pivotal position in a world order whose hallmark is the ban on force and coercion".[408]

The 1970 Declaration on Principles of International Law Concerning Friendly Relations and Co-operation Among States in Accordance with the Charter of the United Nations, adopted on the occasion of the 25th anniversary the UN, also placed the peaceful settlement of disputes among the basic principles of international law.[409] In addition, it is stated in the Declaration that in "their interpretation and application the (...) principles are interrelated and [that] each principle should be construed in the context of the other principles".[410] The UN Charter did so from its very beginning, for Article 33 (1) does not indicate any order in which the methods should be used:

> The parties to any dispute, the continuance of which is likely to endanger the maintenance of international peace and security, shall, first of all, seek a solution by negotiation, enquiry, mediation, conciliation, arbitration, judicial settlement, resort to regional agencies or arrangements, or other peaceful means of their own choice.

These methods do not perform specific functions, but have in common that they encourage communication between the parties in order to settle their dispute either through direct negotiation or through alternatives to it – good offices, mediation, conciliation or inquiry – or attempts to institutionalize the willingness of states to negotiate a settlement when a dispute arises: arbitration and judicial settlement. The option of "other peaceful means of their own choice" wholly corresponds to the context of the principle of sovereign equality. The same applies for Article 36 (3) of the UN Charter in respect of the prohibition on the UN to intervene in matters which essentially fall under the domestic jurisdiction of a state. In fact, it merely urges that:

> ...in making recommendations under this Article the Security Council should also take into consideration that legal disputes should as a general rule be referred by the parties to the International Court of Justice in accordance with the provisions of the Statute of the Court.

During the preparatory discussions in San Francisco in 1945, the delegations of the then great powers strongly objected to the compulsory jurisdiction of the ICJ with regard to legal disputes, which could not be settled in any other way.[411]

The preference of small states for judicial settlement as a protection against power politics resulted in the reference to justice in Article 2(3) of the UN Charter. Nevertheless, negotiations between states is still the only universally accepted means of dispute settlement.[412] Most treaties and treaty provisions on the settlement of disputes between states aim to fill the gap when negotiations fail. These provisions either reserve for the states the acceptance of the decision of third parties – enquiry (fact finding), good offices, mediation, conciliation – or entrust the binding decision to impartial third parties: arbitration, judicial settlement. However, even in the latter case, the parties remain responsible themselves for the implementation of the binding decision. According to the UN Charter, it is up to a state to turn to the Security Council when the other state fails to obey the judgment of the ICJ. The Security

Council can only make recommendations or decide upon measures to be taken to give effect to the judgment if a state appeals to it, and then only if it deems this to be necessary.[413] Up till now, this has happened only once. Nicaragua had recourse to the Security Council in 1986 when the USA rejected the decision of the ICJ. The USA then blocked a decision with its' veto. It goes without saying that the "importance of Article 94 (2) [of the UN Charter, relating to the role the Security Council should play in case a state does not live up to an ICJ judgment[414]] has been considerably prejudiced as a result of this case".[415] However, it should not be forgotten that in general, the final judgments of the ICJ have been observed to a reasonable degree.[416] Aside from the merits of each case, it is striking that the ICJ mainly gave judgment for the claimant in cases where the acceptance of its' jurisdiction was clearly established. In other words, judicial settlement can be considered as a form of 'institutionalization of negotiation' between the parties. This explains why, unless otherwise decided, each party bears its own costs.[417] Moreover, any party may make a request to the Court for the interpretation of the judgment by application or by notification of a special agreement. In the former case the other party is entitled to file written observations.[418]

The key question is whether the UN Charter has not put up a barrier to the 'institutionalization of negotiation' between the parties by stating that in the event of conflict between the obligations of the members under the UN Charter and their obligations under any other international agreement, their obligations under the Charter shall prevail.[419] In the dispute between Libya and the USA and the UK on whether – acting under Chapter VII of the Charter – the Council could set aside provisions on the peaceful settlement of disputes in the 1971 Montreal Convention for the Suppression of Unlawful Acts against the Safety of Civil Aviation, the ICJ failed to put a check on the self-proclaimed room of manoeuvre of the Security Council:

Whereas both Libya and the United States [respectively the United Kingdom], as Members of the United Nations, are obliged to accept and carry out the decisions of the Security Council in accordance with Article 25 of the Charter; whereas the Court, which is at the stage of proceedings on provisional measures, considers that prima facie this obligation extends to the decision contained in resolution 748 (1992); and whereas in accordance with Article 103 of the Charter, the obligations of the Parties in that respect prevail over their obligations under any other international agreement, including the Montreal Convention.[420]

Only the judges from the US, the UK and Italy supported the judgment without an explanation of their vote. The other judges added an explanatory declaration (6), a separate opinion (2) or a dissenting opinion (5) on the relationship between the ICJ and the Security Council. This seems to indicate that the interpretation and application of such decisions will remain controversial.[421] This applies particularly as the UN Charter is recognized as the constitution of the international community and this inherently implies the powers of UN organs, particularly the Security Council, even if these powers may not be submitted to a judicial review. Unfortunately, the millennium intentions do not show any willingness of heads of state and government to declare themselves in that respect.

10.2.3 Millennium intentions

Since 1946 the ICJ has delivered 90 judgments on disputes concerning, *inter alia*, land frontiers and maritime boundaries, territorial sovereignty, the non-use of force, non-interference in the internal affairs of states, diplomatic relations, hostage taking, the right of asylum, nationality, guardianship, rights of passage and economic rights. It has also given 25 advisory opinions, concerning, *inter alia*, admission to United Nations membership, reparation for injuries suffered in the service of the United Nations, the territorial status of South West Africa (Namibia) and Western Sahara, judgments rendered by international administrative tribunals, the expenses of certain United Nations operations, the applicability of the United Nations Headquarters Agreement, the status of human rights rapporteurs, the legality of the threat or use of nuclear weapons, and the legal consequences of the construction of a wall in the occupied Palestinian territory. Twelve contentious cases are currently pending.[422] All in all, the average workload of the ICJ has not increased substantially in comparison with that of the PCIJ, although by virtue of the UN Charter, the former Court is not only one of the six main organs of the organization, but also its principal judicial organ and the only international judicial body open to all states.[423]

The good intentions of the heads of state and government in the Millennium Declaration and the Outcome Document of the 2005 World Summit provide little hope for change, as they reject compulsory jurisdiction and insist on the sovereign equality of states. In the Millennium Declaration they re-dedicate themselves "to support all efforts to uphold the sovereign equality of all states, territorial integrity and political independence, resolution of disputes by peaceful means and in conformity with the principles of justice and international law, the right to self-determination of peoples which remain under colonial domination and foreign occupation, non-interference in the internal affairs of states, respect for human rights and fundamental freedoms, respect for the equal rights of all without distinction as to race, sex, language or religion and international cooperation in solving international problems of an economic, social, cultural or humanitarian character."[424]

Moreover, they resolved to strengthen respect for the rule of law in both international and national affairs and, in particular, to ensure compliance by member states with the decisions of the International Court of Justice, in accordance with the UN Charter, in cases to which they are parties, and to strengthen the International Court of Justice, in order to ensure justice and the rule of law in international affairs.[425] The 2005 Outcome Document only adds a little extra when it emphasizes in the chapter on peace and collective security "the obligation of states to settle their disputes by peaceful means in accordance with Chapter VI of the Charter, including, when appropriate, by the use of the International Court of Justice. All states should act in accordance with the Declaration on Principles of International Law concerning Friendly Relations and Cooperation among States in accordance with the Charter.[426]

The same applies for the recognition of the important role of the International Court of Justice, the principal judicial organ of the United Nations, in adjudicating disputes between states and the value of its' work. The world leaders call upon states that have not yet done so to consider accepting the jurisdiction of the Court in accordance with its' Statute, and to consider means of strengthening the Court's work, amongst other things, by supporting the Secretary-General's Trust Fund to Assist States in the Settlement of Disputes through the International Court of Justice on a voluntary basis.[427]

Moreover, the important function of the ICJ as the principal judicial organ of the UN to give advisory opinions on legal questions to the UNGA and the Security Council, as well as other UN organs and specialized agencies, authorized by the UNGA, is conspicuous by its absence. In our view, this is a lost opportunity to fill the gap which is not provided for in the UN Charter for the peaceful settlement of disputes between the UN organs – particularly the Security Council – and members or other states, on the interpretation and application of the UN Charter.

Neither the Millennium Declaration nor the Outcome Document of the 2005 World Summit do justice to the judicial functions of the ICJ as the principal judicial organ, by virtue of which this Court is not only entitled but also has the duty to interpret the UN Charter. This aspect of its activities relates first of all to advisory opinions at the request of the GA.[428] The Millennium intentions of the heads of state and government do not bode well for the adoption of recent proposals by none other than presidents of the ICJ "to use the advisory function of the ICJ in order to avoid conflicting jurisprudence due to the proliferation of international courts".[429]

Moreover, these intentions do not look at disputes between peoples and states resulting from balancing the rights and obligations which arise from the right to self-determination in the context of the prohibition of secession. For the settlement of such disputes it may be helpful for the UNGA to request an advisory opinion from the ICJ or to consider the option of arbitration by the PCA under its Rules of Arbitration and Conciliation for the settlement of disputes between two parties of which only one is a state.[430] We believe that the more authority UN organs assume within the scope of their activities in this century, the greater the need will be for these organs – particularly the Security Council – to guarantee members and other states good governance and the maintenance of the rule of law within the UN system itself through a wider use of the advisory opinions of the ICJ and/or arbitration between UN organs and states, as well as states and non-state actors.

10.3 Sanctions

Based on Article 41 if the UN Charter, the Security Council can decide to start "measures not involving the use of armed force" which are "to be employed to give effect to its decisions (...) and [which] may include complete or partial interruption of economic relations and of rail, sea, air, postal, telegraphic, radio, and other means of communication and the severance of diplomatic relations". Taken together, these measures are often labeled as 'sanctions'.

Over the years, the United Nations have imposed multilateral sanctions against a number of countries. They did so for various reasons and with different objectives, such as the termination of a war, the introduction of democratic institutions, the extradition of alleged criminals, or the establishment of internal policies favoring human rights. In addition, several states have imposed sanctions on a unilateral basis, while it can also be observed that private citizens or groups of consumers have boycotted products from certain countries to protest against human rights violations, including the non-observation of internationally recognized human rights and labor standards.

According to the former UN Secretary-General Boutros Boutros-Ghali, sanctions are a blunt instrument with a series of negative side-effects especially in the human rights field:

> *They raise the ethical question of whether suffering inflicted on vulnerable groups in the target country is a legitimate means of exerting pressure on political leaders whose behaviour is unlikely to be affected by the plight of their subjects. Sanctions also always have unintended or unwanted effects. They can complicate the work of humanitarian agencies by denying them certain categories of supplies and by obliging them to go through arduous procedures to obtain the necessary exemptions. They can conflict with the development objectives of the Organization and do long-term damage to the productive capacity of the target country. They can have a severe effect on other countries that are neighbours or major economic partners of the target country. They can also defeat their own purpose by provoking a patriotic response against the international community, symbolized by the United Nations, and by rallying the population behind the leaders whose behaviour the sanctions are intended to modify.*[431]

Since then, several UN bodies have further examined the issue. The UN Committee on Economic, Social and Cultural Rights, for instance, underlined in its 1997 General Comment on The Relationship between Economic Sanctions and Respect for Economic, Social and Cultural Rights the extremely negative consequences sanctions normally have in the field of economic, social and cultural human rights. The Committee did so in the following, well chosen words:

> *While the impact of sanctions varies from one case to another, the Committee is aware that they almost always have a dramatic impact on the rights recognized in the Covenant [on Economic, Social and Cultural Rights]. Thus, for example, they often cause significant dis-*

ruption in the distribution of food, pharmaceuticals and sanitation supplies, jeopardise the quality of food and the availability of clean drinking water, severely interfere with the functioning of basic health and education systems, and undermine the right to work. In addition, their unintended consequences can include reinforcement of the power of oppressive elites, the emergence, almost invariably, of a black market and the generation of huge windfall profits for the privileged elites which manage it, enhancement of the control of the governing elites over the population at large, and restriction of opportunities to seek asylum or to manifest political opposition. While the phenomena mentioned in the preceding sentence are essentially political in nature, they also have a major additional impact on the enjoyment of economic, social and cultural rights.[432]

In short: is it fair and ethical for countries and citizens, not guilty of the circumstances that caused the adoption of sanctions, and who have conscientiously followed the UN resolutions, to bear huge material and moral damage, thus risking the destabilization of their own economic and political development?

The problems related to sanctions did lead to the notion of smart sanctions, *i.e.*, sanctions that according to Kofi Annan "seek to pressure regimes rather than peoples and thus reduce humanitarian costs".[433] According to the present Secretary-General, this "increasing interest in more targeted sanctions was evident in the recent measures applied by the Security Council against the military junta in Sierra Leone and against UNITA in Angola". But, he adds, "although sanctions regimes established by the Security Council normally do include humanitarian exemptions, some human rights treaty-monitoring bodies have stressed the need for such regimes to include specific measures protecting the human rights of vulnerable groups".[434] In saying so, he refers to, for instance, the previously mentioned General Comment by the UN Committee on Economic, Social and Cultural Rights.

At a conference at Tilburg University, in 1999, the question was addressed by what means sanctions can be made more successful – or at least tolerable – from a human rights perspective.

The conference came up with seven elements that in that context should be taken into consideration. The elements relate to the specificity of objectives, the proportionality between objective and instrument, the possibility to influence the position of the rulers, the linkage between external and internal pressure, the ways of minimizing and monitoring humanitarian damage, including the damage for neighboring countries, the period of time sanctions take, and, finally, the preference for a multilateral basis for sanctions.[435]

One of the conclusions of the book that came out after the conference, is that much of the criticism of the use of sanctions is based on the lack of focus and precision in many Security Council resolutions as well as in the decisions taken by states to start unilateral sanctions. Political considerations (showing the world that decisive steps are taken) are often more important than a strict definition of objectives and indicators to measure progress towards those objectives. Independent monitoring mechanisms are therefore indispensable and should be an integral part of every sanctions regime.[436]

In addition, it is said that for a monitoring operation to be successful, a clear definition of the objectives is a first priority, while the sanctioning organizations and individual states "should also in any case make an in-depth evaluation of the political situation in the target country, before embarking upon sanctionary measures: How about the possibility to tackle the position of the rulers through combined external and internal pressure, how about the possibilities to strengthen the local civil society? These are important factors as well as indicators to determine whether sanctions will eventually be a success."[437]

Further to that it is stated that the negative impact of sanctions on third parties (civilian population, neighboring countries) should be objectively assessed and considered as an integral part of any resolution adopted by the Security Council. The Security Council itself as well as other 'sanctioners' should avoid violating exactly the same standards of international law they would like to see adhered to by the targeted state. Some 'collateral damage' is un-avoidable and acceptable, but the balance should not be over-looked. And monitoring the consequences of sanctions should be based on serious, systematic and independent research. Here one can think of specialized agencies such as the World Health Orga-nization and the Food and Agriculture Organization, as well as of the UN High Commissioners on Human Rights and Refugees and the UN Special Rapporteurs in the field of human rights. Further to this, one can think of the research capacity of the International Committee of the Red Cross and other NGOs.[438]

Despite all this, one should not be too optimistic on the possi-bilities of 'smart sanctions'. In the words of Kofi Annan:

> *The international community should be under no illusion: these humanitarian and human rights policy goals cannot easily be recon-ciled with those of a sanctions regime. It cannot be too strongly emphasized that sanctions are a tool of enforcement and, like other methods of enforcement, they will do harm. This should be borne in mind when the decision to impose them is taken, and when the results are subsequently evaluated.*[439]

It may be clear that even if human rights concerns are included in the decision to impose or maintain sanctions and even in the case one is prepared to monitor and 'repair' the humanitarian damage, this might not be enough. There will always be a diversity of rea-sons to start sanctions, and by some of these 'sanctioners', human-itarian damage will be considered to be 'collateral'. It is a reality one cannot ignore.

According to the UN, in the meantime a great number of states and humanitarian organizations have clear views of and expressed concerns at the possible adverse impact of sanctions on the most vulnerable segments of the population, such as women and chil-dren, while many of them also have expressed concerns at the neg-ative impact sanctions can have on the economy of third coun-tries. And in response to these concerns, relevant Security Council decisions have reflected a more refined approach to the design, application and implementation of mandatory sanctions.[440] These refinements have included measures targeted at specific actors, as well as humanitarian exceptions embodied in Security Council resolutions. The targeted sanctions, for instance, involve the freezing of assets and blocking the financial transactions of political elites or entities whose behavior triggered sanctions in the first place. That type of sanctions have recently been applied to African countries, where wars are funded in part by the trade of illicit diamonds for arms and related materials.[441]

In the September 2005 document sanctions are also extensively dealt with. So it is stated that "sanctions remain an important tool under the Charter in our efforts to maintain international peace and security without recourse to the use of force", but also that the states want to ensure "that sanctions are carefully targeted in support of clear objectives, comply with sanctions established by the Security Council and are implemented in ways that balance effectiveness to achieve the desired results against the possible adverse consequences, including socio-economic and humanitarian consequences, for populations and third states."[442]

Further to that it is stated that sanctions "should be implemented and monitored effectively with clear benchmarks", that they "should be periodically reviewed, as appropriate", and "remain for as limited a period as necessary to achieve the objectives of the sanctions and should be terminated once their objectives have been achieved".[443] In addition, the Security Council is asked, *inter alia*, "to improve its monitoring of the implementation and effects of sanctions, in order to ensure that sanctions are implemented in an accountable manner", and to develop "a mechanism to address special economic problems arising from the application of sanctions in accordance with the Charter".[444] And last but not least, the member states "call upon the Security Council, with the support of the Secretary-General, to ensure that fair and clear procedures exist for placing individuals and entities on sanctions lists and for removing them, as well as for granting humanitarian exemptions".[445]

10.4 International criminal prosecution

10.4.1 The Yugoslavia Tribunal

The decision of the Security Council to establish the International Criminal Tribunal for the former Yugoslavia (ICTY, 1993) is often explained as a judicial 'placebo'.[446] Following its creation, there has been no serious discussion whether or not the Security Council acted *ultra vires* when it established the ICTY as its subsidiary organ under Article 29 of the UN Charter. Neither the Security Council nor the General Assembly deemed it obviously fit to ask an advisory opinion of the ICJ or to enable the ICTY to ask such an opinion when the question was raised before the ICTY in the Tadic case.[447] It is common knowledge that the Security Council – and particularly one of its' permanent members, the USA – is not fond of accepting international law as the proper framework for putting a check on international politics. On the other hand, the story goes that the ICJ and the ICTY could not get on from the very beginning.[448] Be that as it may, the discussion on the competence of the Security Council to establish ad hoc tribunals as auxiliary agencies and force states to cooperate with these has gone quiet since the Yugoslavia Tribunal confirmed its own lawfulness in appeal and since the UN General Assembly agreed to the financing and appointment of judges, clerks of the court and public prosecutors. It is worth noting that the latest edition of Bruno Simma's authoritative commentary on the Charter of the UN states that the lawfulness of the ad hoc tribunals has now been fairly generally recognized. In this respect the edition refers to the judgment of the Yugoslavia tribunal itself, without questioning, however, whether the tribunal was competent to judge on its own right to exist.[449] The commentary does add that the establishment of the ICC and of mixed international/national tribunals as in Sierra Leone and Cambodia place a question mark next to the future viability of such ad hoc tribunals as an auxiliary agency of the Security Council. Doubts about the ultimately useful effect of these tribunals on the sustainability and justice of peace no doubt play a part in this. A recent investigation into the combination of peace and justice concluded that the establishment of the Yugoslavia Tribunal has already had an impressive influence on the development of international law.[450] The ultimate useful effect of the Yugoslavia Tribunal on the length and justice of peace in the Balkans will still have to be proved.

So far the ICTY has indicted 161 persons for serious violations of international humanitarian law. 56 accused are currently in custody at the Detention Unit, while 37 accused have been transferred to serve their sentence/released following completion of their proceedings. In the meantime, 15 persons have served their sentence.[451]

10.4.2 The Rwanda Tribunal

The Rwanda Tribunal (ICTR) has been established in 1994. The Rwanda Tribunal was the first international tribunal to apply the international law definition of genocide, as provided in the 1948 Genocide Convention. In this respect, the Rwanda Tribunal has played a pioneering role in the explanation of the legal concept of genocide. The Tribunal stated that large-scale rape can also be an act of genocide. In addition, the Tribunal answered specific questions which arose with regard to the application of the concept of crimes against humanity and war crimes. According to the Statute of the Rwanda Tribunal, crimes against humanity are acts committed on discriminatory grounds as part of a widespread or systematic attack on a civilian population. The fact that the Statute did not insist that crimes against humanity are committed in the context of an armed conflict, as was required in the statute of the Yugoslavia Tribunal, was an important step forward. Another important innovation was the fact that the Statute of the Rwanda Tribunal made war crimes committed in an internal armed conflict punishable, while most rules of international humanitarian war are concerned with international conflicts. However, while recognizing the significant contribution which the Rwanda Tribunal made in various fields to the development of international law, Larissa van den Herik states in her doctoral dissertation published in 2005, that in its' judgments the Rwanda Tribunal often failed to provide adequate motives for these new developments and did not provide a sound legal basis for it.[452] Nevertheless, a number of new developments resulting from the Statute and the jurisprudence of the ICTR were subsequently consolidated in the Statute of the International Criminal Court. Therefore, from a legal point of view, the Rwanda Tribunal helped to smooth the path for the Rome Statute for the International Criminal Court.

It is striking that Secretary-General Annan sees the role of international and internationalized criminal tribunals in relative terms. Apart from the fact that they take up a substantial proportion of the UN budget – currently approximately 10% –, he states that they generally appear to contribute little to a lasting national improvement in legal capacity. Therefore he considers that the time is now ripe, taking into account the international standards, to invest more in strengthening the professionalism, integrity, impartiality and effectiveness of national legal systems.[453]

As of mid 2005, the ICTR has handed down 19 judgments involving 25 accused. Another 25 accused are on trial.[454] Both the ICTY and the ICTR should be ready by 2008 with "all trial activities at first instance" and by 2010 with "all their work", thereby transferring "cases involving intermediate- and lower-rank accused to competent national jurisdictions".[455]

10.4.3 The International Criminal Court

This latter approach fits into the basic notion of complementarity or subsidiarity which is central to the 1998 Statute of the International Criminal Court. In the words of its Preamble, "the International Criminal Court established under this Statute shall be complementary to national criminal jurisdictions", which means that national jurisdictions have priority. The ICC can only take over a case in the field of genocide (Article 6 of the Statute), crimes against humanity (Article 7) or war crimes (Article 8), if a state is "unwilling or unable genuinely to carry out the investigation or prosecution" itself. Unwillingness relates to amongst other things the fact that national decisions were made "for the purpose of shielding the person concerned from criminal responsibility for crimes within the jurisdiction of the Court (...)", the existence of "an unjustified delay in the proceedings which in the circumstances is inconsistent with an intent to bring the person concerned to justice", or the situation in which "proceedings were not or are not being conducted independently or impartially (...)". In addition, the inability to prosecute on the national level relates to situations in which states "due to a total or substantial collapse or unavailability of its national judicial system (...) [are] unable to obtain the accused or the necessary evidence and testimony or otherwise unable to carry out its proceedings".[456]

The public prosecutor may institute an investigation on his own initiative ('*proprio motu*') on the basis of information on crimes within the jurisdiction of the ICC.[457] In order to determine the seriousness of this information he can ask states, UN organs, Intergovernmental Organizations (IGOs), NGOs and other sources for further information.[458] The ICC operates under the responsibility of the states which are a party to the 1998 Statute. These states, which constitute the Assembly of States Parties, appoint and dismiss the judges, the clerk of the court and the public prosecutor. Furthermore, a state can withdraw as a party with a period of notice of one year, and in the case of an amendment of the Statute, even with immediate effect, although the possibility of amendment only enters into effect after seven years, *i.e.*, from 1 July 2009.

One of the relatively speaking innovative aspects of the ICC Statute relates to the attention paid to the victims of the violations of core crimes in the field of international criminal law, as covered by the ICC Statute. See for instance Article 68 in relation to "Protection of the victims and witnesses and their participation in the proceedings" and, especially, Article 75 in relation to "Reparations to victims".[459] The attention paid to the position of victims has many sources of inspiration and persons coming up for them. One of these persons is, no doubt, the Dutch professor of International Law and former Director of the (then) UN Division of Human Rights

(1977-1982), Theo van Boven, who time and again has stressed the need not to forget them.[460]

Unlike the two ad hoc tribunals the ICC is not a UN agency. It was even opposed by the Security Council in 2002 and 2003, with resolutions on criminal immunity for American soldiers.[461] Fortunately this came to an end in 2004, albeit with the risk of a possible reduced effort of the USA for peace operations and humanitarian interventions. It is telling that the Security Council decision to refer the situation in Darfur since 1 July 2002 to the prosecutor of the ICC refers to Article 16 of the Rome Statute instead of to its Article 13.[462] According to the latter article, the ICC may exercise jurisdiction if a situation in which one or more crimes appear to have been committed is referred to the Prosecutor by the Security Council acting under Chapter VII of the Charter of the United Nations. In contrast, Article 16 prohibits the Court from commencing or proceeding with an investigation or prosecution under its Statute "for a period of 12 months after the Security Council, in a resolution adopted under Chapter VII of the Charter of the United Nations, has requested the Court to that effect; that request may be renewed by the Council under the same conditions". The convoluted argument behind this solution seems to be that the Security Council, in order to avoid the veto of the US, did not refer the situation in Darfur positively to the ICC, which would imply a recognition of the jurisdiction of the Court, but negatively lifted the possibility of prohibiting an investigation, which by itself, might not have such a consequence. Moreover, the USA had already accepted the reference to Article 16 in the above resolution on criminal immunity for American officials or personnel.

As of October 2005, the public prosecutor, Luis Moreno Ocampo from Argentina, has decided to open investigations into three situations: Darfur/Sudan, the Republic of Uganda, the Democratic Republic of Congo, the first case being referred to him by the Security Council (see above), the second and the third by these states themselves. The latter also goes for the case of the Central African Republic.[463] The very existence and the operation of the

International Criminal Court continue to remain a source of controversy as exemplified by the absence of any reference to the ICC
in the 2005 Outcome Document.

CHAPTER 11
Globalisation with a Human Face; a Few Final Observations

The first objective of the UN is the freedom from fear by maintaining international peace and security. Together with the freedom from want, it is the cornerstone of the political and social international order for achieving the civil, cultural, economic, political and social rights for all. Roosevelt's aim was that the UN, as a social and international order, would achieve the freedom from fear by enforcing the prohibition on violence, and the freedom from want by promoting the principle of equal rights and the self-determination of peoples on the basis of respect, for social progress and development, by finding solutions for international economic and social problems, by realizing a universal respect for and taking into account of human rights and the fundamental freedoms, without distinction of race, gender, language or religion. Taken together and expressed in today's words, he would probably have spoken of 'human security for all'.

The future UN will have to find its strength in co-operation with the civil society and the private sector on the basis of shared responsibilities, thereby accepting the latter as co-constituencies ('stakeholders') of the organization, while, of course, not forgetting that not all responsibilities will or should fully overlap: the partners will have to play separate roles too, based on specific competences and strengths. Allowing full participation rights and duties to the civil society and the private sector is needed, amongst other things, because they can form a bridge between the international civil and social order of sovereign states and the world market. As such, their contribution is essential, both for the sustainable production of prosperity and for the fair distribution of that prosperity. In addition, these partnerships are highly relevant from the perspective of peace and security, sustainable development, and, for instance, the international distribution of labor and the need to live up to internationally recognized core labor standards (the 'human rights conventions' of the ILO). Further to this, states will have to be more accountable to the international community of states, peoples, civil society and the market. The UN must provide a platform for this on the basis of co-operation and, indeed, a distribution of roles between the participants. However, as the primary layers of governance, states will continue to be essential for the time being to put the international rules in all these fields into practice in reality.

There is no doubt, that, despite all kinds of non-state actors knocking on the UN door (NGOs) or asked to fulfill parts of the UN purposes (the private sector), maintaining and effectively realizing international law is still primarily in the hands of sovereign states. It is thereby good to note, that many states still find it difficult to accept that they may not be the only steersmen any more. Many of them will not even consider passing on the sword of government in internal conflicts, with regard to maintaining public order and national security or allowing their political and military leaders to be tried in an international criminal court. On the other hand, 'public opinion' might not be sufficiently aware that there is not a single provision in the UN Charter which gives the UN the competence to intervene in matters which essentially fall under the national jurisdiction of a state (Article 2, par. 7 of the UN Charter), a provision which in practice has been sidelined for human rights and human rights related matters ('perforated sovereignty'), but which in other fields is still highly relevant. Nor does the UN Charter require member states to resolve these domestic matters, with the exception of the application of compulsory measures imposed by the Security Council in the case of a threat to the peace, a breach of the peace and acts of aggression (Chapter VII). Therefore maintaining international law still lies primarily in the hands of sovereign states and 'their' international organizations.

Finally: The Universal Declaration of Human Rights gives everyone an entitlement "to a social and international order in which the rights and freedoms set forth in this Declaration can be fully realized" (Article 28). For the 40th anniversary of the Declaration, Christian Tomuschat suggested that Article 28 should be set aside as being utopian and unrealistic.[464] In his recent book, *Human Rights between Idealism and Realism,* he maintains his vision of the article, though with slightly more understanding of the drafters:

> *As a lawyer, one cannot appreciate such a provision which promises just anything without indicating how that goal might possibly be reached. Before blaming the drafters, however, one should remind oneself of the political character of the UDHR. It was enacted as a resolution of the General Assembly. Being thus legally classifiable as a recommendation, it originally lacked any binding force and could therefore transcend boundary lines which a true legal instrument could not have crossed.*[465]

That is at least something. Nevertheless, the author seems to ignore the fact that Article 28 of the UDHR attempts to underline the connections between, on the one hand, civil and political rights and, on the other hand, economic, social and cultural rights. Roosevelt's world view, expressed in his Four Freedoms, may still be a utopian perspective, but as such it nevertheless forces states and peoples, both individually and in the UN context, to continue to endeavor to achieve them. Every age and every decade will have to interpret the freedoms in its own way in order to bring an end to such things as oppression, intra- and interstate conflicts and absolute poverty. The UN of the future will have to play a major role in all these fields, in order to create a better world for human beings worldwide.

Notes

Chapter 1

1 Article 1, UN Charter. See *Annex 1* to this book for some core articles of the Charter, as far as relevant from the perspective of this book.

2 UN Doc. A/RES/2625 (XXV), Annex of 24 October 1970. See *Annex 3* to this book for the text of the resolution.

3 *Ibid.*, passim.

4 *Ibid.*, substantive part of the resolution.

5 UN Doc. A/CONF/166/9, 19 April 1995.

6 *Ibid.*, par. 6.

7 *Ibid.*, par. 29, Commitment 2, sub b.

8 *Ibid.*, par. 100.

9 UN Doc. A/RES/55/2, 18 September 2000, par. 5.

10 UN Doc. A/RES/60/1, 24 October 2005.

11 Kofi A. Annan, 'A Glass At Least Half Full', written statement published after the September 2005 Summit at <www.un.org>

12 See *Annex 12* to this book for a summary of the Summit outcome.

13 'Admission of a State to the United Nations', Advisory Opinion, *ICJ Reports*, 1948, p. 62, par. 63 and 64.

14 *Case concerning Military and Paramilitary Activities in and around Nicaragua* (Nicaragua v. United States of America), *ICJ Reports*, 1986, p. 133, par. 263. See H. Hohmann and P.J.I.M. de Waart, 'Compulsory Jurisdiction and the Use of Force as a Legal issue: the Epoch-making Judgment of the International Court of Justice', *NILR* 34 (1987), p. 162-191.

15 UN Doc. A/CONF/157/23, 12 July 1993, par. 8: "Democracy, development and respect for human rights and fundamental freedoms are interdependent and mutually reinforcing. (...) The international community should support the strengthening and promoting of democracy, development and respect for human rights and fundamental freedoms in the entire world."

16 See, *inter alia*, the supplement to the UN Docs A/50/332 and A/51/512, 17 December 1996.

17 See *Annex 6* to this book for the text of the Millennium Declaration.

18 *A Fair Globalization: Creating Opportunities for All*, Geneva: International Labour Organization, 2004, p. XII and 142. See *Annex 9* to this book for the synopsis of the report.

19 The UNSG Kofi Annan appointed in February 2003 a Panel of Eminent Persons on United-Nations-Civil Society Relations and asked it to "review existing guidelines, decisions and practices that affect civil society organizations' access to and participation in United Nations deliberations and processes; to identify best practices in the United Nations system and in other international organizations with a view to identifying new and better ways to interact with non-governmental organizations and other civil society organizations; to identify ways of making it easier for civil society actors from developing countries to participate fully in United Nations activities; and to review how the Secretariat is organized; to facilitate, manage and evaluate the relationships of the United Nations with civil society and to learn from experience gained in different parts of the system". It led to the report *We the peoples: civil society, the United Nations and global governance*, UN Doc. A/58/817, 11 June 2004. Quote: p. 8. See *Annex 8* to this book for the executive summary of the report.

20 Resolution No. 1/2004 on 'Accountability of International Organisations', unanimously adopted by the 71st Conference of the International Law Association, held in Berlin, Germany, 16-21 August 2004. The Final Report of the committee of the same name based its recommended rules and procedures for international organizations on the principle of good governance as their cornerstone: "In fulfilling its mandate in the years since its establishment [1996], the Committee has become more than ever convinced that there is no necessary incompatibility between, on the one hand autonomy which international organizations require in their decision-making processes and, on the other hand, the requirements of an accountable regime which functions well and leaves no loopholes." *Report of the Seventy-First Conference*, London: ILA, 2004, p. 230.

21 UN Doc. A/RES/60/1, 24 October 2005, par. 135.

22 John Rawls, *The Law of Peoples*, Cambridge/London: Harvard University Press, 1999.

23 John Rawls, *A Theory of Justice*, Oxford/London/New York: Oxford University Press, 1971.

24 See out of many publications on this issue: Philip Alston (ed.), *Peoples' Rights*, Oxford: Oxford University Press, 2001, and Anna Meijknecht, *Towards International Personality: The Position of Minorities and Indigenous Peoples in International Law*, Antwerp/Groningen/Oxford: Intersentia/Hart, 2001. In relation to defining states, an attempt was made in Article 1 of the Montevideo Convention in the Rights and Duties of States of 1933, which reads: "The State as a person of international law should possess the following qualifications: (a) a permanent population; (b) a defined territory; (c) a government; and (d) capacity to enter into relations with other States." 165 *LNTS*, p. 19. Since then, this definition of a state is by and large accepted.

25 The word 'people' stems from the Latin word populus, which in its turn derives from the Greek word polis (city). This origin indicates a link of citizens with a specific territory. This may explain that in UN parlance the relationship with a specific territory has emerged as an element of a definition of peoples in relation to the right of self-determination. See A. Critescu, 'The historical and current development of the right to self-determination on the basis of the Charter of the United Nations and other instruments adopted by the United Nations organs, with particular reference to the promotion and protection of human rights and fundamental freedoms', UN Doc. E/CN.4/Sub.2/L.641, 8 July 1976; H. Gross Espiell, 'The right of self-determination - implementation of United Nations resolutions', UN Doc: E/CN.4/Sub.2/405/Rev.1.; Paul J.I.M. de Waart, 'Participants and their role in the development of international development law', in International Development Law, *Encyclopedia of Life Support Systems (EOLSS)*, Developed under the Auspices of the UNESCO, Oxford: EOLSS Publishers, 2005, [http://www.eolss.net], par. 3.1: "Identification of peoples."

26 *Op. cit.*, passim.

27 *Ibid.*, p. 72, par. 185 and 186.

28 Nico Schrijver, 'September 11th and Challenges to International Law', in J. Boulden and T.G. Weiss (eds), *Terrorism and the UN: Before and After September 11*, Bloomington: Indiana University Press, 2004, p. 55-76.

29 President Roosevelt's State of the Union to the US Congress on 6 January 1941.

30 Adam Smith, *The Wealth of Nations* [1776], New York: The Modern Library (The Cannan edition 1937), passim.

31 See Tammo Hoeksema and Jan ter Laak (eds), *Human Rights and Terrorism, Seminar in the Hall of the Knights*, A reflection of the seminar's speeches and debates supplemented with concise summaries, The Hague, The Netherlands, 17-18 September 2003; Wolfgang Benedek and Alice Yotopoulos-Marangopoulos (eds), *Anti-terrorist Measures and Human Rights*, Dordrecht/Boston/London: Martinus Nijhoff Publishers, 2004.

Chapter 2

32 F.H. Hinsley, 'International Law and International Organisation in the Development of International Relations Since the 18th Century', *NILR* 26 (1979), p. 37-45.

33 Emery de Vattel, *Le droit des gens ou principes de la loi naturelle appliqués à la conduite & aux affaires des Nations et des Souverains*, A Leyde, Aux dépens de la Compagnie, MDCCLVIII, par. 18.

34 Smith, *op. cit.*, p. 121.

35 *Ibid.*, passim.

36 'Reparations for Injuries suffered in the service of the United Nations', Advisory Opinion, *ICJ Reports*, 1949, p. 185.

37 See Article 108 of the UN Charter: "Amendments to the present Charter shall come into force for all Members of the United Nations when they have been adopted by a vote of two thirds of the members of the General Assembly and ratified in accordance with their respective constitutional processes by two thirds of the Members of the United Nations, including all the permanent members of the Security Council".

38 Michel Cosnard, 'Sovereign Equality', in Michael Byers and Georg Nolte (eds), *United States Hegemony and the Foundations of International Law*, Cambridge: Cambridge University Press, 2003, p. 127.

39 *Ibid.*, p. 135-176.

40 *Ibid.*, p. 232-264.

41 UN Doc. A/RES/55/2, 8 September 2000, par. 6.

42 *Op. cit.*, p. 5, par. 20.

43 UN Doc. A/59/565, 29 November 2004. See *Annex 10* to this book for the executive summary of the report.

44 UN Doc. A/59/2005, 21 March 2005. See *Annex 11* to this book for the summary of the report.

45 UN Doc. A/57/387, 9 September 2002, p. 24.

46 See recently: C. Flinterman and W. van Genugten (eds), *Niet-statelijke actoren en de rechten van de mens; gevestigde waarden, nieuwe wegen*, [Non-state actors and human rights: vested values, new ways], The Hague: Boom Juridische Uitgevers, 2003, and De Waart, *op. cit.*, 2005.

47 W.J.M. van Genugten, R.A.J. van Gestel, J.E.J. Prins and A. Vedder, *NGO's als 'nieuwe toezichthouders' op de naleving van mensenrechten door multinationale ondernemingen* [NGOs as the new supervisors of the observance of human rights by multinational enterprises], The Hague: Boom Juridische Uitgevers, 2004.

48 Paul de Waart, UN 21: 'Social Science of the Global Market', in *Thesaurus Acroasium*, vol. XXIX, *Human Rights and Democracy in the 21st Century*, Athens-Thessaloniki: Sakkoulas Publications, 2000.

49 *Op. cit.*, p. 13.

50 UN Doc. A/RES/60/1, 24 October 2005, par. 22, sub e.

51 *Ibid.*, par. 172.

52 Philippe Sands, *Lawless World: America and the Making and Breaking of Global Rules*, London: Penguin Books, 2005.

53 *Ibid.*, p. 239.

54 *Ibid.*, p. 15.

55 *Ibid.*, p. xix.

56 *Ibid.*, p. 22.

57 <http://www.eseu.be/Categories/Global-Affairs/Iraq/Decl1203 IraqBids.html>

58 Sands, *op. cit.*, p. 204.

59 <http://www.washingtonpost.com/wp-srv/nation/documents/ dojinterrogation-memo20020801.pdf> Memorandum for Alberto R. Gonzales, Counsel to the President: Re: Standards for Conduct of Interrogation under 18 U.S.C. §§ 2340-2340A.

60 *Ibid.*, p. 39.

61 *Ibid.*, p. 46.

62 Sands, *op. cit.*, p. 213.

63 *Ibid.*, p. 171-172.

64 *Ibid.*, p. 239.

Chapter 3

65 See Th .C. van Boven, *De volkenrechtelijke bescherming van de godsdienstvrijheid* [International Protection of Religious Liberty], Assen: Van Gorcum, 1967, p. 19-22, 34 and 271.

66 Articles 1, par. 3; 13, par. 1; 55; 56; 62, par. 2; 68 and 76, UN Charter. See *Annex 1* to this book.

67 See for many details as to the process of drafting: J.P. Humphrey (the first director of the UN Division of Human Rights), *Human Rights and the United Nations: a Great Adventure*, New York, 1984.

68 See *Annex 2* to this book for the full text of the Universal Declaration of Human Rights.

69 It is outside the scope of this book to delineate the whole structure of the UN involvement in human rights. In addition, such a delineation is available in quite a number of publications. See, for example, Magdalena Sepulveda, Theo van Banning, Gudrún D. Gudmundsdóttir, Christine Chamoun and Willem van Genugten, *Human Rights Reference Handbook*, fully revised third edition, Costa Rica: University for Peace, 2004, 513 p. (also on CD, available free of charge for educational purposes).

70 Also see the Dutch Advisory Council on International Affairs, *The United Nations and Human Rights*, The Hague, September 2004, p. 13.

71 *United Nations Yearbook 1948-1949*, p. 535. Of the then 58 UN members, eight abstained from voting and two were absent. The remaining 48 members voted in favor of the UDHR.

72 UN Doc A/CONF.157/23, 12 July 1993, Preamble and par. 5.

73 UN Doc. A/RES/60/1, 24 October 2005, par. 121.

74 Advisory Council on International Affairs, *Universality of Human Rights and Cultural Diversity*, The Hague, June 1998, passim, esp. par. II d.

75 See Article 4, par. 2, ICCPR.

76 UN doc. A/RES/60/1, 24 October 2005, par. 121.

77 UN Doc. CCPR/C/21/Rev.1/Add.6, 2 November 1994.

78 *Ibid.*, par. 8.

79 *Ibid.*. par. 9.

80 *Ibid.*, par. 19. Also see UN Doc. CERD/C/62/Misc.20/Rev.3, 12 March 2003.

81 UN Doc. A/RES/60/1, 24 October 2005, par. 125.

82 *Op. cit.*, p. 624-630.

83 *Ibid.*, p. 626-627.

84 See UN Doc. A/RES/ES-10/14, 8 December 2003, and 'Legal Consequences of the Construction of a Wall in the Occupied Palestinian Territory', Advisory Opinion, *ICJ Reports*, 2004.

85 *Ibid.*, par. 110 and 111.

86 *Ibid.*, par. 12 and 113.

87   UN Doc. A/RES/60/1, 24 October 2005, par. 24. Italics added.
88   *Op. cit.*, par. 16.
89   *Op. cit.*, par. 182.
90   *Ibid*, par. 183.
91   Advisory Council on International Affairs, *Reforming the United Nations: a closer look at the Annan report*, The Hague, May 2005, no. 41, p. 25.
92   *Ibid.*, par. 157-159.
93   *Ibid.*, par. 160.

Chapter 4

94   See on this issue: Malcolm N. Shaw, 'The Definition of Minorities in International Law', in Yoram Dinstein and Mala Tabory (eds), *The Protection of Minorities and Human Rights*, Dordrecht/Boston/London: Martinus Nijhoff Publishers, 1992, p. 1-31. Also see Kristin Henrard, *Devising an Adequate System of Minority Protection; Individual Human Rights, Minority Rights and the Right to Self-Determination*, The Hague/Boston/London: Martinus Nijhoff Publishers, 2000, p. 16-55, and, most recently, Rianne Letschert, *The Impact of Minority Rights Mechanisms*, The Hague: T.M.C. Asser Press, 2005, passim (see the index to her book).
95   See M. van der Stoel, 'Conflictvoorkoming in Europa' [Conflict Prevention in Europe], *Internationale Spectator*, Vol. 48, No.3, March 1994, p. 104.
96   See the report of the first session of the Working Group: UN Doc. E/CN.4/Sub.2/1996/2, 30 November 1995, p. 19.
97   Predecessor of the present Committee on Human Rights of the Dutch Advisory Council on International Affairs.
98   Advisory Report, National Minorities, with special reference to Central and Eastern Europe, The Hague, March 1997, p. 27.
99   Yoram Dinstein, 'Collective Human Rights of Peoples and Minorities', *International and Comparative Law Quarterly*, 1976, p. 113.
100   See for a detailed overview: Eduardo Ruiz Vieytez, *The History of Legal Protection of Minorities in Europe (XVIIth - XXth Centuries)*, Derby: University of Derby Press, 1999. Also see Natan Lerner, 'The Evolution of Minority Rights in International Law', in Catherine Brölmann, René Lefeber and Marjoleine Zieck (eds), *Peoples and Minorities in International Law*, Dordrecht/Boston/London: Martinus Nijhoff Publishers, 1993, p. 77-101.

101   See for instance the Advisory Opinion on the Western Sahara of the International Court of Justice, 3 January 1975, *ICJ Reports*, 1975, p. 31.
102   UN Doc. E/CN.4/Res/1999/S-4/1, 27 September 1999.
103   UN Doc. GA/Res./217 C (III), 10 December 1948.
104   *The Prosecutor v. Jean-Paul Akayesu*, Case No. ICTR-96-4-0T, judgment of 2 September 1998. See for this case and other cases: <http://www.ictr.org/English/factsheets> Extensively about another 'genocide case' (against mr. Rutaganda), including the arguments used by the Tribunal, see *International Legal Materials*, Vol. 39, 2000, esp. p. 617-620.
105   Patrick Thornberry, *International Law and the Rights of Minorities*, Oxford: Clarendon Press, 1991, p. 215.
106   *Ibid.*, p. 216.
107   UN Doc. CCPR/C/21/Rev.1/Add.5, 26 April 1994, p. 1-2.
108   See on this and other issues in relation to the *locus standi* for minorities and indigenous peoples, Anna Meijknecht, *Towards International Legal Personality: The Position of Minorities and Indigenous Peoples in International Law*, Antwerpen/Groningen/Oxford: Intersentia-Hart, 2001, passim.
109   See on this concept and related questions, as discussed in this section: Marianne van den Bosch and Willem van Genugten, 'International legal protection of migrant workers, national minorities and indigenous peoples; comparing underlying concepts', *The International Journal on Minority and Group Rights* 9, 2002, p. 195-233.
110   For an overview of cases until 1995, see Ralph Czarnecki, *The Protection of Minorities Under Article 27 CCPR and the Individual Complaint Procedure*, Bochum: UVB Universitätsverlag Dr. N. Brockmeyer, 1995. For an overview of recent cases, see Henrard, *op. cit.*, p. 174-185 and Rianne Letschert, *op. cit.*, p. 129-134.
111   *Lubicon Lake Band vs Canada*, Case 167/1984, view of 26 March 1990. UN Doc. Supp. No. 40 (A/45/40). This point of view has been repeated several times, amongst others in the case *Apirana Mahuika et al. vs New Zealand Zealand*, Case 547/1993, view of 20 October 2000. UN Doc. CCPR/C/70/D/547/1993 (2000).
112   UN Doc. CCPR/C/21/Rev.1/Add.5, 26 April 1994, p. 3.

113 Manfred Nowak, commenting upon Natan Lerner's, 'The Evolution of Minority Rights in International Law', in Catherine Brölmann, René Lefeber and Marjoleine Zieck (eds), *op. cit.*, p. 106.

114 UN Doc. A/Res/47/135, 3 February 1993.

115 UN Doc. E/CN.4/Sub.2/AC.5/1999/WP.1, 13 May 1998, p. 3-4.

116 *Ibid.* See by the same author: 'Protection of Minorities, Possible Ways and Means of Facilitating the Peaceful and Constructive Solution of Problems Involving Minorities', UN Doc. E/CN.4/Sub.2/1993/34, 10 August 1993.

117 See for an overview of the relevant procedures and mechanisms: Gudmundur Alfredsson, Erika Ferrer and Kathryn Ramsay, *Minority Rights: A Guide to United Nations Procedures and Institutions*, London/Lund: Minority Rights Group and Raoul Wallenberg Institute, 2004 (2nd ed.).

118 <http://www.ohchr.org/english/issues/minorities/group. htm>

119 Rianne Letschert, *op. cit.*, p. 95-144, and passim.

120 *Ibid.*, p. 433-434.

121 Case 24/1977, UN Doc. A/36/40, 29 December 1977, p. 166.

122 Article 1, par. 1, sub b, ILO C. 169, adopted 27 June 1989.

123 *Ibid.*, Article 2, par. 3.

124 UN Doc. E/CN.4/Sub.2/1985/31, 14 May 1985, par. 181.

125 See, for example, UN Doc. E/CN.4/2004/81, 7 January 2004.

126 See Willem van Genugten and Camilo Perez-Bustillo, 'The Emerging International Architecture of Indigenous Rights: the Interaction between Global, Regional, and National Dimensions', *The International Journal on Minority and Group Rights* 11, 2004, p. 379-409, passim.

127 UN Doc. CCPR/C/21/Rev.1/Add.5, 26 April 1994, par. 7.

128 UN Doc. A/CONF.157/23, 12 July 1993, Part I, sect. II, par. 32.

129 UN Doc. GA/RES/50/157, 21 December 1995, annex.

130 UN Doc. E/CN.4/RES/2000/87, 28 April 2000.

131 <http://www.un.org/News/Press/docs/2002/HR4589.doc.htm>

132 <http://www.unhcr.ch/indigenous/main>, <http://www.un.org/esa/socdev/unpfii/index.html>

133 UN Doc. E/CN.4/RES/2001/57, 24 April 2001.

134 *Ibid.*

135 UN Doc. E/CN.4/2002/97 and Add.1, 6 March 2002.

136 <http://www.ohchr.org/english/issues/indigenous/rapporteur/e.>

137 <http://www.unhchr.ch/huricane/huricane.nsf/0/078A4495ADBC5D43C1257057005 1338B?opendocument>

138 Article 1, par. 1, ICCPR and ICESCR.

139 UN Doc. A/RES/1514 (XV), 14 December 1960.

140 UN Doc. A/CONF/157/23, 12 July 1993, par. 2.

141 T.M. Franck, 'Postmodern Tribalism and the right to secession', in Catherine Brölmann, René Lefeber, Marjoleine Zieck (eds), *op. cit.*, p. 3-35; Peter Malanczuk, 'Minorities and Self-determination: Reflections on International Law in General, Including Some Recent Development in Ethiopia', in Neri-Sybesma-Knol and Jef van Bellingen (eds), *Naar een nieuwe interpretatie van het Recht op Zelfbeschikking* [Towards a new interpretation of the right to self-determination], Brussels: VUB-Press, 1995, p. 169-183; Paul J.I.M. de Waart, *Dynamics of Self-determination in Palestine: Protection of Peoples as a Human Right*, Leiden: E.J. Brill, 1994, p. 72-74.

142 Article 22, Covenant of the League of Nations.

143 'Legal Consequences of the Construction of a Wall in the Occupied Palestinian Territory', Advisory Opinion ICJ, *ICJ Reports*, 2004, par. 118.

144 *Ibid.*, par. 122: "In other words, the route chosen for the wall gives expression *in loco* to the illegal measures taken by Israel with regard to Jerusalem and the settlements, as deplored by the Security Council (...). There is also a risk of further alterations to the demographic composition of the Occupied Palestinian Territory resulting from the construction of the wall inasmuch as it is contributing (...) to the departure of Palestinian populations from certain areas. That construction, along with measures taken previously, thus severely impedes the exercise by the Palestinian people of its right to self-determination, and is therefore a breach of Israel's obligation to respect that right."

145 Paul de Waart, 'ICJ Firmly Walled in the Law of Power in the Israeli-Palestinian Peace Process', *LJIL*, 18-3 (2005), p. 467-487.

146 Article 4, ICCPR.

147 P.J.I.M. de Waart, 'Arbitration on Self-Determination: a Code of Conduct for Peoples',

197

in K. Boele Woelki et al. (eds), *Comparability and Evaluation: Essays on Comparative Law and International Commercial Arbitration in Honour of Dimitra Kokkini-Iatridou*, Dordrecht/Boston/ London: Martinus Nijhoff Publishers 1994, p. 383-397. According to the 1970 UN Declaration on Principles of International Law and the 1993 Vienna Declaration secession constitutes one of the modes of implementing the right to self-determination. This may never be construed, however, "as authorizing or encouraging any action which would dismember or impair, totally or in part, the territorial integrity or political unity of sovereign and independent States conducting themselves in compliance with the principle of equal rights and self-determination of peoples as described above and thus possessed of a government representing the whole people belonging to the territory without distinction as to race, creed or colour." UN Docs. A/RES/2625 (XXV), 24 October 1970 and A/CONF.157/23, 12 July 1993.

Chapter 5

148 UN Doc. A/RES/2542 (XXIV), 11 December 1969. Philip Alston, 'Ratification of the Covenant on Economic, Social and Cultural Rights: The Need for an Entirely New Strategy', *AJIL*, 1990/2, p. 372-377.

149 Immanuel Wallerstein, *The Capitalist World Economy*, Cambridge/London: Cambridge University Press, 1979, p. 272-273.

150 John Kenneth Galbraith, *Economics, Peace& Laughter – A Contemporary Guide*, New York/London: Penguin Books, 1971, p. 67-69, and *The Culture of Contentment*, Boston/New York/London: Houghton Mifflin Company, 1992, p. 133-135.

151 J. Boyle, 'A Theory of Law and Information', *California Law Review* (1992), p. 1501. This issue also repeatedly returns in, for example, the successive *Human Development Reports* of the Development Program of the United Nations (UNDP). See most recently UNDP, *Human Development Report 2005*, New York, 2005, passim.

152 UN Doc. A/RES/55/2, 18 September 2000, Chapter VI, par. 26.

153 UN Doc. A/RES/60/1, 24 October 2005, par. 143.

154 UN Doc. A/48/935, May 1994, 'An Agenda for Development', par. 101. Also see, amongst many other recent reports, UN Doc. A/59/565, 29 November 2004 (*op. cit.*).

155 *Ibid.*, (1994 Doc.), par. 110 and 111.

156 UN Doc. A/CONF.166/9, 19 April 1995, Annex I, Commitment 4.

157 *Ibid.*, Annex II, par. 66.

158 Asbjørn Eide, Catarina Krause and Alan Rosas (eds), *Economic, Social and Cultural Rights, a Text Book*, Dordrecht/ Boston/London: Martinus Nijhoff Publishers, 1995, Part IV: "Selected Beneficiaries and Situations", p. 273-355. Also see Kathleen E. Mahoney and Paul Mahoney, *Human Rights in the Twenty-First Century: a Global Challenge*, Dordrecht/Boston/ London: Martinus Nijhoff, 1993; UN Doc. A/177/13, 13 September 1994, "Programme of Action of the International Conference on Population and Development", Part VI: "Population Growth and Structure", dealing with children and young people, the elderly and the disabled.

159 Eberhard Jahn, 'Refugees', in R. Bernhardt (ed.), *Encyclopaedia of Public International Law*, Elsevier, Volume IV, p. 72-76.

160 Labor Conventions Nrs. 21 (1926): 'Inspection of Emigrants Convention'; 97 (1949): 'Migration for Employment Convention'; and 143 (1975): 'Migrant Workers (Supplementary Provisions) Convention'. See ILO, *International Labour Conventions and Recommendations 1919-1981*, Geneva: ILO, 1982.

161 United Nations, *Basic Facts about the United Nations*, New York, 2000, p. 42 and 181.

162 UN Doc. A/RES/1386 (XIV), 20 November 1959, and UN Doc. A/44/25, 20 November 1989. The protocols are annexed to UN Doc. A/RES/54/263, 25 May 2000.

163 Articles 1, 23 and 43, Convention on the Rights of the Child. The Committee consists of ten independent experts. It cannot consider individual complaints. However, child rights may be raised before other committees with competence to consider such complaints.

164 UN Doc. A/CONF/157/23, 12 July 1993, par. II, 45.

165 UN Doc. UN Doc. A/55/2, 18 September 2000

166 UN Doc. A/55/2, 18 September 2000, par. 2, 19 and 21.

167 UN Doc. A/RES/60/1, 24 October 2005, par. 117, 118, 128, 141 and 142.

168 UN Doc. A/RES/646 (VII), 20 December 1952.

169 UN Doc. A/RES/34/180, 18 December 1979.

170 UN Doc. A/RES/48/104, 20 December 1993.

171 UN Doc. A/RES/54/49, 6 October 1999.

172 UN Doc. A/55/2, 18 September 2000, par. 20.

173 UN Doc. A/RES/60/1, 24 October 2005, par. 59 and 116.
174 UN Doc. A/RES/33/52, 14 December 1978.
175 UN Doc. A/RES/45/106, 14 December 1990.
176 UN Doc. A/RES/46/91, 16 December 1991.
177 UN Doc. A/RES/47/5, 16 October 1992.
178 Alfred-Maurice de Zayas, 'United Nations Relief and Rehabilitation Administration', in R. Bernhardt (ed.), *op. cit.*, p. 1149-1152.
179 UN Doc. A/RES/428 (v), 14 December 1950, par. 1: "The United Nations High Commissioner for Refugees, acting under the authority of the General Assembly, shall assume the function of providing international protection, under the auspices of the United Nations, to refugees who fall within the scope of the present Statute and of seeking permanent solutions for the problem of refugees by assisting governments, and subject to the approval of the governments concerned, private organizations to facilitate the voluntary repatriation of such refugees, or their assimilation within the new communities."
180 Benny Morris, *The birth of the Palestinian refugee problem, 1947-1949*, Cambridge: Cambridge University Press, 1987, p. 297-298; A. Takkenberg, *The Status of Palestinian Refugees in International Law*, Oxford: Clarendon Press, 1998, par. 469, p. 353: "It should be stressed again that the international community did not *exclude* Palestinian refugees from the general refugee regime, as is often assumed, but rather *suspended* the application of the 1951 Convention and the involvement of the UNHCE in respect of those refugees being assisted by UNRWA."
181 UN Doc. A/RES/194 (III), 11 December 1949, par. 11, and Morris, *op. cit.*, Chapter 4, "Deciding against a return of refugees, April-December 1948", p. 153: "Henceforward, while lip-service was still occasionally paid to the concept of 'the right to return', the international community was to focus more and more on the necessity or desirability and on the possibility of a partial repatriation couples with the re-settlement on the bulk of the refugees in Arab lands. Israel, it would be later seen, had successfully rebuffed the pressures for a mass return."; Takkenberg, *op. cit.*, par. 20, p. 14-15.
182 Article 1.D, Convention relating to the Status of Refugees, 1951.
183 UN Doc. A/RES/302 (IV), 8 December 1949. See Peter Macalister-Smith, 'United Nations Relief and Works Agency for Palestinians in the Near East', in Bernhardt, *op. cit.*, Volume IV, p. 1152-1164.
184 Protocol relating to the Status of Refugees of 31 January 1967.
185 Atle Grahl-Madsen, 'Asylum, Territorial', in Bernhardt (ed.), *op. cit.*, Volume I, 1992, p. 285.
186 'Programme of Action of the United Nations International Conference on Population and Development', Cairo September 1994, UN Doc. A/CONF/171, 13 September 1994, par. 10.21: "The institution of asylum is under severe strain in industrialized countries for a variety of reasons, including the growing numbers of refugees and asylum-seekers and the misuse of asylum procedures by migrants attempting to circumvent immigration restrictions. While two thirds of all countries in the world have ratified the 1951 Convention relating to the Status of Refugees or the 1967 Protocol, which establish standards for the protection of refugees, there is a need to strengthen the support for international protection of and assistance to refugees, especially refugee women and refugee children, who are particularly vulnerable. Displaced persons, who do not qualify for refugee status and are in some cases outside their country, are also vulnerable and need international assistance. Regional agreements to provide protection to persons fleeing war should be considered."
187 *Ibid.*, par. 10.23.
188 UNHCR, *Basic Facts: Refugees by Numbers* (2005 edition), < http://www.unhcr.ch/cgi-bin/texis/vtx/basics>
189 The authors would like to thank Laura van Waas-Hayward, Ph.D. candidate, Tilburg University, for providing them with this succinct information on stateless persons.
190 Maureen Lynch, *Lives on hold: The human cost of statelessness*, Washington: Refugees International, 2005.
191 Advisory Board on Human Security, *Denial of citizenship: A challenge to human security*, 2004; UNHCR, 'Statelessness and citizenship', in *The state of the world's refugees – A humanitarian agenda*, Oxford: Oxford University Press, 1997.

192 UNHCR, 'Information and accession package: the 1954 Convention relating to the status of stateless persons and the 1961 Convention on the reduction of statelessness', UNHCR, Geneva 1999.

193 UNHCR, *The Status of the World's Refugees in search of solutions*, Oxford: Oxford University Press, 1995, Chapter 5, "Managing Migration; International Organization for Migration (IOM)", *World Migration 2005: Costs and Benefits of International Migration*, <http://www.iom.int/en/news/pr882_en.shtml>

194 UN Doc. A/RES/45/158, 18 December 1990.

195 The Committee consists of 10 independent experts. Under article 76, a State party may recognize the competence of the Committee to receive and consider communications from one State party alleging that another State party is not fulfilling its obligations under the Convention. Such communications may be received only from States parties which have so recognized the competence of the Committee. The Committee will deal with a matter referred to it in this way only after all available domestic remedies have been exhausted, and may then propose its good offices in an effort to reach a friendly solution. Under article 77, a State party may recognize the competence of the Committee to receive and consider communications from or on behalf of individuals within that State's jurisdiction who claim that their rights under the Convention have been violated. Such communications may be received only if they concern a State party which has so recognized the competence of the Committee. If the Committee is satisfied that the matter has not been, and is not being, examined in another international context, and that all domestic remedies have been exhausted, it may call for explanations, and express its views.

196 UN Doc. A/RES/55/2, 18 September 2000, par. 25.

197 UN Doc. A/RES/60/1, 24 October 2005, par. 61-64.

198 ECOSOC/ RES/663 C (XXIV), 31 July 1957 and 2076 (LXII), 13 May 1977.

199 UN Doc. A/RES/34/169, 17 December 1979 and UN Doc. A/RES/40/33, 29 November 1985.

200 UN Doc. A/RES/40/32, 29 December 1985 and UN Doc. A/RES/40/146, 13 December 1985.

201 UN Doc. A/RES/39/46, 10 December 1984. Also see UN Doc. A/RES/3453 (XXX), 9 December 1975.

202 UN Doc. A/RES37/194, 18 December 1982

203 UN Doc. A/CONF.166/9, 19 April 1995, Annex I, par. 15 (h): "One of the world's largest minorities, more than 1 in 10, are people with disabilities, who are too often forced into poverty, unemployment and social isolation."

204 UN Doc. A/RES/2856 (XXVI), 20 December 1971, 'Declaration on the Rights of the Mentally Retarded Persons'.

205 UN Doc. A/RES/36/77, 8 December 1981.

206 UN Doc. A/CONF.157/23, 12 July 1993, par. II (64). Also see UN Doc. A/CONF.166/9, 19 April 1995, Annex I, par. 29, commitment 6 sub (n).

207 UN Doc. A/RES/48/96, 20 December 1993, par. 14.

208 UN Doc. A/RES/60/1, 24 October 2005, par. 129.

209 UN Doc. A/CONF.177/13, 18 October 1994, Annex 1, par. 2.1 and UN Doc. A/CONF/177/20, 17 October 1995, 'Report of the Fourth World Conference on Women', Annex II, par. 9.

210 UN Doc. A/CONF/197/20, 17 October 1995, Chapter VI: 'Adoption of the Beijing Declaration and Platform of Action. B Reservations and interpretative statements on the Beijing Declaration and Platform for Action', par. 11: "(...) the Holy See cannot accept ambiguous terminology concerning unqualified control over sexuality and fertility, particularly as it could be interpreted as a societal endorsement of abortion and homosexuality"; par. 20: "Third, we wish to state that the adoption of paragraph 96 does not signify endorsement by the Government of Malaysia of sexual promiscuity, any form of sexual perversion or sexual behaviour that is synonymous with homosexuality and lesbianism"; par. 26: "The representative of Peru submitted the following statement: (...) It is understood that sexual rights refer solely to heterosexual relationships."

211 Earth Negotiations Bulletin, 'A Daily Report of the Fourth World Conference on Women', Vol. 14 nr, 21, 18 September 1995.

212 UN Doc. A/CONF.197/20, 17 October 1995, par. 46 (Italics added).

213 Ibid., Chapter V, par. 16: "Israel would have preferred that explicit reference be made to the particular barriers faced by women because of sexual orientation. However, in the light of the interpretation given to the words 'other status' by, inter alia, the United Nations Human Rights Committee, we interpret the words 'other status' to include sexual orientation"; par. 28: "The South African delegation interprets paragraph 96 (...), to include the right to be free from coercion, discrimination and violence based on sexual orientation"; par. 30: "The United States has a firm policy of non-discrimination on the basis of sexual orientation and considers that the omission of this reference in paragraph 46 and elsewhere in the Platform for Action in no way justifies such discrimination in any country."

214 Articles 28 and 29, UDHR.

215 Article 28, ICCPR.

216 UN Doc. CHR/Resolution 2000/63, 26 April 2000. The Sub-Commission appointed Mr. Miguel Alfonso Martinez as Special Rapporteur to undertake the study. The ECOSOC approved the appointment on 24 July 2001. According to its outline the study will elaborate upon the study of Erica-Irene A. Daes, *Freedom of the individual under law: an analysis of article 29 of the Universal Declaration of Human Rights*, Geneva: UN Centre for Human Rights, Human Rights study series no. 3, 1990.

217 See, for example, 'A Universal Declaration on Human Responsibilities', proposed by the InterAction Council of 25 former heads of state and government in 1997, published in Henry J. Steiner and Philip Alston, *International Human Rights in Context: Law, Politics, Morals*, Oxford: Oxford University Press, Second Edition, 2000, p. 351-353, as part of the text and materials on "Rights, Duties and Cultural Relativism" (Chapter 5, p. 351-403). Also see, 'The Trieste Declaration of Human Duties – a Code of Ethics of Shared Responsibilities', of the International Council of Human Duties, 1993, <http://www.univ.trieste.it/~ichd/>

218 UN Doc. A/RES/55/2, 18 september 2000, par. 6.

219 UN Doc. A/RES/60/1, 24 October 2005, par. 4.

220 Wolfgang Benedek and Alice Yotopoulos-Marangopoulos (eds), *Anti-terrorist Measures and Human Rights*, Leiden/Boston: Martinus Nijhoff Publishers, 2004, p. 6-7.

221 Robert D. Kaplan, *Warrior Politics: Why Leadership Demands a Pagan Ethos*, New York: First Vintage Book Edition, 2003, p. 118.

222 Ibid., p. 9.

223 Caleb Carr, *The Lessons of Terror: a History of Warfare against Civilians*, New York: Random House Paperback Edition, 2003, p. 212.

224 Ibid., p. 121.

225 Ibid., p. 6.

226 Ibid., p. 17-18.

227 Ibid., p. 262.

228 OEA Doc. A/SER.L/V/II.116, 22 October 2002, Preface.

229 Ibid.

230 Kevin Boyle, 'Terrorism, States of Emergency and Human Rights', in Wolfgang Benedek and Alice Yotopoulos-Marangopoulos (eds), *op. cit.*, p. 100.

231 ICJ Reports, 2004, par. 106.

232 Article 18, par. 3, ICCPR: "Freedom to manifest one's religion or beliefs may be subject only to such limitations as are prescribed by law and are necessary to protect public safety, order, health, or morals or the fundamental rights of others."

Chapter 6

233 Article 55, UN Charter.

234 UN Doc. A/RES/1514 (XV), 14 December 1960.

235 A.A. Fatouros, 'Developing States', in Bernhardt (ed.), *op. cit.*, Vol. I (1992), p. 1017-1018. Also see Jaap van Soest, *The Start of International Development Cooperation in the United Nations 1945-1952*, Assen: Van Gorcum, 1978.

236 Paul de Waart, 'Sustainable Development through a Socially Responsible Trade and Investment Regime', in Nico Schrijver and Friedl Weiss (eds), *International Law and Sustainable Development: Principles and Practice*, Dordrecht/Boston/London: Martinus Nijhoff Publishers, 2004, p. 273-294.

237 Op. cit., p. 636.

238 De Waart, *op. cit.*, LJIL, 18-3 (2005), p. 467-487.

239 See, for example, the epoch-making report of Raúl Prebisch, *Transformación y desarollo La gran tarea de la América Latina*, Mexico: Fondo de Cultura Económica, 1971.

240 UN Doc. A/RES/1995 (XIX), 30 December 1964; Branislav Gosovic, *UNCTAD Conflict and Compromise: The Third World's Quest for an Equitable Order through the United Nations*, Leiden: Sijthoff, 1972.

241 See Pieter VerLoren van Themaat, *The Changing Structure of International Economic Law: a contribution of legal theory on the debate on a new international economic order*, Dordrecht/Boston/London/The Hague: Martinus Nijhoff Publishers/T.M.C Asser Institute, 1981.

242 See Karin Arts, *Integrating Human Rights and Development Cooperation: the Case of the Lomé Convention*, Dordrecht/Boston/London: Martinus Nijhoff Publishers, 2000.

243 See Y. Li, *Transfer of Technology for Deep Seabed Mining: The 1982 Law of the Sea Convention and Beyond*, Dordrecht/Boston/London: Martinus Nijhoff Publishers, 1994.

244 UN Doc. A/RES/55/2, 18 September 2000. See *Annex 6* to this book and the website <www.un.org/millennium>

245 In 2004, the development assistance by the US rose to 0.17% ODA (with Iraq as the top recipient), while the average of the EU countries was at 0.36%. The average of the total of the DAC countries was in 2004 at 0.26%. See the annual report of the Development Assistance Committee of the OECD at <www.oecd.org/dac>

246 Jeffrey D. Sachs, *Investing in development; a practical plan to achieve the Millennium Development Goals*, London/Sterling: Earthscan, Millennium Project, UNDP, 17 January 2005, p. xi.

247 *Ibid*, p. 1.

248 *Ibid.*, p. 7.

249 *Ibid.*, p. 64.

250 *Ibid.*, p. 110 and 112.

251 *Op. cit.*, p. 137.

252 *Ibid.*

253 UN Doc. A/RES/60/1, 24 October 2005, par. 26 and par. 68, respectively.

254 Singapore Ministerial Declaration, adopted on 13 December 1996. (No WTO-code available.)

255 The 2003 meeting in Cancún was finalised with a ministerial *statement* only, due to the lack of progress and consensus during the conference, to put it mildly; see WT/MIN(03)/20, 23 September 2003.

256 WT/MIN(01)/DEC/1, adopted on 14 November 2001.

257 See for other examples of overlapping standards: W.J.M. van Genugten, 'Linking the power of economics to the realisation of human rights, with the WTO as a special case', paper presented in Hong Kong, May 2005 (publication forthcoming in 2006).

258 The so-called 'human rights conventions' of the ILO: C.29 (1930) on 'Forced Labor', C.87 (1948) on 'Freedom of Association and Protection of the Right to Organize', C.98 (1949) on 'The Right to Organize and Collective Bargaining', C.100 (1951) on 'Equal Remuneration', C.105 (1957) on 'Abolition of Forced Labor', C.111 (1958) on 'Discrimination', C.138 (1973) on 'Minimum Age', and C.182 (1999) on the 'Worst Forms of Child Labor'.

259 See for parallels, the discussion on the human rights obligations of the IMF and the World Bank: Mac Darrow, *Between Light and Shadow. The World Bank, the International Monetary Fund and International Human Rights Law*, Oxford: Hart, 2003, esp. Chapter IV; Willem van Genugten, Paul Hunt and Susan Mathews (eds), *World Bank, IMF and Human Rights*, Nijmegen: Wolf Legal Publishers, 2003.

260 WT/MIN(01)/DEC/1, 20 November 2001.

261 *Op. cit.*, par. 62.

262 *Ibid.*, par. 58.

263 *Op. cit.*, p. 212.

264 *Ibid.*

265 *Ibid.*

266 *Ibid.*

267 WT/MIN(01)/DEC/1, adopted on 14 November 2001.

268 *Op. cit.*, p. 212.

269 *Ibid.*, passim.

270 *Ibid.*

271 UN Doc. A/RES/60/1, 24 October 2005, par. 27-32.

272 <http://www.wto.org/english/thewto_e/minist_e/min05_ e/min05_18dec_e.htm> The full document – WT/MIN(05)/ W/3/Rev.2, 18 December 2005 – can be found at <http:// www.wto.org/english/thewto_e/minist_e/mi n05_e/min05_18dec_e.htm>

273 UN doc. E/CN.4/Sub.2/1992/16, 3 July 1992 p. 14.

274 UN doc. E/CN.4/Sub.2/1999/11, 17 June 1999 p. 13.

275 *Ibid.*, p. 15.

276 *Ibid.*, p. 14-15.

277 See Mac Darrow, *op. cit.*

278 'Report of the Secretary-General on the Work of the Organization', United Nations, New York, 1998, UN doc. A/53/1, 27 August 1998, p. 23.

279 UN Doc. E/CN.4/Sub.2/1999/11, 17 June 1999, p. 14.

280 See in great detail, Willem van Genugten, Paul Hunt and Susan Mathews (eds), *World Bank, IMF and Human Rights*, Nijmegen: Wolf Legal Publishers, 2003, p. 247-255.

281 ILO Tripartite Declaration of Principles, par. 8, *Official Bulletin* ILO, Geneva, 1978, Vol. LXI, Series A, No. 1.

282 See W.J.M. van Genugten, "Companies and Human Rights: the Binding Character of Voluntary Codes of Conduct", in Wybo P. Heere (ed.), *From Government to Governance, Proceedings of the 2003 Hague Joint Conference on Contemporary Issues of International Law*, The Hague: T.M.C. Asser Press, 2004, p. 187-193.

283 Also see the ILO Declaration on Fundamental Principles and Rights at Work of June 1998, par. 22: "Declares that all Members, even if they have not ratified the Conventions in question, have an obligation arising from the very fact of membership in the Organization to respect, to promote and to realize, in good faith and in accordance with the Constitution, the principles concerning the fundamental rights which are the subject of those Conventions, namely:
(a) freedom of association and the effective recognition of the right to collective bargaining;
(b) the elimination of all forms of forced or compulsory labour;
(c) the effective abolition of child labour; and
(d) the elimination of discrimination in respect of employment and occupation."

284 See Nicola Jägers, *Corporate Human Rights Obligations: in Search of Accountability*, Antwerp/Oxford/New York: Intersentia, 2002, Chapter VII.

285 UN doc. E/CN.4/2005/L.87, 15 April 2005, par. 1.

286 *Ibid.*, par. 3.

287 *Op. cit.*, par. 20.

288 UN Doc. A/60/124, 10 August 2005, par. 8.

289 *Ibid.*, par. 11.

290 *Ibid.*, par. 12.

291 *Ibid.*, par. 13.

292 Sachs, *op. cit.*

293 *Ibid.*, p. 137.

294 *Ibid.*, p. 31.

295 Cancelled.

296 UN Doc. A/RES/41/128, 4 December 1986.

297 See for instance UN Doc. A/CONF/157/23, 12 July 1993, par. I, 10.

298 See for instance its vote against the 2004 Resolution on the Right to Development (Res. 2004/7), adopted by the Commission on Human Rights by 49 votes against 3. See UN Doc. E/2004/23, 15 October 2004 p. 368.

299 Report of the Commission on Human Security, *Human Security Now*, New York, 2003, p. 4. The executive summary of the report has been added to this book, as *Annex 7*.

Chapter 7

300 See the preliminary reports of E. Hey and N.J. Schrijver on 'Volkenrecht en duurzame ontwikkeling' [International law and sustainable development], in *Mededelingen van de Nederlandse Vereniging voor Internationaal Recht* [Proceedings of the Netherlands Society of International Law] Nr. 127, The Hague: Asser Press, 155 p.; Antoinette Hildering, *International law, Sustainable Development and Water Management*, dissertation, Vrije Universiteit Amsterdam, Delft: Eburon Academic Publishers, 2004, Annex 2 'Principles per policy level', p. 193-201; the Earth Charter Initiative on "Values and Principles for a Sustainable Future": <http://www.earthcharter.org>

301 See UN Doc. A/57/329, 31 August 2002, 'Letter of the governments of Bangladesh and the Netherlands enclosing the New Delhi Declaration'; also see International Law Association, *Report of the 70th Conference New Delhi*, London: ILA, 2003, p. 22 and p. 380, and ILA Report of the Seventy-First Conference, *op. cit.*, p. 566-567.

302 UN Doc. A/Res. 2997 (XXVII), 15 December 1972.

303 World Commission on Environment and Development, *Our Common Future*, Oxford: Oxford University Press, 1987.

304 *Ibid.*, p. 43.

305 See A/CONF.151/26 (Vol. I), 12 August 1992, Annex 1. See *Annex 4* to this book for the full text of the Rio Declaration.

306 UN Doc. A/CONF. 199/20, 4 December 2002. See for an interesting recent study: Susan M. Mathews, 'Imperial Imperatives: Ecodevelopment and the Resistance of Adivasis of Nagarhole National Park, India', <http://www2.warwick.ac.uk/fac/soc/law/elj/lgd/2005_1/mathews/.>

307 UN Doc. A/RES/60/1, 24 October 2005, par. 48.

Chapter 8

308 S.D. Bailey and S. Daws, *The Procedure of the UN Security Council*, Oxford: Oxford University Press, 3rd ed., 1998.

309 Chapter VII of the UN Charter, Art. 41. See *Annex 1* to this book.

310 Article 108, UN Charter.

311 Bruno Simma, *The Charter of the United Nations: A Commentary*, Oxford: Oxford University Press, 2002, p. 31.

312 On the concepts of negative and positive peace, see B.V.A. Röling, *Volkenrecht en Vrede* [International Law and Peace], Deventer: Kluwer, 3rd ed., 1985, p. 18-19.

313 Article 27, UN Charter.

314 B. Fassbender, *UN Security Council Reform and the Right of Veto. A Constitutional Perspective*, The Hague: Kluwer Law International, 1998, p. 301-305.

315 UN Doc. A/RES. 377 A (V), 3 November 1950.

316 See Articles 12, 14 and 24, UN Charter.

317 UN Doc. A/RES/1991 A (XVIII), 17 December 1963.

318 See *United Nations Yearbook 1965*, New York: United Nations, p. 232.

319 *Op. cit.*, Preamble.

320 *Ibid.*

321 B. Fassbender, 'All Illusions Shattered? Looking Back on a Decade of Failed Attempts to reform the UN Security Council', in 7 *Max Planck Yearbook of United Nations Law* (2003), p. 183-228; Kenneth W. Manusama, *The Principle of Legality in the Law and Post-Cold War Practice of the United Nations Security Council*, dissertation, Free University of Amsterdam, 2004, p. 347-349.

322 Articles 23 and 108, UN Charter.

323 Op. cit.

324 *Op. cit.*, par. 256.

325 *Op. cit.*, par. 252.

326 *Op. cit.*, par. 168, referring to UN Doc. A/Res./55/2, 18 September 2000.

327 *Ibid.*, par. 170.

328 UN Doc. A/RES/60/1, 24 October 2005, par. 153.

329 This question is also at the center of the report issued jointly by the Dutch Advisory Council on International Affairs and the Advisory Committee on Issues of Public International Law, *Pre-emptive Action*, The Hague, July 2004.

330 Richard N. Gardner, 'Neither Bush nor the "Jurisprudes"', *American Journal of International Law*, 2003, 97/3, p. 590.

331 *Op. cit.*, par. 191 and 192.

332 *Op. cit.*, par. 122 and 126.

333 See N.J. Schrijver, 'September 11th and Challenges to International Law', in J. Boulden and T.G. Weiss (eds), *Terrorism and the UN: Before and After September 11*, Bloomington: Indiana University Press, 2004, p. 55-76.

334 UN Doc. A/59/2005, 21 March 2005, par. 91: "(…) the right to resist occupation must be understood in its true meaning. It cannot include the right to deliberately kill or maim civilians". Also see UN Doc. A/59/565, 29 November 2004, par. 164.

335 See, *e.g.*, Art. 2 of the International Convention for the Suppression of the Financing of Terrorism, United Nations, 1999.

336 UN Doc. SC/Res./1566, 8 October 2004.

337 UN Doc. A/RES/60/1, 24 October 2005, par. 81-83.

338 *Ibid.*, par. 85.

Chapter 9

339 For a survey of current peace operations, see <http://www.un.org/Depts/dpko/dpko/text.htm>

340 The term 'peace operations' is an umbrella concept, including quite a variety of operations. The *SIPRI Yearbook 2004* mentions a total of 52 multilateral peace missions all over the world, including small observations missions. An example of a non-UN led but UN-mandated peace operation, is the International Security Assistance Force (ISAF) in Afghanistan, at the moment under the command of NATO. A large number of peace missions, which have not been mandated by the UN, are performed by regional organizations such as NATO, the EU, the Community of Independent States (CIS) and the African Union (AU). A small number of peace missions are under the command of other organizations or ad hoc coalitions of states.

341 The most frequent type of conflict is the intrastate conflict. The *SIPRI Yearbook 2004* states that only two out of 19 conflicts in 2003 resulting in many thousands of deaths each, were between states: the conflict between India and Pakistan in Kashmir and the American-British invasion of Iraq.

342 UN Doc. A/Res/109 (II), 21 October 1947.

343 UN Doc. A/Res/1000 (ES-1), 5 November 1956.

344 *Ibid.*

345 S. Tharoor, 'Should UN Peacekeeping Go Back to Basics?', *Survival*, Winter 1995-1996, p. 56.

346 An example is the United Nations Transitional Authority in Cambodia (UNTAC), whose mandate included a human rights component, as well as governmental, electoral, military, police, repatriating and rehabilitation components.

347 For a detailed description of this matter, see Rob de Wijk, *Vechten met één hand op de rug? Vredesondersteuning in escalerende conflicten* [Fighting with one hand behind your back? Supporting peace in escalating conflicts], The Hague: Netherlands Institute of International Relations 'Clingendael', March 1998.

348 See UN Doc. A/55/305, 21 August 2000, foreword by UN Secretary-General Kofi Annan.

349 See *Annex 5* to this book for the executive summary of the report.

350 *Ibid.*, passim.

351 See Dick A. Leurdijk (ed.), *A UN Rapid Deployment Brigade, Strengthening the Capacity for Quick Response*, The Hague: Netherlands Institute of International Relations 'Clingendael', 1995.

352 See H. Peter Langille, 'Renewing Partnerships for the Prevention of Armed Conflict: Options to Enhance Rapid Deployment and Initiate A UN Standing Emergency Capability', A Policy Option Paper Prepared for the Canadian Centre for Foreign Policy Development, Global Human Security Ideas and Initiatives, see <http://www.worldfederalistscanada.org/langille1.pdf>.

353 UN Doc. A/50/60/-S/1995/1, 3 January 1995.

354 See Gerard Quille, '"Battle Groups" to strengthen EU military crisis management?', *European Security Review*, April 2004, p. 1-2.

355 UN Doc. A/47/277-S/24111, 17 June 1992.

356 See *A European initiative to strengthen the role of the United Nations in promoting peace and security*, Document A/1839, 'Assembly of Western European Union, The Interparliamentary European Security and Defence Assembly', 1 December 2003, p. 8-9.

357 See 'Remarks of Mr. Jean-Marie Guéhenno, Under-Secretary-General for Peacekeeping Operations', to the Fourth Committee of the General Assembly, 20 October 2005, p. 4.

358 See 'African peacekeeping, Revival or relapse?', *Strategic Comments*, Volume 5, June 2004; and Cedric de Coning, 'Peacekeeping in Africa, the next decade', *Conflict Trends*, 3/2002, p. 46-56.

359 'African peacekeeping, Revival or relapse?', *Strategic Comments*, Volume 10 Issue 5, June 2004, p. 2.

360 'Can Africans keep their own peace?', *The Economist*, 17 June 2004, p. 46.

361 'Into the breach, Peacekeeping in Africa', *The Economist*, 17 June 2004.

362 *Ibid.*

363 See Rizal Sukma, *The Future of ASEAN: Towards a Security Community*, Jakarta: CSIS, 3 June 2003; Leonard C. Sebastian and Chong Ja Ian, 'Towards an ASEAN Security Community at Bali', *Perspectives*, Singapore: Institute of Defence and Strategic Studies, October 2003; and Adianto P. Simamora, 'UN welcomes ASEAN Peacekeeping Force', *Jakarta Post*, 27 February 2004.

364 Adrian Kuah, 'The ASEAN Security Community', *IDDS Commentaries*, Singapore, 15 June 2004.

365 Jean-Marie Guéhenno, 'United Nations Peacekeeping', *Conflict Trends*, 3/2003, p. 15-16. Also see Bertrand G. Ramcharan, *The Security Council and the Protection of Human Rights*, Dordrecht/Boston/London: Martinus Nijhoff Publishers, 2002, p. 111-115. Ramcharan concludes – p. 213 – that "in the future work of the Security Council, it will be important to accentuate the principle of justice and the protection principle. A Security Council that is moved by considerations of justice and by a willingness to act for protection of those at risk will be faithful to the Charter's vision of peace grounded in economic and social justice and respect for human rights".

366 UN Doc. A/RES/60/1, 24 October 2005, par. 92.

367 *Ibid.*

368 *Ibid.*, par. 93.

369 *Ibid.*, par. 94-95.

370 *Ibid.*, par. 97.

371 *Ibid.*, par. 98.

372 *Ibid.*

373 *Ibid.*, par. 100.

374 *Ibid.*, par. 101-102.

375 *Ibid.*, par. 103.

Chapter 10

376 See, for example, W.J.M. van Genugten, 'Mensenrechten tussen staatssoevereiniteit en internationale jurisdictie' [Human rights between state sovereignty and international jurisdiction], *Rechtsfilosofie en Rechtstheorie*, 1992/3, p. 204-223; Nico Schrijver, 'Soevereiniteit versus humaniteit? Het hek raakt van de dam' [Sovereignty v. humanity? Things are getting out of hand], *Internationale Spectator*, May 2000, p. 227-332, with a summary in English; and Paul de Waart, 'Rechtmatigheid van humanitaire interventie' [Legitimacy of humanitarian intervention], *Ibid.*, p. 232-238. Also see N.M. Blokker and N.J. Schrijver (eds), *The Security Council and the Use of Force. Theory and Reality-A Need for Change?*, Leiden: Martinus Nijhoff, 2005.

377 G. Molier, *De (on)rechtmatigheid van humanitaire interventie* [The (il)legality of humanitarian interventions], The Hague: Boom Juridische Uitgevers, 2003, with a summary in English. The doctoral research was supervised by W. Verwey, whose essay 'Humanitarian Intervention under International Law', *NILR* (32), 1985, p. 357-418, placed the subject on the agenda in the Netherlands.

378 Articles 27, par. 3 and 39, UN Charter.

379 The Hague, April 2000.

380 *Ibid.*, p. 35.

381 *Ibid.*

382 *Ibid.*

383 *Ibid.*

384 UN Doc. A/RES/56/83, 28 January 2002.

385 UN Doc. A/RES /59/35, 16 December 2004, on 'Responsibility of States for Internationally Wrongful Acts'.

386 *ICJ Reports*, 1970, par. 33.

387 See N.J. Schrijver, 'The Changing Nature of State Sovereignty', *British Yearbook of International Law 1999*, vol. 70, Oxford, 2000, p. 65-98.

388 Michael Ignatieff, *Whose Universal Values? The Crisis in Human Rights*, Praemium Erasmianum Essay 1999, The Hague: Foundation Praemium Erasmianum, 1999, written on the occasion of the presentation of the Erasmus award to Mary Robinson, the then UN High Commissioner for Human Rights.

389 'The burden', *New York Times Magazine*, 5 January 2003.

390 Ignatieff, *op. cit.*, (1999), p. 18.

391 UN Doc. A/RES/60/1, 24 October 2005, par. 138.

392 *Ibid.*, par. 139.

393 Art. 14 of the Covenant of the League of Nations, 1919.

394 Arthur Eyffinger, *The International Court of Justice 1946-1996*, The Hague/London/Boston: Kluwer Law International, 1996, p. 80.

395 Article 36, PCIJ Statute.

396 Articles 92 and 93 (1), UN Charter.

397 *Ibid.*, Article 1.

398 Articles XXIII – XXIV, Hague Conventions of 29 July 1899, and Articles XLIV ff. of the Hague Conventions of 18 October 1907.

399 Eyffinger, *op. cit.*, p. 64-64.

400 *Ibid.*, p. 74.

401 *Ibid.*, p. 80-81. National groups of the PCA may nominate through their governments candidates to the UNGA and the Security Council.

402 *Ibid.*, p. 91.

403 In its active period 1922-1940 the PCIJ dealt with 29 contentious cases and gave 27 advisory opinions. See Hermann Mosler and Karin Oellers-Frahm, 'The World Court of the League of Nations', in Simma, *op. cit.*, p. 1142.

404 Eyffinger, *op. cit.*, p. 76.

405 Preamble, par. 3, UN Charter.

406 See Article 2, UN Charter, incorporated in *Annex 1* to this book.

407 Bardo Fassbender and Albert Bleckmann, 'Article 2 (1)', in Simma, *op. cit.*, p. 70.

408 Christian Tomuschat, 'Article 2 (3)', in Simma, *op. cit.*, p. 103.

409 See *Annex 3* to this book.

410 UN Doc. A/RES/2625 (XXV), 24 October 1970, General Part sub 2. At present the only veto-power, which accepted the 'compulsory clause' is the UK. France withdrew its acceptance in 1974 after the submission to the ICJ by Australia and New Zealand of the legality of its nuclear tests in the South Pacific, and the US did so in 1985 after the submission of the dispute on the legality of (para)military activities by the US in Nicaragua. The USSR/Russia and China never accepted the compulsory jurisdiction of the Court. See Eyffinger, *op. cit.*, p. 131.

411 P.J.I.M. de Waart, *The Element of Negotiation in the Pacific Settlement of Disputes between States: an analysis of provisions made and/or applied since 1918 in the field of the pacific settlement if international disputes*, The Hague: Martinus Nijhoff, 1973, p. 1.

412 Eyffinger, *op. cit.*, p. 21.

413 Article 94 (2), UN Charter.

414 See *Annex 1* to this book for the full text of the Article.

415 Hermann Mosler and Karin Oellers-Frahm, 'Article 94', in Simma, *op. cit.*, p. 1178.

416 Alain Pillepich, 'Article 94', in , in Jean-Pierre Cot, Alain Pellet, Mathias Forteau (eds), *La Charte des Nations Unies Commentaire article par article*, 3rd ed., Paris: Economica, 2005, p. 1996.

417 Article 64, ICJ Statute.

418 Article 98, Rules of Court. See Eyffinger, *op. cit.*, p. 145.

419 Article 103, UN Charter.

420 *ICJ Reports*, 1992, p. 26. Paul J.I.M. de Waart, 'The UN System at Crossroads: People's Centre or Big Brothers' Small Club', in Niels Blokker & Sam Muller, *Towards More Effective Supervision by International organizations*, Dordrecht/Boston/London: Martinus Nijhoff Publishers, 1994, Volume I, p. 61-62.

421 Rudolf Bernhardt, 'Article 103', in Simma, *op. cit.*, p. 1302.

422 <http://www.icj-cij.org/icjwww/igeneralinformation/icjgnnot.html>.

423 Hermann Mosler and Karin Oellers-Frahm, 'Article 92', in Simma, *op. cit.*, p. 1146.

424 UN Doc. A/RES/55/2, 18 September 2000, par. 4.

425 *Ibid.*, par. 9 and 30.

426 UN Doc. A/RES/60/1, 24 October 2005, par. 73.

427 *Ibid.*, par. 134 sub (f).

428 Hermann Mosler and Karin Oellers-Frahm, 'Article 92', in Simma, *op. cit.*, p. 1146-1147.

429 Mosler/Oellers-Frahm, 'Article 96', *Ibid.* p. 1182.

430 P.J.I.M. de Waart, 'Arbitration on Self-determination: a Code of Conduct for Peoples', in K. Boele-Woelki, et al. (eds), *Comparability and Evaluation: Essays on Comparative Law, Private International Law and International Commercial Arbitration in hounour of Dimitri Kokkini-Iatridou*, Dordrecht/Boston/London: Martinus Nijhoff Publishers, p. 383-398.

431 UN Doc. A/50/60-S/1995/1, 3 January 1995, par. 70.

432 UN Doc. E/C.12/1997/8, CESCR, 'General Comment No. 8 (1997)', 12 December 1997, par. 3.

433 UN Doc. A/53/1, 27 August 1998, Supplement No. 1, p. 7.

434 *Ibid.*

435 W.J.M. van Genugten and G.A de Groot (eds), *United Nations Sanctions; Effectiveness and Effects, Especially in the Field of Human Rights*,

Antwerpen/Groningen/Oxford: Intersentia, 1999, p. 135-152.

436 *Ibid.*, p. 150.

437 *Ibid.*, p. 150-151.

438 *Ibid.*, p. 151.

439 UN Doc. A/53/1, 27 August 1998, p. 7.

440 <http://www.un.org/Docs/sc/committees/INTRO.htm>

441 *Ibid.*

442 UN Doc. A/RES/60/1, 24 October 2005, par. 106.

443 *Ibid.*, par. 107.

444 *Ibid.*, par. 108.

445 *Ibid.*, par. 109.

446 Paul R. Williams and Michael P. Scharf, *Peace with Justice? War Crimes and Accountability in the Former Yugoslavia*, Lanham/Boulder/New York/Boston: Rowman & Littlefield Publishers, 2002, p. 91-112.

447 Paul de Waart, 'Legal protection of defendants against the UN Security Council', in *Contemporary International Law Issues: New Forms, Ned Applications*, 1997, Hague Joint Conference ASIL/NVIR, The Hague: T.M.C. Asser Institute, 1998, p. 14-17.

448 The first registrar of the ICTY, Theo van Boven, recalled that the judges of the ICJ did not want to share the Peace Palace with the ICTY, because of the very fact that the latter Tribunal was established by the Security Council and the fear that the ICTY would endanger the independent position of the ICJ. See Cees Banning and Petra de Koning, *Balkan aan de Noordzee: Over het Joegoslavië-tribunaal, over recht en onrecht* [Balkan at the North Sea: About the Yugoslavia Tribunal, about justice and injustice], Amsterdam/Rotterdam: Prometheus/NRC Handelsblad, 2005, p. 32 (in Dutch, English edition forthcoming].

449 Simma, *op. cit.*, p. 555; Laurence Boisson de Chazournes, 'Les Nations Unies et les juridictions penales internationales', in Cot, Pellet, Forteau, *op. cit.*, p. 217-225. Also see Göran Sluiter, *International Criminal Adjudication and the Collection of Evidence: Obligations of States*, Antwerp/Groningen/Oxford: Intersentia, 2005, p. 22-23.

450 Williams/Scharf, *op. cit.*, p. 104.

451 <http://www.un.org/icty/glance/index.htm> These and other figures are presented by the ICTY itself (last update: 12 September 2005).

452 L.J. van den Herik, *The Contribution of the Rwanda Tribunal to the Development of International Law*, Leiden: Nijhoff, 2005.

453 UN Doc. S/2004/616, 23 August 2004.

454 <http://www.ictr.org/default.htm>. Figures presented by the ICTR itself (last update: May 2005).

455 UN Doc. SC/RES/1503 (2003), 28 August 2003.

456 Article 17, ICC Statute.

457 Article 15, par. 1, ICC Statute.

458 Article 15, par. 3, ICC Statute.

459 See for more information on the position of (specific) victims of violations of core crimes of inter-/supranational criminal law: Anne-Marie L.M. de Brouwer, *Supranational Criminal Prosecution of Sexual Violence; The ICC, and the Practice of the ICTY and the ICTR*, Antwerp/Groningen/Oxford: Intersentia, 2005. Also see the resolution on 'Basic Principles and Guidelines on the Right to a Remedy and Reparation for Victims of Gross Violations of International Human Rights Law and Serious Violations of International Humanitarian Law', UN Doc. A/C.3/60/L.24, 24 October 2005.

460 See out of many sources, Fons Coomans, Fred Grünfeld, Ingrid Westendorp and Jan Willems, *Rendering Justice to the Vulnerable, Liber amicorum in Honour of Theo van Boven*, The Hague/London/Boston: Kluwer Law International, 2000.

461 UN Docs S/RES/1422(2002), 12 July 2002, and S/RES/1486, 12 June 2003, requesting, "consistent with the provisions of Article 16 of the Rome Statute, that the ICC, if a case arises involving current or former officials or personnel from a contributing State not a Party to the Rome Statute over acts or omissions relating to a United Nations established or authorized operation, shall for a 12-month period starting 1 July 2003 not commence or proceed with investigation or prosecution of any such case, unless the Security Council decides otherwise".

462 UN Doc. S/RES/1593 (2005), 31 March 2005.

463 <http://www.icc-cpi.int/cases.html>

Chapter 11

464 Christian Tomuschat, 'The Universal Declaration of Human Rights of 1948: Does it need any Updating?', SIM Special, No. 9, Utrecht: SIM, 1989, p. 79.

465 Christian Tomuschat, Human Rights between Idealism and Realism, Oxford: Oxford University Press, 2003, p. 29.

Selected Bibliography on the United Nations

General international law and organization studies

C.F. Amerasinghe, *Principles of the Institutional Law of International Organizations*, Cambridge (2nd ed., 2005)

I. Brownlie, *Principles of Public International Law*, Oxford (6th ed., 2003)

M. Byers and G. Nolte (eds), *United States Hegemony and the Foundations of International Law*, Cambridge (2003)

A. Cassese, *International Law*, Oxford (2nd ed., 2005)

I. Claude, *Swords into Plowshares. The Problems and Progress of International Organization*, New York (4th ed., 1971)

H.K. Jacobson, *Networks of Interdependence: International Organizations and the Global Political System*, New York (2nd ed., 1984)

C.W. Jenks, *The Proper Law of International Organisations*, London (1962)

J. Rawls, *The Law of Peoples*, Cambridge/London (1999)

J.G. Ruggie (ed.), *Multilateralism Matters: The Theory and Praxis of an Institutional Form*, New York (1993)

P. Sands, *Lawless World: America and the Making and Breaking of Global Rules*, London (2005)

H.G. Schermers and N. Blokker, *International Institutional Law: Unity within diversity*, Leiden (4th ed., 2003)

M.N. Shaw, *International Law*, Cambridge (5th ed., 2003)

M. Virally, *L'Organisation mondiale*, Paris (1972)

O. Young, *International Governance: Protecting the Environment in a Stateless Society*, New York (1994)

League of Nations

P.F. Brugière, *La sécurité collective, 1919-1945*, Paris (1952)

UN Library Geneva/Graduate Institute of International Studies, *The League of Nations in retrospect: proceedings of the symposium*, Berlin (1983)

F.S. Northedge, *The League of Nations: Its Life and Times 1920-1946*, Leicester (1988)

F.P. Walters, *A History of the League of Nations*, London, 2 volumes (1952)

History of the United Nations

L. Emmerij, R. Jolly and T.G. Weiss, *Ahead of the Curve? UN Ideas and Global Challenges*, Bloomington (2001)

L.M. Goodrich and E. Hambro, *Charter of the United Nations: Commentary and Documents*, New York (3rd ed., 1969)

R. Jolly, L. Emmerij and T.G. Weiss, *The Power of UN Ideas. Lessons from the First 60 Years*, New York (2005)

R.B. Russell and J.E. Muther, *A History of the United Nations. The Role of the United States 1940-1945*, Washington (1958)

S.C. Schlesinger, *Act of Creation. The Founding of the United Nations*, Boulder (2003)

United Nations, *Documents of the United Nations Conference on International Organization*, New York (the UNCIO Documents, 22 vols, 1945-1955)

Works of reference

R. Bernhardt (ed.), *Encyclopedia of Public International Law*, Amsterdam, vol. I (1992); vol. II (1995); vol. III (1997); vol. IV (2000); vol. V (2003), in particular volume IV on the UN

E.J. Osmanczyk (ed.), *The Encyclopedia of the United Nations and International Relations*, New York (2nd ed., 1994)

H. Volger, *A Concise Encyclopedia of the United Nations*, The Hague (2002)

T.G. Weiss and S. Daws (eds), *The Oxford Handbook on the United Nations*, Oxford (forthcoming)

R. Wolfrum (ed.), *Handbuch der Vereinte Nationen*, München (1991)

Main textbooks

P.R. Baehr and L. Gordenker, *The United Nations: Reality and Ideal*, Basingstoke (4th ed., 2005)

M. Bedjaoui, *Towards a new international economic order*, Paris (1979)

Ch. Chaumont, *L'organisation des Nations Unies*, Paris (1990)

I. Claude, *The Changing United Nations*, New York (1967)

A. Knight, *A Changing United Nations: Multilateral Evolution and the Quest for Global Governance*, Basingstoke (2000)

K.A. Mingst and M.P. Karns, *The United Nations in the Post-Cold War Era*, Boulder (3rd ed., 2005)

A. Roberts and B. Kingsbury (eds), *United Nations, Divided World: The UN's Roles in International Relations*, Oxford (2nd ed., 1993)

K.P. Saksena, *Reforming the United Nations: The Challenge of Relevance*, New Delhi (1995)

T.G. Weiss, D.P. Forsythe and R.A. Coate, *The United Nations and Changing World Politics*, Boulder (4th ed., 2004)

N.D. White, *The United Nations System – Toward International Justice*, Boulder (2002)

United Nations law

B. Conforti, *The Law and Practice of the United Nations*, Leiden (3rd ed., 2005)

J-P. Cot et A. Pellet, *La Charte des Nations Unies. Commentaire article par article*, Paris (3rd ed., 2005)

R. Higgins, *The Development of International Law Through the Political Organs of the United Nations*, London (1963)

H. Kelsen, *The Law of the United Nations: a critical analysis of its fundamental problems*, New York (1951)

O. Schachter and C. Joyner (eds), *United Nations Legal Order*, Cambridge, 2 vols (1995)

O. Schachter, "The Relation of Law, Politics and Action in the United Nations", RdC, vol. 109, 1963-II, pp. 185-256

B. Simma (ed.), *The Charter of the United Nations. A Commentary*, Oxford (2nd ed., 2002)

R. Wolfrum and C. Philipp (eds), *United Nations: Law, Policies and Practice*, Dordrecht (1995)

Studies on the principal UN organs

General

P. Taylor and A.J.R. Groom (eds), *The United Nations at the Millennium: the principal organs*, London (2000)

General Assembly

S.D. Bailey, *The General Assembly of the United Nations. A Study of Procedure and Practice*, London (1960)

B. Finley, *The Structure of the United Nations General Assembly*, New York (2nd ed., 1990)

M.J. Peterson, *The General Assembly in World Politics*, Boston (1986)

F.A. Vallat, "The Competence of the United Nations General Assembly", *RdC*, vol. 79, 1959-II, pp. 203-292

Security Council

S.D. Bailey and S. Daws, *The Procedure of the UN Security Council*, Oxford (3rd ed., 1998)

M. Bedjaoui, *The New World Order and the Security Council: Testing the Legality of its Acts*, Dordrecht (1994)

B. Fassbender, *UN Security Council Reform and the Right of Veto: A Constitutional Perspective*, The Hague (1998)

O. Fleurence, *La réforme du Conseil de sécurité. L'état du débat depuis la fin de la guerre froide*, Brussels (2000)

K. Herndl, "Reflections on the Role, Functions and Procedures of the Security Council", *RdC* vol. 206, 1987-VI, pp. 289-395.

D.M. Malone (ed.), *The U.N. Security Council: from the Cold War to the 21st Century*, Boulder (2004)

B. G. Ramcharan, *The Security Council and the Protection of Human Rights*, The Hague (2002)

D. Sarooshi, *The United Nations and the Development of Collective Security: the delegation by the Security Council of its Chapter VII powers*, Oxford (1999)

E. de Wet, *The Chapter VII Powers of the UN Security Council*, Oxford (2004)

Economic and Social Council

D. P. Forsythe (ed.), *The United Nations in the World Political Economy: Essays in Honour of Leon Gordenker*, Basingstoke (1989)

J.P. Renninger, *ECOSOC: Options for Reform*, New York (1981)

C. Rucz, *Le Conseil économique et social de l'ONU et la coopération pour le développement*, Paris (1983)

W.R. Sharp, *The United Nations Economic and Social Council*, New York (1969)

D. Williams, *The Specialized Agencies and the United Nations: the system in crisis*, London (1987)

Trusteeship Council

S.R. Chowdhuri, *International Mandates and Trusteeship Systems: A Comparative Study*, The Hague (1955)

J.N. Murray, *The United Nations Trusteeship System*, Urbana (1957)

C.E. Toussaint, *The Trusteeship System of the United Nations*, Westport (1976)

International Court of Justice

M. Bedjaoui, *The International Court of Justice in its Heyday*, The Hague (1996)

P.H.F. Bekker, *World Court Decisions at the Turn of the Millennium (1997-2001)*, The Hague (2002)

L. Damrosch, *The International Court of Justice at a Crossroads*, New York (1987)

T.O. Elias, *The United Nations Charter and the World Court*, Lagos (1989)

A. Eyffinger, *The International Court of Justice: 1946-1996*, The Hague (1999)

V. Lowe and M. Fitzmaurice (eds), *Fifty Years of the International Court of Justice: Essays in Honour of Sir Robert Jennings*, Cambridge (1996)

B.N. Patel, *The World Court Reference Guide (1992-2000)*, The Hague (2002)

S. Rosenne, *The Law and Practice of the International Court (1920-1996)*, 4 vols, The Hague (3rd ed., 1997)

S. Rosenne, *The World Court: What It Is and How It Works*, updated by T. Gill *et al.*, Leiden (6th ed., 2003)

M. Sameh M. Amr, *The Role of the International Court of Justice as the Principal Organ of the United Nations*, The Hague (2003)

Secretariat

L. Gordenker, *The UN Secretary-General and Secretariat*, London (2005)

G. Langrod, *The International Civil Service: its origins, its nature, its evolution*, Leiden (1963)

J. Lemoine, *The International Civil Servant – an Endangered Species*, The Hague (1995)

T. Meron, *The United Nations Secretariat: the rules and the practice*, Lexington (1977)

B. Rivlin and L. Gordenker (eds), *The Challenging Role of the UN Secretary-General: Making the Most Impossible Job in the World Possible*, Westport (1993)

S.M. Schwebel, *The Secretary-General of the United Nations: His Political Powers and Practice*, Cambridge (1952)

J. Siotis, *Essai sur Le Secrétariat International*, Genève (1963)

M.-C. Smouts, *Le Secrétaire Général des Nations Unies: son rôle dans la solution des conflits internationaux*, Paris (1971)

B. Urquhardt, *Hammarskjöld*, New York (1972)

International criminal tribunals

M.C. Bassiouni and P. Manikas, *The Law of the International Criminal Tribunal for the Former Yugoslavia*, New York (1996)

M. Boot, *Nullem Crimen sine Lege and the Subject Matter Jurisdiction of the International Criminal Court: Genocide, Crimes against Humanity and War Crimes*, Antwerp/Oxford/New York (2002)

A.-M. de Brouwer, *Supranational Criminal Prosecution of Sexual Violence. The ICC and the Practice of the ICTY and the ICTR*, Antwerp (2005)

A. Cassese, *International Criminal Law*, Oxford (2003)

A. Cassese, P. Gaeta and J.R.W.D. Jones (eds), *The Rome Statute of the International Criminal Court: A Commentary*, 3 vols., Oxford (2002)

L.J. van den Herik, *The Contribution of the Rwanda Tribunal to the Development of International Law*, Leiden (2005)

J.R.W.D. Jones and S. Powles, *International Criminal Practice: the International Criminal Tribunal for the Former Yugoslavia, the International Criminal Tribunal for Rwanda, the International Criminal Court, the Special Court for Sierra Leone, the East Timor Special Panel for Serious Crimes, War crimes prosecutions in Kosovo*, New York/Oxford (3rd ed., 2003)

R. May *et al.* (ed.), *Essays on ICTY procedure and evidence in honour of Gabrielle Kirk McDonald*, The Hague (2001)

F. Mégret, *Le Tribunal Pénal International pour le Rwanda*, Paris (2002)

G. Robertson, *Crimes against Humanity*, London (1999)

C.P.R. Romano/A. Nollkaemper/J.K. Kleffner (eds), *Internationalized Criminal Courts and Tribunals: Sierra Leone, East Timor, Kosovo, and Cambodia*, Oxford (2004)

W.A. Schabas, *An Introduction to the International Criminal Court*, Cambridge (3rd ed., 2004)

O. Triffterer (ed.), *Commentary on the Rome Statute of the International Criminal Court; Observers' Notes, Article by Article*, Baden-Baden (1999)

P. R. Williams and Michael P. Scharf, *Peace with Justice? War Crimes and Accountability in the Former Yugoslavia*, Lanham (2002)

Human rights and protection of minorities

P. Alston (ed.), *The United Nations and Human Rights: a Critical Reappraisal*, Oxford (2nd ed., 2005)

Th. C. van Boven, *People Matter*, Amsterdam (1982)

A. Cassese, *Self-determination of Peoples: A Legal Reappraisal*, Cambridge (1995)

Y. Dinstein and Mala Tabory (eds), *The Protection of Minorities and Human Rights*, Dordrecht (1992)

A. Eide, C. Krause and A. Rosas (eds), *Economic, Social and Cultural Rights, a Text Book*, Dordrecht (1995)

S. Foster, *Human Rights and Civil Liberties*, Harlow (2003)

K. Henrard, *Devising an Adequate System of Minority Protection; Individual Human Rights, Minority Rights and the Right to Self-Determination*, The Hague (2000)

J.P. Humphrey, *Human Rights and the United Nations: a Great Adventure*, New York (1983)

R.M. Leschert, *The Impact of Minority Rights Mechanisms*, The Hague (2005)

B.G. Ramcharan, *The United Nations High Commissioner for Human Rights*, The Hague (2002)

A.H. Robertson, rev. by J.G. Merrills, *Human Rights in the World*, Manchester/New York (3rd ed., 1992)

M. Sepulveda, Th. van Banning, G.D. Gudmundsdóttir, C. Chamoun and W.J.M. van Genugten, *Human Rights Reference Handbook*, Costa Rica (3rd ed., 2004)

H.J. Steiner and P. Alston, *International human rights in context: law, politics, morals: texts and materials*, Oxford (2nd ed., 2000)

P. Thornberry, *International Law and the Rights of Minorities*, Oxford (1991)

C. Tomuschat, *Human Rights: Between Idealism and Realism*, Oxford (2003)

P.J.I.M. de Waart, Dynamics of Self-determination in Palestine: Protection of Peoples as a Human Right, Leiden (1994)

Peace-keeping

Roméo Dallaire, *Shake Hands with the Devil. The Failure of Humanity in Rwanda*, New York (2004)

P.F. Diehl, *International Peacekeeping*, Baltimore (1993)

W. Durch, *The Evolution of UN Peacekeeping: Case Studies and Comparative Analysis*, London (1993)

S.M. Hill and Sh.P. Malik, *Peacekeeping and the United Nations*, Aldershot (1996)

Royal Netherlands Army, *Peace Operations, Army Doctrine Publication III*, The Hague (1999)

W. Shawcross, *Deliver Us From Evil. Peacekeepers, Warlords and a World of Endless Conflict*, New York (2000)

D.S. Sörenson, *The Politics of peacekeeping in the Post-Cold War Era*, London (2005)

J. Whitman, *Peacekeeping and the UN Agencies*, London (1999)

M. Zwanenburg, *Accountability of Peacesupport Operation*, Leiden (2005)

Collective sanctions

W.J.M. van Genugten and G.A. de Groot (eds), *United Nations sanctions: effectiveness and effects, especially in the field of human rights: a multi-disciplinary approach*, Antwerp (1999)

V. Gowlland-Debbas, *Collective responses to illegal acts in international law: United Nations action in the question of Southern Rhodesia*, Dordrecht (1990)

V. Gowlland-Debbas, *United Nations Sanctions and International Law*, The Hague (2001)

P. Wallersteen, *International Sanctions: Between words and wars in the global system*, London (2005)

Use of force

N.M. Blokker and N.J. Schrijver (eds), *The Security Council and the Use of Force. Theory and reality - a need for change?*, Leiden (2005)

W. Clarke and Jeffrey Herbst (eds), *Learning from Somalia; The Lessons of Armed Humanitarian Intervention*, Boulder/Oxford (1997)

T.M. Franck, *Recourse to Force: State action against threats and armed attacks*, Cambridge (2002)

J.L. Holzgrefe and R.O. Keohane (eds), *Humanitarian Intervention. Ethical, Legal, and Political Dilemmas*, Cambridge (2003)

F.R. Téson, *Humanitarian Intervention: An Inquiry into Law and Morality*, New York (1988)

M. Walzer, *Arguing About War*, New Haven/London (2004)

Terrorism

W. Benedek and A. Yotopoulos-Marangopoulos (eds), *Anti-terrorist Measures and Human Rights*, Leiden (2004)

J. Boulden and T.G. Weiss (eds), *Terrorism and the UN: Before and After September 11*, Bloomington (2004)

H. Duffy, *The "War on Terror" and the Framework of International Law*, Cambridge (2005)

Criticisms and caricatures of the United Nations

Y.Z. Blum, *Eroding the United Nations Charter*, Dordrecht (1993)

W.F. Buckley Jr, *United Nations Journal. A Delegate's Odyssey*, New York (1977)

J. Harrod and N.J. Schrijver (eds), *The UN Under Attack*, Aldershot (1988)

D.P. Moynihan, *The United Nations: A Dangerous Place*, Boston (1978)

R. Righter, *Utopia Lost: The United Nations and World Order*, New York (1995)

Alternative visions on and reform of the United Nations

M. Bertrand, *The Third Generation World Organization*, Dordrecht (1989)

H. Gherari and S. Szurek (dir.), *L'émergence de la société civile internationale – Vers la privatisation du droit international?*, Paris (2003)

John Keane, *Global Civil Society?*, Cambridge (2003)

J. Müller (ed.), *Reforming the United Nations: New Initiatives and Past Efforts*, Vol. I-III, The Hague (1997)

J. Müller (ed.), *Reforming the United Nations: the Quiet Revolution*, The Hague (2001)

T.G. Weiss and L. Gordenker (eds), *NGO's, the UN and Global Governance*, Boulder (1996)

Annexes

Introductory note

Quotations have been taken from important UN legal instruments, documents and reports throughout this book. Some deserve special attention because of their landmark character or because they are otherwise important or interesting for a better understanding of the United Nations. The annexes have also been included in the main contents of the book, in order to make them easily accessible to the reader.

Index to the annexes

Charter of the United Nations*

(selection of articles)

PREAMBLE

We the peoples of the United Nations determined

- to save succeeding generations from the scourge of war, which twice in our lifetime has brought untold sorrow to mankind, and
- to reaffirm faith in fundamental human rights, in the dignity and worth of the human person, in the equal rights of men and women and of nations large and small, and
- to establish conditions under which justice and respect for the obligations arising from treaties and other sources of international law can be maintained, and
- to promote social progress and better standards of life in larger freedom, and for these ends
- to practice tolerance and live together in peace with one another as good neighbours, and
- to unite our strength to maintain international peace and security, and
- to ensure, by the acceptance of principles and the institution of methods, that armed force shall not be used, save in the common interest, and
- to employ international machinery for the promotion of the economic and social advancement of all peoples,

Have resolved to combine our efforts to accomplish these aims. Accordingly, our respective Governments, through representatives assembled in the city of San Francisco, who have exhibited their full powers found to be in good and due form, have agreed to the present Charter of the United Nations and do hereby establish an international organization to be known as the United Nations.

CHAPTER I

Purposes and principles

Article 1

The Purposes of the United Nations are:

1. To maintain international peace and security, and to that end: to take effective collective measures for the prevention and removal of threats to the peace, and for the suppression of acts of aggression of other breaches of the peace, and to bring about peaceful means, and in conformity with the principles of justice and international law, adjustment or settlement of international disputes or situations which might lead to a breach of the peace;

---

* Adopted in San Francisco, 26 June 1945; entry into force: 24 October 1945.

2. To develop friendly relations among nations based on respect for the principle of equal rights and self-determination of peoples, and to take other appropriate measures to strengthen universal peace;
3. To achieve international cooperation in solving international problems of an economic, social, cultural, or humanitarian character, and in promoting and encouraging respect for human rights and for fundamental freedoms for all without distinction as to race, sex, language, or religion; and
4. To be a center for harmonizing the actions of nations in the attainment of these common ends.

Article 2
The Organization and its Members, in pursuit of the Purposes stated in Article 1, shall act in accordance with the following Principles.
1. The Organization is based on the principle of the sovereign equality of all its Members.
2. All Members, in order to ensure to all of them the rights and benefits resulting from membership, shall fulfil in good faith the obligations assumed by them in accordance with the present Charter.
3. All Members shall settle their international disputes by peaceful means in such a manner that international peace and security, and justice, are not endangered.
4. All Members shall refrain in their international relations from the threat or use of force against the territorial integrity or political independence of any state, or in any other manner inconsistent with the Purposes of the United Nations.
5. All Members shall give the United Nations every assistance in any action it takes in accordance with the present Charter, and shall refrain from giving assistance to any state against which the United Nations is taking preventive or enforcement action.
6. The Organization shall ensure that states which are not Members of the United Nations act in accordance with these Principles so far as may be necessary for the maintenance of international peace and security.
7. Nothing contained in the present Charter shall authorize the United Nations to intervene in matters which are essentially within the domestic jurisdiction of any state or shall require the Members to submit such matters to settlement under the present Charter; but this principle shall not prejudice the application of enforcement measures under Chapter VII.

CHAPTER II
Membership

Article 4
1. Membership in the United Nations is open to all other peace-loving states which accept the obligations contained in the present Charter and, in the judgment of the Organization, are able and willing to carry out these obligations.
2. (...)

Article 5
A Member of the United Nations against which preventive or enforcement action has been taken by the Security Council may be suspended from the exercise of the rights and privileges of membership by the General Assembly upon the recommendation of the Security Council. The exercise of these rights and privileges may be restored by the Security Council.

Article 6
A Member of the United Nations which has persistently violated the Principles contained in the present Charter may be expelled from the Organization by the General Assembly upon the recommendation of the Security Council.

CHAPTER IV
The General Assembly
Functions and Powers

Article 11
1. The General Assembly may consider the general principles of cooperation in the maintenance of international peace and security, including the principles governing disarmament and the regulation of armaments, and may make recommendations with regard to such principles to the Members or to the Security Council or to both.
2. The General Assembly may discuss any questions relating to the maintenance of international peace and security brought before it by any Member of the United Nations, or by the Security Council, or by a state which is not a Member of the United Nations (...) and (...) may make recommendations with regard to any such questions to the state or states concerned or to the Security Council or to both. Any such question on which action is necessary shall be referred to the Security Council by the
3. General Assembly either before or after discussion. The General Assembly may call the attention of the Security Council to situations which are likely to endanger international peace and security.
4. (....)

Article 13
1. The General Assembly shall initiate studies and make recommendations for the purpose of:
a. promoting international cooperation in the political field and encouraging the progressive development of international law and its codification;
b. promoting international cooperation in the economic, social, cultural, educational, and health fields, and assisting in the realization of human rights and fundamental freedoms for all without distinction as to race, sex, language, or religion.
2. (...)

Article 14

(...) the General Assembly may recommend measures for the peaceful adjustment of any situation, regardless of origin, which it deems likely to impair the general welfare or friendly relations among nations, including situations resulting from a violation of the provisions of the present Charter setting forth the Purposes and Principles of the United Nations.

Voting

Article 19

A Member of the United Nations which is in arrears in the payment of its financial contributions to the Organization shall have no vote in the General Assembly if the amount of its arrears equals or exceeds the amount of the contributions due from it for the preceding two full years. The General Assembly may, nevertheless, permit such a Member to vote if it is satisfied that the failure to pay is due to conditions beyond the control of the Member.

CHAPTER V
The Security Council
Composition

Article 23

1. The Security Council shall consist of fifteen Members of the United Nations. The Republic of China, France, the Union of Soviet Socialist Republics, the United Kingdom of Great Britain and Northern Ireland, and the United States of America shall be permanent members of the Security Council. The General Assembly shall elect ten other Members of the United Nations to be non-permanent members of the Security Council, due regard being specially paid, in the first instance to the contribution of Members of the United Nations to the maintenance of international peace and security and to the other purposes of the Organization, and also to equitable geographical distribution.
2. The non-permanent members of the Security Council shall be elected for a term of two years. In the first election of the non-permanent members after the increase of the membership of the Security Council from eleven to fifteen, two of the four additional Members shall be chosen for a term of one year. A retiring member shall not be eligible for immediate re-election.
3. Each member of the Security Council shall have one representative.

Functions and Powers

Article 24

1. In order to ensure prompt and effective action by the United Nations, its Members confer on the Security Council primary responsibility for the maintenance of international peace and security, and agree that in carrying out its duties under this responsibility the Security Council acts on their behalf.

2. (...)
3. (...)

Article 25
The Members of the United Nations agree to accept and carry out the decisions of the Security Council in accordance with the present Charter.

Voting

Article 27
1. Each member of the Security Council shall have one vote.
2. Decisions of the Security Council on procedural matters shall be made by an affirmative vote of nine members.
3. Decisions of the Security Council on all other matters shall be made by an affirmative vote of nine members including the concurring votes of the permanent members; provided that, in decisions under Chapter VI, and under paragraph 3 of Article 52, a party to a dispute shall abstain from voting.

CHAPTER VI
Pacific settlement of disputes

Article 33
1. The parties to any dispute, the continuance of which is likely to endanger the maintenance of international peace and security, shall, first of all, seek a solution by negotiation, enquiry, mediation, conciliation, arbitration, judicial settlement, resort to regional agencies or arrangements, or other peaceful means of their own choice.
2. The Security Council shall, when it deems necessary, call upon the parties to settle their dispute by such means.

Article 34
The Security Council may investigate any dispute, or any situation which might lead to international friction or give rise to a dispute, in order to determine whether the continuance of the dispute or situation is likely to endanger the maintenance of international peace and security.

Article 36
1. The Security Council may, at any stage of a dispute of the nature referred to in Article 33 or of a situation of like nature, recommend appropriate procedures or methods of adjustment.
2. The Security Council should take into consideration any procedures for the settlement of the dispute which have already been adopted by the parties.
3. In making recommendations under this Article the Security Council should also take into consideration that legal disputes should as a general rule be referred by the parties to the International Court of Justice in accordance with the provisions of the Statute of the Court.

CHAPTER VII
Action with respect to threats to the peace, breaches of the peace, and acts of aggression

Article 39
The Security Council shall determine the existence of any threat to the peace, breach of the peace, or act of aggression and shall make recommendations, or decide what measures shall be taken in accordance with Articles 41 and 42, to maintain or restore international peace and security.

Article 40
In order to prevent an aggravation of the situation, the Security Council may, before making the recommendations or deciding upon the measures provided for in Article 39, call upon the parties concerned to comply with such provisional measures as it deems necessary or desirable. Such provisional measures shall be without prejudice to the rights, claims, or position of the parties concerned. The Security Council shall duly take account of failure to comply with such provisional measures.

Article 41
The Security Council may decide what measures not involving the use of armed force are to be employed to give effect to its decisions, and it may call upon the Members of the United Nations to apply such measures. These may include complete or partial interruption of economic relations and of rail, sea, air, postal, telegraphic, radio, and other means of communication and the severance of diplomatic relations.

Article 42
Should the Security Council consider that measures provided for in Article 41 would be inadequate or have proved to be inadequate, it may take such action by air, sea, or land forces as may be necessary to maintain or restore international peace and security. Such action may include demonstrations, blockade, and other operations by air, sea, or land forces of Members of the United Nations.

Article 43
1. All Members of the United Nations, in order to contribute to the maintenance of international peace and security, undertake to make available to the Security Council, on its call and in accordance with a special agreement or agreements, armed forces, assistance, and facilities, including rights of passage, necessary for the purpose of maintaining international peace and security.
2. Such agreement or agreements shall govern the numbers and types of forces, their degree of readiness and general location, and the nature of the facilities and assistance to be provided.
3. The agreement or agreements shall be negotiated as soon as possible on the initiative of the Security Council. They shall be concluded between the Security Council and Members or between the Security Council and

groups of Members and shall be subject to ratification by the signatory states in accordance with their respective constitutional processes.

Article 45
In order to enable the United Nations to take urgent military measures, Members shall hold immediately available national air force contingents for combined international enforcement action. The strength and degree of readiness of these contingents and plans for their combined action shall be determined, within the limits laid down in the special agreement or agreements referred to in Article 43, by the Security Council with the assistance of the Military Staff Committee.

Article 50
If preventive or enforcement measures against any state are taken by the Security Council, any other state, whether a Member of the United Nations or not, which finds itself confronted with special economic problem arising from the carrying out of those measures shall have the right to consult the Security Council with regard to a solution of those problems.

Article 51
Nothing in the present Charter shall impair the inherent right of individual or collective self-defence if an armed attack occurs against a Member of the United Nations, until the Security Council has taken the measures necessary to maintain international peace and security. Measures taken by Members in the exercise of this right of self-defence shall be immediately reported to the Security Council and shall not in any way affect the authority and responsibility of the Security Council under the present Charter to take at any time such action as it deems necessary in order to maintain or restore international peace and security.

CHAPTER VIII
Regional arrangements

Article 52
1. Nothing in the present Charter precludes the existence of regional arrangements or agencies for dealing with such matters relating to the maintenance of international peace and security as are appropriate for regional action, provided that such arrangements or agencies and their activities are consistent with the Purposes and Principles of the United Nations.
2. The Members of the United Nations entering into such arrangements or constituting such agencies shall make every effort to achieve pacific settlement of local disputes through such regional arrangements or by such regional agencies before referring them to the Security Council.
3. The Security Council shall encourage the development of pacific settlement of local disputes through such regional arrangements or by such regional agencies either on the initiative of the states concerned or by reference from the Security Council.
4. (...)

Article 53
1. The Security Council shall, where appropriate, utilize such regional arrangements or agencies for enforcement action under its authority. But no enforcement action shall be taken under regional arrangements or by regional agencies without the authorization of the Security Council, with the exception of measures against any enemy state, as defined in paragraph 2 of this Article, provided for pursuant to Article 107 or in regional arrangements directed against renewal of aggressive policy on the part of any such state until such time as the Organization may, on request of the Governments concerned, be charged with the responsibility for preventing further aggression by such a state.
2. The term enemy state as used in paragraph 1 of this Article applies to any state which during the Second World War has been an enemy of any signatory of the present Charter.

CHAPTER IX
International Economic and Social Cooperation

Article 55
With a view to the creation of conditions of stability and well-being which are necessary for peaceful and friendly relations among nations based on respect for the principle of equal rights and self-determination of peoples, the United Nations shall promote:
a. higher standards of living, full employment, and conditions of economic and social progress and development;
b. solutions of international economic, social, health, and related problems; and international cultural and educational cooperation; and
c. universal respect for, and observance of, human rights and fundamental freedoms for all without distinction as to race, sex, language, or religion.

Article 56
All Members pledge themselves to take joint and separate action in cooperation with the Organization for the achievement of the purposes set forth in Article 55.

Article 57
1. The various specialized agencies, established by intergovernmental agreement and having wide international responsibilities, as defined in their basic instruments, in economic, social, cultural, educational, health, and related fields, shall be brought into relationship with the United Nations in accordance with the provisions of Article 63.
2. Such agencies thus brought into relationship with the United Nations are hereinafter referred to as specialized agencies.

CHAPTER X
The Economic and Social Council
Functions and Powers

Article 62
1. The Economic and Social Council may make or initiate studies and reports with respect to international economic, social, cultural, educational, health, and related matters and may make recommendations with respect to any such matters to the General Assembly, to the Members of the United Nations, and to the specialized agencies concerned.
2. It may make recommendations for the purpose of promoting respect for, and observance of, human rights and fundamental freedoms for all.
3. It may prepare draft conventions for submission to the General Assembly, with respect to matters falling within its competence.
4. (...)

Procedure

Article 68
The Economic and Social Council shall set up commissions in economic and social fields and for the promotion of human rights, and such other commissions as may be required for the performance of its functions.

Article 71
The Economic and Social Council may make suitable arrangements for consultation with non-governmental organizations which are concerned with matters within its competence. Such arrangements may be made with international organizations and, where appropriate, with national organizations after consultation with the Member of the United Nations concerned.

CHAPTER XIV
The International Court of Justice

Article 92
The International Court of Justice shall be the principal judicial organ of the United Nations. It shall function in accordance with the annexed Statute, which is based upon the Statute of the Permanent Court of International Justice and forms an integral part of the present Charter.

Article 93
1. All Members of the United Nations are ipso facto parties to the Statute of the International Court of Justice.
2. (...)

Article 94
1. Each Member of the United Nations undertakes to comply with the decision of the International Court of Justice in any case to which it is a party.
2. If any party to a case fails to perform the obligations incumbent upon it under a judgment rendered by the Court, the other party may have recourse to the Security Council, which may, if it deems necessary, make recommendations or decide upon measures to be taken to give effect to the judgment.

Article 95

Nothing in the present Charter shall prevent Members of the United Nations from entrusting the solution of their differences to other tribunals by virtue of agreements already in existence or which may be concluded in the future.

Article 96

1. The General Assembly or the Security Council may request the International Court of Justice to give an advisory opinion on any legal question.
2. Other organs of the United Nations and specialized agencies, which may at any time be so authorized by the General Assembly, may also request advisory opinions of the Court on legal questions arising within the scope of their activities.

CHAPTER XV
The Secretariat

Article 97

The Secretariat shall comprise a Secretary-General and such staff as the Organization may require. The Secretary-General shall be appointed by the General Assembly upon the recommendation of the Security Council. He shall be the chief administrative officer of the Organization.

Article 98

The Secretary-General shall act in that capacity in all meetings of the General Assembly, of the Security Council, of the Economic and Social Council, (...), and shall perform such other functions as are entrusted to him by these organs. (...)

Article 99

The Secretary-General may bring to the attention of the Security Council any matter which in his opinion may threaten the maintenance of international peace and security.

Article 100

1. (...)
2. Each Member of the United Nations undertakes to respect the exclusively international character of the responsibilities of the Secretary-General and the staff and not to seek to influence them in the discharge of their responsibilities.

CHAPTER XVI
Miscellaneous provisions

Article 103

In the event of a conflict between the obligations of the Members of the United Nations under the present Charter and their obligations under any other international agreement, their obligations under the present Charter shall prevail.

Article 105
1. Organization shall enjoy in the territory of each of its Members such privileges and immunities as are necessary for the fulfilment of its purposes.
2. Representatives of the Members of the United Nations and officials of the Organization shall similarly enjoy such privileges and immunities as are necessary for the independent exercise of their functions in connection with the Organization.
3. (...)

Article 108
Amendments to the present Charter shall come into force for all Members of the United Nations when they have been adopted by a vote of two thirds of the members of the General Assembly and ratified in accordance with their respective constitutional processes by two thirds of the Members of the United Nations, including all the permanent members of the Security Council.

Universal Declaration of Human Rights[*]
(full text)

PREAMBLE
- Whereas recognition of the inherent dignity and of the equal and inalienable rights of all members of the human family is the foundation of freedom, justice and peace in the world,
- Whereas disregard and contempt for human rights have resulted in barbarous acts which have outraged the conscience of mankind, and the advent of a world in which human beings shall enjoy freedom of speech and belief and freedom from fear and want has been proclaimed as the highest aspiration of the common people,
- Whereas it is essential, if man is not to be compelled to have recourse, as a last resort, to rebellion against tyranny and oppression, that human rights should be protected by the rule of law,
- Whereas it is essential to promote the development of friendly relations between nations,
- Whereas the peoples of the United Nations have in the Charter reaffirmed their faith in fundamental human rights, in the dignity and worth of the human person and in the equal rights of men and women and have determined to promote social progress and better standards of life in larger freedom,
- Whereas Member States have pledged themselves to achieve, in co-operation with the United Nations, the promotion of universal respect for and observance of human rights and fundamental freedoms,
- Whereas a common understanding of these rights and freedoms is of the greatest importance for the full realization of this pledge,
Now, therefore, the General Assembly
- Proclaims this Universal Declaration of Human Rights as a common standard of achievement for all peoples and all nations, to the end that every individual and every organ of society, keeping this Declaration constantly in mind, shall strive by teaching and education to promote respect for these rights and freedoms and by progressive measures, national and international, to secure their universal and effective recognition and observance, both among the peoples of Member States themselves and among the peoples of territories under their jurisdiction.

Article 1
All human beings are born free and equal in dignity and rights. They are endowed with reason and conscience and should act towards one another in a spirit of brotherhood.

---

[*] UN Doc. GA/RES/217 A (III), 10 December 1948.

Article 2
- Everyone is entitled to all the rights and freedoms set forth in this Declaration, without distinction of any kind, such as race, colour, sex, language, religion, political or other opinion, national or social origin, property, birth or other status.
- Furthermore, no distinction shall be made on the basis of the political, jurisdictional or international status of the country or territory to which a person belongs, whether it be independent, trust, non-self-governing or under any other limitation of sovereignty.

Article 3
Everyone has the right to life, liberty and security of person.

Article 4
No one shall be held in slavery or servitude; slavery and the slave trade shall be prohibited in all their forms.

Article 5
No one shall be subjected to torture or to cruel, inhuman or degrading treatment or punishment.

Article 6
Everyone has the right to recognition everywhere as a person before the law.

Article 7
All are equal before the law and are entitled without any discrimination to equal protection of the law. All are entitled to equal protection against any discrimination in violation of this Declaration and against any incitement to such discrimination.

Article 8
Everyone has the right to an effective remedy by the competent national tribunals for acts violating the fundamental rights granted him by the constitution or by law.

Article 9
No one shall be subjected to arbitrary arrest, detention or exile.

Article 10
Everyone is entitled in full equality to a fair and public hearing by an independent and impartial tribunal, in the determination of his rights and obligations and of any criminal charge against him.

Article 11
1. Everyone charged with a penal offence has the right to be presumed innocent until proved guilty according to law in a public trial at which he has had all the guarantees necessary for his defence.
2. No one shall be held guilty of any penal offence on account of any act or omission which did not constitute a penal offence, under national or

international law, at the time when it was committed. Nor shall a heavier penalty be imposed than the one that was applicable at the time the penal offence was committed.

Article 12
No one shall be subjected to arbitrary interference with his privacy, family, home or correspondence, nor to attacks upon his honour and reputation. Everyone has the right to the protection of the law against such interference or attacks.

Article 13
1. Everyone has the right to freedom of movement and residence within the borders of each State.
2. Everyone has the right to leave any country, including his own, and to return to his country.

Article 14
1. Everyone has the right to seek and to enjoy in other countries asylum from persecution.
2. This right may not be invoked in the case of prosecutions genuinely arising from non-political crimes or from acts contrary to the purposes and principles of the United Nations.

Article 15
1. Everyone has the right to a nationality.
2. No one shall be arbitrarily deprived of his nationality nor denied the right to change his nationality.

Article 16
1. Men and women of full age, without any limitation due to race, nationality or religion, have the right to marry and to found a family. They are entitled to equal rights as to marriage, during marriage and at its dissolution.
2. Marriage shall be entered into only with the free and full consent of the intending spouses.
3. The family is the natural and fundamental group unit of society and is entitled to protection by society and the State.

Article 17
1. Everyone has the right to own property alone as well as in association with others.
2. No one shall be arbitrarily deprived of his property.

Article 18
Everyone has the right to freedom of thought, conscience and religion; this right includes freedom to change his religion or belief, and freedom, either alone or in community with others and in public or private, to manifest his religion or belief in teaching, practice, worship and observance.

Article 19
Everyone has the right to freedom of opinion and expression; this right
includes freedom to hold opinions without interference and to seek,
receive and impart information and ideas through any media and regardless of frontiers.

Article 20
1. Everyone has the right to freedom of peaceful assembly and association.
2. No one may be compelled to belong to an association.

Article 21
1. Everyone has the right to take part in the government of his country,
   directly or through freely chosen representatives.
2. Everyone has the right of equal access to public service in his country.
3. The will of the people shall be the basis of the authority of government; this will shall be expressed in periodic and genuine elections
   which shall be by universal and equal suffrage and shall be held by
   secret vote or by equivalent free voting procedures.

Article 22
Everyone, as a member of society, has the right to social security and is
entitled to realization, through national effort and international co-operation and in accordance with the organization and resources of each State,
of the economic, social and cultural rights indispensable for his dignity
and the free development of his personality.

Article 23
1. Everyone has the right to work, to free choice of employment, to just
   and favourable conditions of work and to protection against unemployment.
2. Everyone, without any discrimination, has the right to equal pay for
   equal work.
3. Everyone who works has the right to just and favourable remuneration
   ensuring for himself and his family an existence worthy of human dignity, and supplemented, if necessary, by other means of social protection.
4. Everyone has the right to form and to join trade unions for the protection of his interests.

Article 24
Everyone has the right to rest and leisure, including reasonable limitation of working hours and periodic holidays with pay.

Article 25
1. Everyone has the right to a standard of living adequate for the health
   and well-being of himself and of his family, including food, clothing,
   housing and medical care and necessary social services, and the right to
   security in the event of unemployment, sickness, disability, widow-

hood, old age or other lack of livelihood in circumstances beyond his control.
2. Motherhood and childhood are entitled to special care and assistance. All children, whether born in or out of wedlock, shall enjoy the same social protection.

Article 26

1. Everyone has the right to education. Education shall be free, at least in the elementary and fundamental stages. Elementary education shall be compulsory. Technical and professional education shall be made generally available and higher education shall be equally accessible to all on the basis of merit.
2. Education shall be directed to the full development of the human personality and to the strengthening of respect for human rights and fundamental freedoms. It shall promote understanding, tolerance and friendship among all nations, racial or religious groups, and shall further the activities of the United Nations for the maintenance of peace.
3. Parents have a prior right to choose the kind of education that shall be given to their children.

Article 27

1. Everyone has the right freely to participate in the cultural life of the community, to enjoy the arts and to share in scientific advancement and its benefits.
2. Everyone has the right to the protection of the moral and material interests resulting from any scientific, literary or artistic production of which he is the author.

Article 28

Everyone is entitled to a social and international order in which the rights and freedoms set forth in this Declaration can be fully realized.

Article 29

1. Everyone has duties to the community in which alone the free and full development of his personality is possible.
2. In the exercise of his rights and freedoms, everyone shall be subject only to such limitations as are determined by law solely for the purpose of securing due recognition and respect for the rights and freedoms of others and of meeting the just requirements of morality, public order and the general welfare in a democratic society.
3. These rights and freedoms may in no case be exercised contrary to the purposes and principles of the United Nations.

Article 30

Nothing in this Declaration may be interpreted as implying for any State, group or person any right to engage in any activity or to perform any act aimed at the destruction of any of the rights and freedoms set forth herein.

Declaration on Principles of International Law Concerning Friendly Relations and Co-operation Among States in Accordance with the Charter of the United Nations*

(full text)

The General Assembly,

Recalling its resolutions 1815 (XVII) of 18 December 1962, 1966 (XVIII) of 16 December 1963, 2103 (XX) of 20 December 1965, 2181 (XXI) of 12 December 1966, 2327 (XXII) of 18 December 1967, 2463 (XXIII) of 20 December 1968 and 2533 (XXIV) of 8 December 1969, in which it affirmed the importance of the progressive development and codification of the principles of international law concerning friendly relations and co-operation among States,

Having considered the report of the Special Committee on Principles of International Law concerning Friendly Relations and Co-operation among States, which met in Geneva from 31 March to 1 May 1970,

Emphasizing the paramount importance of the *Charter of the United Nations* for the maintenance of international peace and security and for the development of Friendly relations and Co-operation among States,

Deeply convinced that the adoption of the Declaration on Principles of International Law concerning Friendly Relations and Co-operation among States in accordance with the Charter of the United Nations on the occasion of the twenty-fifth anniversary of the United Nations would contribute to the strengthening of world peace and constitute a landmark in the development of international law and of relations among States, in promoting the rule of law among nations and particularly the universal application of the principles embodied in the Charter,

Considering the desirability of the wide dissemination of the text of the Declaration,

1. Approves the Declaration on Principles of International Law concerning Friendly Relations and Co-operation among States in accordance with the Charter of the United Nations, the text of which is annexed to the present resolution;

2. Expresses its appreciation to the Special Committee on Principles of International Law concerning Friendly Relations and Co-operation among States for its work resulting in the elaboration of the Declaration;

3. Recommends that all efforts be made so that the Declaration becomes generally known.

---

* UN Doc. GA/RES/2625 (XXV), 24 October 1970.

DECLARATION ON PRINCIPLES OF INTERNATIONAL LAW CONCERNING
FRIENDLY RELATIONS AND CO-OPERATION AMONG STATES IN ACCOR-
DANCE WITH THE CHARTER OF THE UNITED NATIONS

The General Assembly,

PREAMBLE

Reaffirming in the terms of the Charter of the United Nations that the maintenance of international peace and security and the development of
friendly relations and co-operation between nations are among the fundamental purposes of the United Nations,

Recalling that the peoples of the United Nations are determined to practise
tolerance and live together in peace with one another as good neighbours,

Bearing in mind the importance of maintaining and strengthening international peace founded upon freedom, equality, justice and respect for
fundamental human rights and of developing friendly relations among
nations irrespective of their political, economic and social systems or the
levels of their development,

Bearing in mind also the paramount importance of the Charter of the
United Nations in the promotion of the rule of law among nations,
Considering that the faithful observance of the principles of international
law concerning friendly relations and co-operation among States and the
fulfilment in good faith of the obligations assumed by States, in accordance with the Charter, is of the greatest importance for the maintenance
of international peace and security and for the implementation of the
other purposes of the United Nations,

Noting that the great political, economic and social changes and scientific
progress which have taken place in the world since the adoption of the
Charter give increased importance to these principles and to the need for
their more effective application in the conduct of States wherever carried
on,

Recalling the established principle that outer space, including the Moon
and other celestial bodies, is not subject to national appropriation by
claim of sovereignty, by means of use or occupation, or by any other
means, and mindful of the fact that consideration is being given in the
United Nations to the question of establishing other appropriate provisions similarly inspired,

Convinced that the strict observance by States of the obligation not to intervene in the affairs of any other State is an essential condition to ensure
that nations live together in peace with one another, since the practice of
any form of intervention not only violates the spirit and letter of the

Charter, but also leads to the creation of situations which threaten international peace and security,

Recalling the duty of States to refrain in their international relations from military, political, economic or any other form of coercion aimed against the political independence or territorial integrity of any State,
Considering it essential that all States shall refrain in their international relations from the threat or use of force against the territorial integrity or political independence of any State, or in any other manner inconsistent with the purpose of the United Nations,

Considering it equally essential that all States shall settle their international disputes by peaceful means in accordance with the Charter,

Reaffirming, in accordance with the Charter, the basic importance of sovereign equality and stressing that the purposes of the United Nations can be implemented only if States enjoy sovereign equality and comply fully with the requirements of this principle in their international relations,

Convinced that the subjection of peoples to alien subjugation, domination and exploitation constitutes a major obstacle to the promotion of international peace and security,

Convinced that the principle of equal rights and self-determination of peoples constitutes a significant contribution to contemporary international law, and that its effective application is of paramount importance for the promotion of friendly relations among States, based on respect for the principle of sovereign equality,

Convinced in consequence that any attempt aimed at the partial or total disruption of the national unity and territorial integrity of a State or country or at its political independence is incompatible with the purposes and principles of the Charter,

Considering the provisions of the Charter as a whole and taking into account the role of relevant resolutions adopted by the competent organs of the United Nations relating to the content of the principles,

Considering that the progressive development and codification of the following principles:
(a) The principle that States shall refrain in their international relations from the threat or use of force against the territorial integrity or political independence of any State, or in any other manner inconsistent with the purpose of the United Nations,
(b) The principle that States shall settle their international disputes by peaceful means in such a manner that international peace and security and justice are not endangered,
(c) The duty not to intervene in matters within the domestic jurisdiction of any State, in accordance with the Charter,

(d) The duty of States to co-operate with one another in accordance with the Charter,

(e) The principle of equal rights and self-determination of peoples,

(f) The principle of sovereign equality of States,

(g) The principle that States shall fulfil in good faith the obligations assumed by them in accordance with the Charter, so as to secure their more effective application within the international community, would promote the realization of the purposes of the United Nations,

Having considered the principles of international law relating to friendly relations and co-operation among States,

1. *Solemnly proclaims* the following principles:
The principle that States shall refrain in their international relations from the threat or use of force against the territorial integrity or political independence of any State, or in any other manner inconsistent with the purpose of the United Nations.

Every State has the duty to refrain in its international relations from the threat or use of force against the territorial integrity or political independence of any State, or in any other manner inconsistent with the purposes of the United Nations. Such a threat or use of force constitutes a violation of international law and the Charter of the United Nations and shall never be employed as a means of settling international issues.

A war of aggression constitutes a crime against the peace, for which there is responsibility under international law.

In accordance with the purposes and principles of the United Nations, States have the duty to refrain from propaganda for wars of aggression.

Every State has the duty to refrain from the threat or use of force to violate the existing international boundaries of another State or as a means of solving international disputes, including territorial disputes and problems concerning frontiers of States.

Every State likewise has the duty to refrain from the threat or use of force to violate international lines of demarcation, such as armistice lines, established by or pursuant to an international agreement to which it is a party or which it is otherwise bound to respect. Nothing in the foregoing shall be construed as prejudicing the positions of the parties concerned with regard to the status and effects of such lines under their special regimes or as affecting their temporary character.

States have a duty to refrain from acts of reprisal involving the use of force.

Every State has the duty to refrain from any forcible action which deprives peoples referred to in the elaboration of the principle of equal rights and self-determination of their right to self-determination and freedom and independence.

Every State has the duty to refrain from organizing or encouraging the organization of irregular forces or armed bands, including mercenaries, for incursion into the territory of another State.

Every State has the duty to refrain from organizing, instigating, assisting or participating in acts of civil strife or terrorist acts in another State or acquiescing in organized activities within its territory directed towards the commission of such acts, when the acts referred to in the present paragraph involve a threat or use of force.

The territory of a State shall not be the object of military occupation resulting from the use of force in contravention of the provisions of the Charter. The territory of a State shall not be the object of acquisition by another State resulting from the threat or use of force. No territorial acquisition resulting from the threat or use of force shall be recognized as legal. Nothing in the foregoing shall be construed as affecting:

(a) Provisions of the Charter or any international agreement prior to the Charter regime and valid under international law; or
(b) The powers of the Security Council under the Charter.

All States shall pursue in good faith negotiations for the early conclusion of a universal treaty on general and complete disarmament under effective international control and strive to adopt appropriate measures to reduce international tensions and strengthen confidence among States.

All States shall comply in good faith with their obligations under the generally recognized principles and rules of international law with respect to the maintenance of international peace and security, and shall endeavour to make the United Nations security system based on the Charter more effective.

Nothing in the foregoing paragraphs shall be construed as enlarging or diminishing in any way the scope of the provisions of the Charter concerning cases in which the use of force is lawful.

The principle that States shall settle their international disputes by peaceful means in such a manner that international peace and security and justice are not endangered

Every State shall settle its international disputes with other States by peaceful means in such a manner that international peace and security and justice are not endangered.

States shall accordingly seek early and just settlement of their international disputes by negotiation, inquiry, mediation, conciliation, arbitration, judicial settlement, resort to regional agencies or arrangements or other peaceful means of their choice. In seeking such a settlement the parties shall agree upon such peaceful means as may be appropriate to the circumstances and nature of the dispute.

The parties to a dispute have the duty, in the event of failure to reach a solution by any one of the above peaceful means, to continue to seek a settlement of the dispute by other peaceful means agreed upon by them.

States parties to an international dispute, as well as other States, shall refrain from any action which may aggravate the situation so as to endanger the maintenance of international peace and security, and shall act in accordance with the purposes and principles of the United Nations.

International disputes shall be settled on the basis of the sovereign equality of States and in accordance with the principle of free choice of means. Recourse to, or acceptance of, a settlement procedure freely agreed to by States with regard to existing or future disputes to which they are parties shall not be regarded as incompatible with sovereign equality.

Nothing in the foregoing paragraphs prejudices or derogates from the applicable provisions of the Charter, in particular those relating to the pacific settlement of international disputes.

The principle concerning the duty not to intervene in matters within the domestic jurisdiction of any State, in accordance with the Charter

No State or group of States has the right to intervene, directly or indirectly, for any reason whatever, in the internal or external affairs of any other State. Consequently, armed intervention and all other forms of interference or attempted threats against the personality of the State or against its political, economic and cultural elements, are in violation of international law.

No State may use or encourage the use of economic, political or any other type of measures to coerce another State in order to obtain from it the subordination of the exercise of its sovereign rights and to secure from it advantages of any kind. Also, no State shall organize, assist, foment, finance, incite or tolerate subversive, terrorist or armed activities directed towards the violent overthrow of the regime of another State, or interfere in civil strife in another State.

The use of force to deprive peoples of their national identity constitutes a violation of their inalienable rights and of the principle of non-intervention.

Every State has an inalienable right to choose its political, economic, social and cultural systems, without interference in any form by another State.

Nothing in the foregoing paragraphs shall be construed as affecting the relevant provisions of the Charter relating to the maintenance of international peace and security.

The duty of States to co-operate with one another in accordance with the Charter

States have the duty to co-operate with one another, irrespective of the differences in their political, economic and social systems, in the various spheres of international relations, in order to maintain international peace and security and to promote international economic stability and progress, the general welfare of nations and international co-operation free from discrimination based on such differences.

To this end:
(a) States shall co-operate with other States in the maintenance of international peace and security;
(b) States shall co-operate in the promotion of universal respect for, and observance of, human rights and fundamental freedoms for all, and in the elimination of all forms of racial discrimination and all forms of religious intolerance;

(c) States shall conduct their international relations in the economic, social, cultural, technical and trade fields in accordance with the principles of sovereign equality and non-intervention;

(d) States Members of the United Nations have the duty to take joint and separate action in co-operation with the United Nations in accordance with the relevant provisions of the Charter.

States should co-operate in the economic, social and cultural fields as well as in the field of science and technology and for the promotion of international cultural and educational progress. States should co-operate in the promotion of economic growth throughout the world, especially that of the developing countries.

The principle of equal rights and self-determination of peoples

By virtue of the principle of equal rights and *self-determination of peoples* enshrined in the Charter of the United Nations, all peoples have the right freely to determine, without external interference, their political status and to pursue their economic, social and cultural development, and every State has the duty to respect this right in accordance with the provisions of the Charter.

Every State has the duty to promote, through joint and separate action, realization of the principle of equal rights and self-determination of peoples, in accordance with the provisions of the Charter, and to render assistance to the United Nations in carrying out the responsibilities entrusted to it by the Charter regarding the implementation of the principle, in order:

(a) To promote friendly relations and co-operation among States; and

(b) To bring a speedy end to colonialism, having due regard to the freely expressed will of the peoples concerned;
and bearing in mind that the subjection of peoples to alien subjugation, domination and exploitation constitutes a violation of the principle, as well as a denial of fundamental human rights, and is contrary to the Charter.

Every State has the duty to promote through joint and separate action universal respect for and observance of human rights and fundamental freedoms in accordance with the Charter.

The establishment of a sovereign and independent State, the free association or integration with an independent State or the emergence into any other political status freely determined by a people constitute modes of implementing the right of self determination by that people.

Every State has the duty to refrain from any forcible action which deprives peoples referred to above in the elaboration of the present principle of their right to self-determination and freedom and independence. In their actions against, and resistance to, such forcible action in pursuit of the exercise of their right to self-determination, such peoples are entitled to seek and to receive support in accordance with the purposes and principles of the Charter.

The territory of a colony or other Non-Self-Governing Territory has, under the Charter, a status separate and distinct from the territory of the State administering it; and such separate and distinct status under the Charter shall exist until the people of the colony or Non-Self-Governing Territory have exercised their right of self-determination in accordance with the Charter, and particularly its purposes and principles.

Nothing in the foregoing paragraphs shall be construed as authorizing or encouraging any action which would dismember or impair, totally or in part, the territorial integrity or political unity of sovereign and independent States conducting themselves in compliance with the principle of equal rights and self-determination of peoples as described above and thus possessed of a government representing the whole people belonging to the territory without distinction as to race, creed, or colour.

Every State shall refrain from any action aimed at the partial or total disruption of the national unity and territorial integrity of any other State or country.

The principle of sovereign equality of States

All States enjoy sovereign equality. They have equal rights and duties and are equal members of the international community, notwithstanding differences of an economic, social, political or other nature.

In particular, sovereign equality includes the following elements:
(a) States are juridically equal;
(b) Each State enjoys the rights inherent in full sovereignty;
(c) Each State has the duty to respect the personality of other States;
(d) The territorial integrity and political independence of the State are inviolable;
(e) Each State has the right freely to choose and develop its political, social, economic and cultural systems;
(f) Each State has the duty to comply fully and in good faith with its international obligations and to live in peace with other States.

The principle that States shall fulfil in good faith the obligations assumed by them in accordance with the Charter

Every State has the duty to fulfil in good faith the obligations assumed by it in accordance with the Charter of the United Nations.

Every State has the duty to fulfil in good faith its obligations under the generally recognized principles and rules of international law.

Every State has the duty to fulfil in good faith its obligations under international agreements valid under the generally recognized principles and rules of international law.

Where obligations arising under international agreements are in conflict with the obligations of Members of the United Nations under the Charter of the United Nations, the obligations under the Charter shall prevail.

2. *Declares* that:
In their interpretation and application the above principles are interrelated and each principle should be construed in the context of the other principles.

Nothing in this Declaration shall be construed as prejudicing in any manner the provisions of the Charter or the rights and duties of Members States under the Charter or the rights of peoples under the Charter, taking into account the elaboration of these rights in this Declaration.

3. *Declares further* that:
The principles of the Charter which are embodied in this Declaration constitute basic principles of international law, and consequently appeals to all States to be guided by these principles in their international conduct and to develop their mutual relations on the basis of the strict observance of these principles.

Rio Declaration on Environment and Development[*]
(full text)

The United Nations Conference on Environment and Development,
- Having met at Rio de Janeiro from 3 to 14 June 1992,
- Reaffirming the Declaration of the United Nations Conference on the Human Environment, adopted at Stockholm on 16 June 1972, a/ and seeking to build upon it,
- With the goal of establishing a new and equitable global partnership through the creation of new levels of cooperation among States, key sectors of societies and people,
- Working towards international agreements which respect the interests of all and protect the integrity of the global environmental and developmental system,
- Recognizing the integral and interdependent nature of the Earth, our home,

Proclaims that:

Principle 1
Human beings are at the centre of concerns for sustainable development. They are entitled to a healthy and productive life in harmony with nature.

Principle 2
States have, in accordance with the Charter of the United Nations and the principles of international law, the sovereign right to exploit their own resources pursuant to their own environmental and developmental policies, and the responsibility to ensure that activities within their jurisdiction or control do not cause damage to the environment of other States or of areas beyond the limits of national jurisdiction.

Principle 3
The right to development must be fulfilled so as to equitably meet developmental and environmental needs of present and future generations.

Principle 4
In order to achieve sustainable development, environmental protection shall constitute an integral part of the development process and cannot be considered in isolation from it.

Principle 5
All States and all people shall cooperate in the essential task of eradicating poverty as an indispensable requirement for sustainable development,

---

[*] Report of the United Nations Conference on Environment and Development (Rio de Janeiro, 3-14 June 1992), UN Doc.

in order to decrease the disparities in standards of living and better meet the needs of the majority of the people of the world.

Principle 6
The special situation and needs of developing countries, particularly the least developed and those most environmentally vulnerable, shall be given special priority. International actions in the field of environment and development should also address the interests and needs of all countries.

Principle 7
States shall cooperate in a spirit of global partnership to conserve, protect and restore the health and integrity of the Earth's ecosystem. In view of different contributions to global environmental degradation, States have common but differentiated responsibilities. The developed countries acknowledge the responsibility that they bear in the international pursuit of sustainable development in view of the pressures their societies place on the global environment and of the technologies and financial resources they command.

Principle 8
To achieve sustainable development and a higher quality of life for all people, States should reduce and eliminate unsustainable patterns of production and consumption and promote appropriate demographic policies.

Principle 9
States should cooperate to strengthen endogenous capacity-building for sustainable development by improving scientific understanding through exchanges of scientific and technological knowledge, and by enhancing the development, adaptation, diffusion and transfer of technologies, including new and innovative technologies.

Principle 10
Environmental issues are best handled with the participation of all concerned citizens, at the relevant level. At the national level, each individual shall have appropriate access to information concerning the environment that is held by public authorities, including information on hazardous materials and activities in their communities, and the opportunity to participate in decision-making processes. States shall facilitate and encourage public awareness and participation by making information widely available. Effective access to judicial and administrative proceedings, including redress and remedy, shall be provided.

Principle 11
States shall enact effective environmental legislation. Environmental standards, management objectives and priorities should reflect the environmental and developmental context to which they apply. Standards applied by some countries may be inappropriate and of unwarranted economic and social cost to other countries, in particular developing countries.

Principle 12
States should cooperate to promote a supportive and open international
economic system that would lead to economic growth and sustainable
development in all countries, to better address the problems of environmental degradation. Trade policy measures for environmental purposes
should not constitute a means of arbitrary or unjustifiable discrimination
or a disguised restriction on international trade. Unilateral actions to deal
with environmental challenges outside the jurisdiction of the importing
country should be avoided. Environmental measures addressing transboundary or global environmental problems should, as far as possible, be
based on an international consensus.

Principle 13
States shall develop national law regarding liability and compensation for
the victims of pollution and other environmental damage. States shall
also cooperate in an expeditious and more determined manner to develop
further international law regarding liability and compensation for adverse
effects of environmental damage caused by activities within their jurisdiction or control to areas beyond their jurisdiction.

Principle 14
States should effectively cooperate to discourage or prevent the reloca-
tion and transfer to other States of any activities and substances that
cause severe environmental degradation or are found to be harmful to
human health.

Principle 15
In order to protect the environment, the precautionary approach shall be
widely applied by States according to their capabilities. Where there are
threats of serious or irreversible damage, lack of full scientific certainty
shall not be used as a reason for postponing cost-effective measures to
prevent environmental degradation.

Principle 16
National authorities should endeavour to promote the internalization of
environmental costs and the use of economic instruments, taking into
account the approach that the polluter should, in principle, bear the cost
of pollution, with due regard to the public interest and without distorting
international trade and investment.

Principle 17
Environmental impact assessment, as a national instrument, shall be
undertaken for proposed activities that are likely to have a significant
adverse impact on the environment and are subject to a decision of a
competent national authority.

Principle 18
States shall immediately notify other States of any natural disasters or
other emergencies that are likely to produce sudden harmful effects on

the environment of those States. Every effort shall be made by the international community to help States so afflicted.

Principle 19
States shall provide prior and timely notification and relevant information to potentially affected States on activities that may have a significant adverse transboundary environmental effect and shall consult with those States at an early stage and in good faith.

Principle 20
Women have a vital role in environmental management and development. Their full participation is therefore essential to achieve sustainable development.

Principle 21
The creativity, ideals and courage of the youth of the world should be mobilized to forge a global partnership in order to achieve sustainable development and ensure a better future for all.

Principle 22
Indigenous people and their communities and other local communities have a vital role in environmental management and development because of their knowledge and traditional practices. States should recognize and duly support their identity, culture and interests and enable their effective participation in the achievement of sustainable development.

Principle 23
The environment and natural resources of people under oppression, domination and occupation shall be protected.

Principle 24
Warfare is inherently destructive of sustainable development. States shall therefore respect international law providing protection for the environment in times of armed conflict and cooperate in its further development, as necessary.

Principle 25
Peace, development and environmental protection are interdependent and indivisible.

Principle 26
States shall resolve all their environmental disputes peacefully and by appropriate means in accordance with the Charter of the United Nations.

Principle 27
States and people shall cooperate in good faith and in a spirit of partnership in the fulfilment of the principles embodied in this Declaration and in the further development of international law in the field of sustainable development.

Report of the Panel on United Nations Peace Operations*
(executive summary)

The United Nations was founded, in the words of its Charter, in order "to save succeeding generations from the scourge of war". Meeting this challenge is the most important function of the Organization, and to a very significant degree it is the yardstick with which the Organization is judged by the peoples it exists to serve. Over the last decade, the United Nations has repeatedly failed to meet the challenge, and it can do no better today. Without renewed commitment on the part of Member States, significant institutional change and increased financial support, the United Nations will not be capable of executing the critical peacekeeping and peace-building tasks that the Member States assign to it in coming months and years. There are many tasks which United Nations peacekeeping forces should not be asked to undertake and many places they should not go. But when the United Nations does send its forces to uphold the peace, they must be prepared to confront the lingering forces of war and violence, with the ability and determination to defeat them.

The Secretary-General has asked the Panel on United Nations Peace Operations, composed of individuals experienced in various aspects of conflict prevention, peacekeeping and peace-building, to assess the shortcomings of the existing system and to make frank, specific and realistic recommendations for change. Our recommendations focus not only on politics and strategy but also and perhaps even more so on operational and organizational areas of need.

For preventive initiatives to succeed in reducing tension and averting conflict, the Secretary-General needs clear, strong and sustained political support from Member States. Furthermore, as the United Nations has bitterly and repeatedly discovered over the last decade, no amount of good intentions can substitute for the fundamental ability to project credible force if complex peacekeeping, in particular, is to succeed. But force alone cannot create peace; it can only create the space in which peace may be built. Moreover, the changes that the Panel recommends will have no lasting impact unless Member States summon the political will to support the United Nations politically, financially and operationally to enable the United Nations to be truly credible as a force for peace.

Each of the recommendations contained in the present report is designed to remedy a serious problem in strategic direction, decision-making, rapid deployment, operational planning and support, and the use of modern information technology. Key assessments and recommendations are highlighted below, largely in the order in which they appear in the body of the text (the numbers of the relevant paragraphs in the

---

* Report of the Panel on United Nations Peace Operations, chaired by Lakhdar Brahimi, UN Doc. A/55/305, 21 August 2000.

main text are provided in parentheses). In addition, a summary of recommendations is contained in the annex.

Experience of the past

It should have come as no surprise to anyone that some of the missions of the past decade would be particularly hard to accomplish: they tended to deploy where conflict had not resulted in victory for any side, where a military stalemate or international pressure or both had brought fighting to a halt but at least some of the parties to the conflict were not seriously committed to ending the confrontation. United Nations operations thus did not *deploy into* post-conflict situations but tried *to create* them. In such complex operations, peacekeepers work to maintain a secure local environment while peacebuilders work to make that environment self-sustaining. Only such an environment offers a ready exit to peacekeeping forces, making peacekeepers and peacebuilders inseparable partners.

Implications for preventive action and peace-building: the need for strategy and support

The United Nations and its members face a pressing need to establish more effective strategies for conflict prevention, in both the long and short terms. In this context, the Panel endorses the recommendations of the Secretary-General with respect to conflict prevention contained in the Millennium Report (A/54/2000) and in his remarks before the Security Council's second open meeting on conflict prevention in July 2000. It also encourages the Secretary-General's more frequent use of fact-finding missions to areas of tension in support of short-term crisis-preventive action.

Furthermore, the Security Council and the General Assembly's Special Committee on Peacekeeping Operations, conscious that the United Nations will continue to face the prospect of having to assist communities and nations in making the transition from war to peace, have each recognized and acknowledged the key role of peace-building in complex peace operations. This will require that the United Nations system address what has hitherto been a fundamental deficiency in the way it has conceived of, funded and implemented peace-building strategies and activities. Thus, the Panel recommends that the Executive Committee on Peace and Security (ECPS) present to the Secretary-General a plan to strengthen the permanent capacity of the United Nations to develop peace-building strategies and to implement programmes in support of those strategies.

Among the changes that the Panel supports are: a doctrinal shift in the use of civilian police and related rule of law elements in peace operations that emphasizes a team approach to upholding the rule of law and respect for human rights and helping communities coming out of a conflict to achieve national reconciliation; consolidation of disarmament, demobilization, and reintegration programmes into the assessed budgets of complex peace operations in their first phase; flexibility for heads of United Nations peace operations to fund "quick impact projects" that make a real difference in the lives of people in the mission area; and better integration of electoral assistance into a broader strategy for the support of governance institutions.

Implications for peacekeeping: the need for robust doctrine and realistic mandates

The Panel concurs that consent of the local parties, impartiality and the use of force only in self-defence should remain the bedrock principles of peacekeeping. Experience shows, however, that in the context of intra-State/transnational conflicts, consent may be manipulated in many ways. Impartiality for United Nations operations must therefore mean adherence to the principles of the Charter: where one party to a peace agreement clearly and incontrovertibly is violating its terms, continued equal treatment of all parties by the United Nations can in the best case result in ineffectiveness and in the worst may amount to complicity with evil. No failure did more to damage the standing and credibility of United Nations peacekeeping in the 1990s than its reluctance to distinguish victim from aggressor.

In the past, the United Nations has often found itself unable to respond effectively to such challenges. It is a fundamental premise of the present report, however, that it must be able to do so. Once deployed, United Nations peacekeepers must be able to carry out their mandate professionally and successfully. This means that United Nations military units must be capable of defending themselves, other mission components and the mission's mandate. Rules of engagement should be sufficiently robust and not force United Nations contingents to cede the initiative to their attackers.

This means, in turn, that the Secretariat must not apply best-case planning assumptions to situations where the local actors have historically exhibited worst-case behaviour. It means that mandates should specify an operation's authority to use force. It means bigger forces, better equipped and more costly but able to be a credible deterrent. In particular, United Nations forces for complex operations should be afforded the field intelligence and other capabilities needed to mount an effective defence against violent challengers.

Moreover, United Nations peacekeepers – troops or police – who witness violence against civilians should be presumed to be authorized to stop it, within their means, in support of basic United Nations principles. However, operations given a broad and explicit mandate for civilian protection must be given the specific resources needed to carry out that mandate.

The Secretariat must tell the Security Council what it needs to know, not what it wants to hear, when recommending force and other resource levels for a new mission, and it must set those levels according to realistic scenarios that take into account likely challenges to implementation. Security Council mandates, in turn, should reflect the clarity that peacekeeping operations require for unity of effort when they deploy into potentially dangerous situations.

The current practice is for the Secretary-General to be given a Security Council resolution specifying troop levels on paper, not knowing whether he will be given the troops and other personnel that the mission needs to function effectively, or whether they will be properly equipped. The Panel is of the view that, once realistic mission requirements have been set and agreed to, the Council should leave its authorizing resolution in draft form until the Secretary-General confirms that he has received troop and other commitments from Member States sufficient to meet those requirements.

Member States that do commit formed military units to an operation should be invited to consult with the members of the Security Council during mandate formulation; such advice might usefully be institutionalized via the establishment of ad hoc subsidiary organs of the Council, as provided for in Article 29 of the Charter. Troop contributors should also be invited to attend Secretariat briefings of the Security Council pertaining to crises that affect the safety and security of mission personnel or to a change or reinterpretation of the mandate regarding the use of force.

New headquarters capacity for information management and strategic analysis

The Panel recommends that a new information-gathering and analysis entity be created to support the informational and analytical needs of the Secretary-General and the members of the Executive Committee on Peace and Security (ECPS). Without such capacity, the Secretariat will remain a reactive institution, unable to get ahead of daily events, and the ECPS will not be able to fulfil the role for which it was created.

The Panel's proposed ECPS Information and Strategic Analysis Secretariat (EISAS) would create and maintain integrated databases on peace and security issues, distribute that knowledge efficiently within the United Nations system, generate policy analyses, formulate long-term strategies for ECPS and bring budding crises to the attention of the ECPS leadership. It could also propose and manage the agenda of ECPS itself, helping to transform it into the decision-making body anticipated in the Secretary-General's initial reforms.

The Panel proposes that EISAS be created by consolidating the existing Situation Centre of the Department of Peacekeeping Operations (DPKO) with a number of small, scattered policy planning offices, and adding a small team of military analysts, experts in international criminal networks and information systems specialists. EISAS should serve the needs of all members of ECPS.

Improved mission guidance and leadership

The Panel believes it is essential to assemble the leadership of a new mission as early as possible at United Nations Headquarters, to participate in shaping a mission's concept of operations, support plan, budget, staffing and Headquarters mission guidance. To that end, the Panel recommends that the Secretary-General compile, in a systematic fashion and with input from Member States, a comprehensive list of potential special representatives of the Secretary-General (SRSGs), force commanders, civilian police commissioners, their potential deputies and potential heads of other components of a mission, representing a broad geographic and equitable gender distribution.

Rapid deployment standards and "on-call" expertise

The first 6 to 12 weeks following a ceasefire or peace accord are often the most critical ones for establishing both a stable peace and the credibility of a new operation. Opportunities lost during that period are hard to regain.

The Panel recommends that the United Nations define "rapid and effective deployment capacity" as the ability to fully deploy traditional peacekeeping operations within 30 days of the adoption of a Security Council resolution establishing such an operation, and within 90 days in the case of complex peacekeeping operations.

The Panel recommends that the United Nations standby arrangements system (UNSAS) be developed further to include several coherent, multinational, brigade-size forces and the necessary enabling forces, created by Member States working in partnership, in order to better meet the need for the robust peacekeeping forces that the Panel has advocated. The Panel also recommends that the Secretariat send a team to confirm the readiness of each potential troop contributor to meet the requisite United Nations training and equipment requirements for peacekeeping operations, prior to deployment. Units that do not meet the requirements must not be deployed.

To support such rapid and effective deployment, the Panel recommends that a revolving "on-call list" of about 100 experienced, well qualified military officers, carefully vetted and accepted by DPKO, be created within UNSAS. Teams drawn from this list and available for duty on seven days' notice would translate broad, strategic-level mission concepts developed at Headquarters into concrete operational and tactical plans in advance of the deployment of troop contingents, and would augment a core element from DPKO to serve as part of a mission start-up team.

Parallel on-call lists of civilian police, international judicial experts, penal experts and human rights specialists must be available in sufficient numbers to strengthen rule of law institutions, as needed, and should also be part of UNSAS. Pre-trained teams could then be drawn from this list to precede the main body of civilian police and related specialists into a new mission area, facilitating the rapid and effective deployment of the law and order component into the mission.

The Panel also calls upon Member States to establish enhanced national "pools" of police officers and related experts, earmarked for deployment to United Nations peace operations, to help meet the high demand for civilian police and related criminal justice/rule of law expertise in peace operations dealing with intra-State conflict. The Panel also urges Member States to consider forming joint regional partnerships and programmes for the purpose of training members of the respective national pools to United Nations civilian police doctrine and standards.

The Secretariat should also address, on an urgent basis, the needs: to put in place a transparent and decentralized recruitment mechanism for civilian field personnel; to improve the retention of the civilian specialists that are needed in every complex peace operation; and to create standby arrangements for their rapid deployment.

Finally, the Panel recommends that the Secretariat radically alter the systems and procedures in place for peacekeeping procurement in order to facilitate rapid deployment. It recommends that responsibilities for peacekeeping budgeting and procurement be moved out of the Department of Management and placed in DPKO. The Panel proposes the creation of a new and distinct body of streamlined field procurement policies and procedures; increased delegation of procurement authority to the field; and greater flexibility for field missions in the management of their budgets. The Panel also urges that the Secretary-General formulate and submit to the General Assembly, for its approval, a global logistics support strategy governing the stockpiling of equipment reserves and standing contracts with the private sector for common goods and services. In the interim, the Panel recommends that additional "start-up kits" of essential equipment be maintained at the United Nations Logistics Base (UNLB) in Brindisi, Italy.

The Panel also recommends that the Secretary-General be given authority, with the approval of the Advisory Committee on Administrative and Budgetary Questions (ACABQ) to commit up to $50 million well in advance of the adoption of a Security Council resolution establishing a new operation once it becomes clear that an operation is likely to be established.

Enhance Headquarters capacity to plan and support peace operations

The Panel recommends that Headquarters support for peacekeeping be treated as a core activity of the United Nations, and as such the majority of its resource requirements should be funded through the regular budget of the Organization. DPKO and other offices that plan and support peacekeeping are currently primarily funded by the Support Account, which is renewed each year and funds only temporary posts. That approach to funding and staff seems to confuse the temporary nature of specific operations with the evident permanence of peacekeeping and other peace operations activities as core functions of the United Nations, which is obviously an untenable state of affairs.

The total cost of DPKO and related Headquarters support offices for peacekeeping does not exceed $50 million per annum, or roughly 2 per cent of total peacekeeping costs. Additional resources for those offices are urgently needed to ensure that more than $2 billion spent on peacekeeping in 2001 are well spent. The Panel therefore recommends that the Secretary-General submit a proposal to the General Assembly outlining the Organization's requirements in full.

The Panel believes that a methodical management review of DPKO should be conducted but also believes that staff shortages in certain areas are plainly obvious. For example, it is clearly not enough to have 32 officers providing military planning and guidance to 27,000 troops in the field, nine civilian police staff to identify, vet and provide guidance for up to 8,600 police, and 15 political desk officers for 14 current operations and two new ones, or to allocate just 1.25 per cent of the total costs of peacekeeping to Headquarters administrative and logistics support.

Establish Integrated Mission Task Forces for mission planning and support

The Panel recommends that Integrated Mission Task Forces (IMTFs) be created, with staff from throughout the United Nations system seconded to them, to plan new missions and help them reach full deployment, significantly enhancing the support that Headquarters provides to the field. There is currently no integrated planning or support cell in the Secretariat that brings together those responsible for political analysis, military operations, civilian police, electoral assistance, human rights, development, humanitarian assistance, refugees and displaced persons, public information, logistics, finance and recruitment.

Structural adjustments are also required in other elements of DPKO, in particular to the Military and Civilian Police Division, which should be reorganized into two separate divisions, and the Field Administration and Logistics Division (FALD), which should be split into two divisions. The Lessons Learned Unit should be strengthened and moved into the DPKO Office of Operations. Public information planning and support at Headquarters also needs strengthening, as do elements in the Department of Political Affairs (DPA), particularly the electoral unit. Outside the Secretariat, the ability of the Office of the United Nations High Commissioner for Human Rights to plan and support the human rights components of peace operations needs to be reinforced.

Consideration should be given to allocating a third Assistant Secretary-General to DPKO and designating one of them as "Principal Assistant Secretary-General", functioning as the deputy to the Under-Secretary-General.

Adapting peace operations to the information age

Modern, well utilized information technology (IT) is a key enabler of many of the above-mentioned objectives, but gaps in strategy, policy and practice impede its effective use. In particular, Headquarters lacks a sufficiently strong responsibility centre for user-level IT strategy and policy in peace operations. A senior official with such responsibility in the peace and security arena should be appointed and located within EISAS, with counterparts in the offices of the SRSG in every United Nations peace operation.

Headquarters and the field missions alike also need a substantive, global, Peace Operations Extranet (POE), through which missions would have access to, among other things, EISAS databases and analyses and lessons learned.

Challenges to implementation

The Panel believes that the above recommendations fall well within the bounds of what can be reasonably demanded of the Organization's Member States. Implementing some of them will require additional resources for the Organization, but we do not mean to suggest that the best way to solve the problems of the United Nations is merely to throw additional resources at them. Indeed, no amount of money or resources can substitute for the significant changes that are urgently needed in the culture of the Organization.

The Panel calls on the Secretariat to heed the Secretary-General's initiatives to reach out to the institutions of civil society; to constantly keep in mind that the United Nations they serve is *the* universal organization. People everywhere are fully entitled to consider that it is *their* organization, and as such to pass judgement on its activities and the people who serve in it.

Furthermore, wide disparities in staff quality exist and those in the system are the first to acknowledge it; better performers are given unreasonable workloads to compensate for those who are less capable. Unless the United Nations takes steps to become a true meritocracy, it will not be able to reverse the alarming trend of qualified personnel, the young among them in particular, leaving the Organization. Moreover, qualified people will have no incentive to join it. Unless managers at all levels, beginning with the Secretary-General and his senior staff, seriously address this problem on a priority basis, reward excellence and remove incompetence, additional resources will be wasted and lasting reform will become impossible.

Member States also acknowledge that they need to reflect on their working culture and methods. It is incumbent upon Security Council members, for example, and the membership at large to breathe life into the words that they produce, as did, for instance, the Security Council delegation that flew to Jakarta and Dili in the wake of the East Timor crisis in 1999, an example of effective Council *action* at its best: *res, non verba*.

We – the members of the Panel on United Nations Peace Operations – call on the leaders of the world assembled at the Millennium Summit, as they renew their commitment to the ideals of the United Nations, to commit as well to strengthen the capacity of the United Nations to fully accomplish the mission which is, indeed, its very *raison d'être*: to help communities engulfed in strife and to maintain or restore peace.

While building consensus for the recommendations in the present report, we have also come to a shared vision of a *United* Nations, extending a strong helping hand to a community, country or region to avert conflict or to end violence. We see an SRSG ending a mission well accomplished, having given the people of a country the opportunity to do for themselves what they could not do before: to build and hold onto peace, to find reconciliation, to strengthen democracy, to secure human rights. We see, above all, a United Nations that has not only the will but also the ability to fulfil its great promise, and to justify the confidence and trust placed in it by the overwhelming majority of humankind.

Millennium Declaration*

(full text)

The General Assembly
Adopts the following Declaration:

UNITED NATIONS MILLENNIUM DECLARATION

I. Values and principles

1. We, heads of State and Government, have gathered at United Nations Headquarters in New York from 6 to 8 September 2000, at the dawn of a new millennium, to reaffirm our faith in the Organization and its Charter as indispensable foundations of a more peaceful, prosperous and just world.
2. We recognize that, in addition to our separate responsibilities to our individual societies, we have a collective responsibility to uphold the principles of human dignity, equality and equity at the global level. As leaders we have a duty therefore to all the world's people, especially the most vulnerable and, in particular, the children of the world, to whom the future belongs.
3. We reaffirm our commitment to the purposes and principles of the Charter of the United Nations, which have proved timeless and universal. Indeed, their relevance and capacity to inspire have increased, as nations and peoples have become increasingly interconnected and interdependent.
4. We are determined to establish a just and lasting peace all over the world in accordance with the purposes and principles of the Charter. We rededicate ourselves to support all efforts to uphold the sovereign equality of all States, respect for their territorial integrity and political independence, resolution of disputes by peaceful means and in conformity with the principles of justice and international law, the right to self-determination of peoples which remain under colonial domination and foreign occupation, non-interference in the internal affairs of States, respect for human rights and fundamental freedoms, respect for the equal rights of all without distinction as to race, sex, language or religion and international cooperation in solving international problems of an economic, social, cultural or humanitarian character.
5. We believe that the central challenge we face today is to ensure that globalization becomes a positive force for all the world's people. For while globalization offers great opportunities, at present its benefits

---

* Adopted at the Millennium Summit of the General Assembly of the United Nations; UN Doc. A/RES/55/2, 18 September 2000.

are very unevenly shared, while its costs are unevenly distributed. We recognize that developing countries and countries with economies in transition face special difficulties in responding to this central challenge. Thus, only through broad and sustained efforts to create a shared future, based upon our common humanity in all its diversity, can globalization be made fully inclusive and equitable. These efforts must include policies and measures, at the global level, which correspond to the needs of developing countries and economies in transition and are formulated and implemented with their effective participation.

6. We consider certain fundamental values to be essential to international relations in the twenty-first century. These include:

- *Freedom.* Men and women have the right to live their lives and raise their children in dignity, free from hunger and from the fear of violence, oppression or injustice. Democratic and participatory governance based on the will of the people best assures these rights.

- *Equality.* No individual and no nation must be denied the opportunity to benefit from development. The equal rights and opportunities of women and men must be assured.

- *Solidarity.* Global challenges must be managed in a way that distributes the costs and burdens fairly in accordance with basic principles of equity and social justice. Those who suffer or who benefit least deserve help from those who benefit most.

- *Tolerance.* Human beings must respect one other, in all their diversity of belief, culture and language. Differences within and between societies should be neither feared nor repressed, but cherished as a precious asset of humanity. A culture of peace and dialogue among all civilizations should be actively promoted.

- *Respect for nature.* Prudence must be shown in the management of all living species and natural resources, in accordance with the precepts of sustainable development. Only in this way can the immeasurable riches provided to us by nature be preserved and passed on to our descendants. The current unsustainable patterns of production and consumption must be changed in the interest of our future welfare and that of our descendants.

- *Shared responsibility.* Responsibility for managing worldwide economic and social development, as well as threats to international peace and security, must be shared among the nations of the world and should be exercised multilaterally. As the most universal and most representative organization in the world, the United Nations must play the central role.

7. In order to translate these shared values into actions, we have identified key objectives to which we assign special significance.

II. Peace, security and disarmament

8. We will spare no effort to free our peoples from the scourge of war, whether within or between States, which has claimed more than 5 million lives in the past decade. We will also seek to eliminate the dangers posed by weapons of mass destruction.

9. We resolve therefore:
- To strengthen respect for the rule of law in international as in national affairs and, in particular, to ensure compliance by Member States with the decisions of the International Court of Justice, in compliance with the Charter of the United Nations, in cases to which they are parties.
- To make the United Nations more effective in maintaining peace and security by giving it the resources and tools it needs for conflict prevention, peaceful resolution of disputes, peacekeeping, post-conflict peace-building and reconstruction. In this context, we take note of the report of the Panel on United Nations Peace Operations and request the General Assembly to consider its recommendations expeditiously.
- To strengthen cooperation between the United Nations and regional organizations, in accordance with the provisions of Chapter VIII of the Charter.
- To ensure the implementation, by States Parties, of treaties in areas such as arms control and disarmament and of international humanitarian law and human rights law, and call upon all States to consider signing and ratifying the Rome Statute of the International Criminal Court.
- To take concerted action against international terrorism, and to accede as soon as possible to all the relevant international conventions.
- To redouble our efforts to implement our commitment to counter the world drug problem.
- To intensify our efforts to fight transnational crime in all its dimensions, including trafficking as well as smuggling in human beings and money laundering.
- To minimize the adverse effects of United Nations economic sanctions on innocent populations, to subject such sanctions regimes to regular reviews and to eliminate the adverse effects of sanctions on third parties.
- To strive for the elimination of weapons of mass destruction, particularly nuclear weapons, and to keep all options open for achieving this aim, including the possibility of convening an international conference to identify ways of eliminating nuclear dangers.
- To take concerted action to end illicit traffic in small arms and light weapons, especially by making arms transfers more transparent and supporting regional disarmament measures, taking account of all the recommendations of the forthcoming United Nations Conference on Illicit Trade in Small Arms and Light Weapons.
- To call on all States to consider acceding to the Convention on the Prohibition of the Use, Stockpiling, Production and Transfer of Anti-personnel Mines and on Their Destruction, as well as the amended mines protocol to the Convention on conventional weapons.
10. We urge Member States to observe the Olympic Truce, individually and collectively, now and in the future, and to support the International Olympic Committee in its efforts to promote peace and human understanding through sport and the Olympic Ideal.

11. We will spare no effort to free our fellow men, women and children from the abject and dehumanizing conditions of extreme poverty, to which more than a billion of them are currently subjected. We are committed to making the right to development a reality for everyone and to freeing the entire human race from want.

12. We resolve therefore to create an environment – at the national and global levels alike – which is conducive to development and to the elimination of poverty.

13. Success in meeting these objectives depends, *inter alia*, on good governance within each country. It also depends on good governance at the international level and on transparency in the financial, monetary and trading systems. We are committed to an open, equitable, rule-based, predictable and nondiscriminatory multilateral trading and financial system.

14. We are concerned about the obstacles developing countries face in mobilizing the resources needed to finance their sustained development. We will therefore make every effort to ensure the success of the High-level International and Intergovernmental Event on Financing for Development, to be held in 2001.

15. We also undertake to address the special needs of the least developed countries. In this context, we welcome the Third United Nations Conference on the Least Developed Countries to be held in May 2001 and will endeavour to ensure its success. We call on the industrialized countries:
   - To adopt, preferably by the time of that Conference, a policy of duty- and quota-free access for essentially all exports from the least developed countries;
   - To implement the enhanced programme of debt relief for the heavily indebted poor countries without further delay and to agree to cancel all official bilateral debts of those countries in return for their making demonstrable commitments to poverty reduction; and
   - To grant more generous development assistance, especially to countries that are genuinely making an effort to apply their resources to poverty reduction.

16. We are also determined to deal comprehensively and effectively with the debt problems of low- and middle-income developing countries, through various national and international measures designed to make their debt sustainable in the long term.

17. We also resolve to address the special needs of small island developing States, by implementing the Barbados Programme of Action and the outcome of the twenty-second special session of the General Assembly rapidly and in full. We urge the international community to ensure that, in the development of a vulnerability index, the special needs of small island developing States are taken into account.

18. We recognize the special needs and problems of the landlocked developing countries, and urge both bilateral and multilateral donors to increase financial and technical assistance to this group of countries to meet their special development needs and to help them overcome

the impediments of geography by improving their transit transport systems.

19. We resolve further:

- To halve, by the year 2015, the proportion of the world's people whose income is less than one dollar a day and the proportion of people who suffer from hunger and, by the same date, to halve the proportion of people who are unable to reach or to afford safe drinking water.
- To ensure that, by the same date, children everywhere, boys and girls alike, will be able to complete a full course of primary schooling and that girls and boys will have equal access to all levels of education.
- By the same date, to have reduced maternal mortality by three quarters, and under-five child mortality by two thirds, of their current rates.
- To have, by then, halted, and begun to reverse, the spread of HIV/AIDS, the scourge of malaria and other major diseases that afflict humanity.
- To provide special assistance to children orphaned by HIV/AIDS.
- By 2020, to have achieved a significant improvement in the lives of at least 100 million slum dwellers as proposed in the "Cities Without Slums" initiative.

20. We also resolve:

- To promote gender equality and the empowerment of women as effective ways to combat poverty, hunger and disease and to stimulate development that is truly sustainable.
- To develop and implement strategies that give young people everywhere a real chance to find decent and productive work.
- To encourage the pharmaceutical industry to make essential drugs more widely available and affordable by all who need them in developing countries.
- To develop strong partnerships with the private sector and with civil society organizations in pursuit of development and poverty eradication.
- To ensure that the benefits of new technologies, especially information and communication technologies, in conformity with recommendations contained in the ECOSOC 2000 Ministerial Declaration, are available to all.

IV. Protecting our common environment

21. We must spare no effort to free all of humanity, and above all our children and grandchildren, from the threat of living on a planet irredeemably spoilt by human activities, and whose resources would no longer be sufficient for their needs.

22. We reaffirm our support for the principles of sustainable development, including those set out in Agenda 21, agreed upon at the United Nations Conference on Environment and Development.

23. We resolve therefore to adopt in all our environmental actions a new ethic of conservation and stewardship and, as first steps, we resolve:

- To make every effort to ensure the entry into force of the Kyoto Protocol, preferably by the tenth anniversary of the United Nations Conference on Environment and Development in 2002, and to embark on the required reduction in emissions of greenhouse gases.
- To intensify our collective efforts for the management, conservation and sustainable development of all types of forests.
- To press for the full implementation of the Convention on Biological Diversity and the Convention to Combat Desertification in those Countries Experiencing Serious Drought and/or Desertification, particularly in Africa.
- To stop the unsustainable exploitation of water resources by developing water management strategies at the regional, national and local levels, which promote both equitable access and adequate supplies.
- To intensify cooperation to reduce the number and effects of natural and manmade disasters.
- To ensure free access to information on the human genome sequence.

V. Human rights, democracy and good governance

24. We will spare no effort to promote democracy and strengthen the rule of law, as well as respect for all internationally recognized human rights and fundamental freedoms, including the right to development.
25. We resolve therefore:
    - To respect fully and uphold the Universal Declaration of Human Rights.
    - To strive for the full protection and promotion in all our countries of civil, political, economic, social and cultural rights for all. • To strengthen the capacity of all our countries to implement the principles and practices of democracy and respect for human rights, including minority rights.
    - To combat all forms of violence against women and to implement the Convention on the Elimination of All Forms of Discrimination against Women.
    - To take measures to ensure respect for and protection of the human rights of migrants, migrant workers and their families, to eliminate the increasing acts of racism and xenophobia in many societies and to promote greater harmony and tolerance in all societies.
    - To work collectively for more inclusive political processes, allowing genuine participation by all citizens in all our countries.
    - To ensure the freedom of the media to perform their essential role and the right of the public to have access to information.

VI. Protecting the vulnerable

26. We will spare no effort to ensure that children and all civilian populations that suffer disproportionately the consequences of natural disasters, genocide, armed conflicts and other humanitarian emergencies are given every assistance and protection so that they can resume normal life as soon as possible. We resolve therefore:

- To expand and strengthen the protection of civilians in complex emergencies, in conformity with international humanitarian law.
- To strengthen international cooperation, including burden sharing in, and the coordination of humanitarian assistance to, countries hosting refugees and to help all refugees and displaced persons to return voluntarily to their homes, in safety and dignity and to be smoothly reintegrated into their societies.
- To encourage the ratification and full implementation of the Convention on the Rights of the Child and its optional protocols on the involvement of children in armed conflict and on the sale of children, child prostitution and child pornography.

VII. Meeting the special needs of Africa

27. We will support the consolidation of democracy in Africa and assist Africans in their struggle for lasting peace, poverty eradication and sustainable development, thereby bringing Africa into the mainstream of the world economy.
28. We resolve therefore:
    - To give full support to the political and institutional structures of emerging democracies in Africa.
    - To encourage and sustain regional and subregional mechanisms for preventing conflict and promoting political stability, and to ensure a reliable flow of resources for peacekeeping operations on the continent.
    - To take special measures to address the challenges of poverty eradication and sustainable development in Africa, including debt cancellation, improved market access, enhanced Official Development Assistance and increased flows of Foreign Direct Investment, as well as transfers of technology.
    - To help Africa build up its capacity to tackle the spread of the HIV/AIDS pandemic and other infectious diseases.

VIII. Strengthening the United Nations

29. We will spare no effort to make the United Nations a more effective instrument for pursuing all of these priorities: the fight for development for all the peoples of the world, the fight against poverty, ignorance and disease; the fight against injustice; the fight against violence, terror and crime; and the fight against the degradation and destruction of our common home.
30. We resolve therefore:
    - To reaffirm the central position of the General Assembly as the chief deliberative, policy-making and representative organ of the United Nations, and to enable it to play that role effectively.
    - To intensify our efforts to achieve a comprehensive reform of the Security Council in all its aspects.
    - To strengthen further the Economic and Social Council, building on its recent achievements, to help it fulfil the role ascribed to it in the Charter.

- To strengthen the International Court of Justice, in order to ensure justice and the rule of law in international affairs.
- To encourage regular consultations and coordination among the principal organs of the United Nations in pursuit of their functions.
  - To ensure that the Organization is provided on a timely and predictable basis with the resources it needs to carry out its mandates.
- To urge the Secretariat to make the best use of those resources, in accordance with clear rules and procedures agreed by the General Assembly, in the interests of all Member States, by adopting the best management practices and technologies available and by concentrating on those tasks that reflect the agreed priorities of Member States.
- To promote adherence to the Convention on the Safety of United Nations and Associated Personnel.
- To ensure greater policy coherence and better cooperation between the United Nations, its agencies, the Bretton Woods Institutions and the World Trade Organization, as well as other multilateral bodies, with a view to achieving a fully coordinated approach to the problems of peace and development.
- To strengthen further cooperation between the United Nations and national parliaments through their world organization, the Inter-Parliamentary Union, in various fields, including peace and security, economic and social development, international law and human rights and democracy and gender issues.
- To give greater opportunities to the private sector, non-governmental organizations and civil society, in general, to contribute to the realization of the Organization's goals and programmes.

31. We request the General Assembly to review on a regular basis the progress made in implementing the provisions of this Declaration, and ask the Secretary-General to issue periodic reports for consideration by the General Assembly and as a basis for further action.

32. We solemnly reaffirm, on this historic occasion, that the United Nations is the indispensable common house of the entire human family, through which we will seek to realize our universal aspirations for peace, cooperation and development. We therefore pledge our unstinting support for these common objectives and our determination to achieve them.

Report of the Commission on Human Security*

(outline)

Human security – now

People's security around the world is interlinked - as today's global flows of goods, services, finance, people and images highlight. Political liberalization and democratization opens new opportunities but also new fault lines, such as political and economic instabilities and conflicts within states. More than 800,000 people a year lose their lives to violence. About 2.8 billion suffer from poverty, ill health, illiteracy and other maladies. Conflict and deprivation are interconnected. Deprivation has many causal links to violence, although these have to be carefully examined. Conversely, wars kill people, destroy trust among them, increase poverty and crime, and slow down the economy. Addressing such insecurities effectively demands an integrated approach.

The report's call for human security is a response to the challenges in today's world. Policies and institutions must respond to these insecurities in stronger and more integrated ways. The state continues to have the primary responsibility for security. But as security challenges become more complex and various new actors attempt to play a role, we need a shift in paradigm. The focus must broaden from the state to the security of people - to human security.

Human security means protecting vital freedoms. It means protecting people from critical and pervasive threats and situations, building on their strengths and aspirations. It also means creating systems that give people the building blocks of survival, dignity and livelihood. Human security connects different types of freedoms - freedom from want, freedom from fear and freedom to take action on one's own behalf. To do this, it offers two general strategies: protection and empowerment. Protection shields people from dangers. It requires concerted effort to develop norms, processes and institutions that systematically address insecurities. Empowerment enables people to develop their potential and become full participants in decision-making. Protection and empowerment are mutually reinforcing, and both are required in most situations.

Human security complements state security, furthers human development and enhances human rights. It complements state security by being people-centered and addressing insecurities that have not been considered as state security threats. By looking at "downside risks", it broadens the human development focus beyond "growth with equity". Respecting human rights are at the core of protecting human security.

---

* Report of the Commission on Human Security, chaired by Sadako Ogata and Amartya Sen, New York 2003, 1 May 2003.

Promoting democratic principles is a step toward attaining human security and development. It enables people to participate in governance and make their voices heard. This requires building strong institutions, establishing the rule of law and empowering people.

Ways to advance the security of people

Human security seeks to strengthen and bring together efforts to address issues such as conflict and deprivation. Attempts are being made, for example, to realize the United Nations' Millennium Declaration and the Millennium Development Goals (MDGs). Achieving human security requires building on and going beyond the MDGs, by undertaking efforts to address the full range of critical and pervasive threats facing people.

Protecting people in violent conflict: Civilians are the main casualties in conflicts. Both norms and mechanisms to protect civilians should be strengthened. This requires comprehensive and integrated strategies, linking political, military, humanitarian and development aspects. The Commission proposes placing human security formally on the agenda of security organizations at all levels. There are critical gaps in how human rights are upheld, in respect for citizenship and humanitarian law. These gaps need to be closed as well as attention given to ending the impunity of perpetrators of human rights violations. Community-based strategies to promote coexistence and trust among people will support these efforts. Equally urgent is meeting the life-saving needs of people through humanitarian assistance. Special attention should be given to protecting women, children, the elderly and other vulnerable groups. Disarming people and fighting crime through preventing the proliferation of weapons and illegal trade in resources and people has to be a priority.

Protecting and empowering people on the move: For the majority of people, migration is an opportunity to improve their livelihood. For others, migrating is the only option to protect themselves, such as those forced to flee because of conflicts or serious human rights violations. Others may also be forced to leave their homes to escape chronic deprivations or sudden downturns. Today, there is no agreed international framework to provide protection or to regulate migration, except for refugees. The feasibility of an international migration framework should be explored, through establishing the basis of high-level and broad-based discussions and dialogues on the need to strike a careful balance between the security and development needs of countries, and the human security of people on the move. Equally important is to ensure the protection of refugees and internally displaced persons, and identify ways to end their plight.

Protecting and empowering people in post-conflict situations: Cease-fire agreements and peace settlements may mark the end of conflict, but not necessarily the advent of peace and human security. The responsibility to protect people in conflict should be complemented by a responsibility to rebuild. A new framework and a funding strategy are necessary to rebuild conflict-torn states – one that focuses on the protection and empowerment of people. Such a human security framework emphasizes the linkages among the many issues affecting people, such as ensuring people's safety through strengthening civilian police and demobilizing combatants; meeting immediate needs of displaced people; launching reconstruction and development; promoting reconciliation and coexistence; and advancing effective governance. To be successful, it requires setting up unified leadership for all actors close to the delivery point of human security. To implement such a framework, a new fundraising strategy should be designed for post-conflict situations, at field level, to ensure coherence in the planning, budgeting and implementation of human security related activities.

Economic insecurity - the power to choose among opportunities: Extreme poverty remains pervasive. The proper functioning of markets as well as development of non market institutions are key to poverty eradication. Efficient and equitable trade arrangements, economic growth reaching the extreme poor and a fair distribution of benefits are essential. Together with addressing chronic poverty, human security focuses on sudden economic downturns, natural disasters and the social impacts of crises. To make people secure when crisis hits or to enable them to move out of poverty, we need social arrangements to meet their basic needs and ensure an economic and social minimum. Three-quarters of the world's people are not protected by social security or do not have secure work. Efforts to ensure sustainable livelihoods and work based security for all need to be strengthened. Access to land, credit, education, and housing, especially for poor women, is critical. An equitable distribution of resources is key to livelihood security and can enhance people's own capacity and ingenuity. Social protection measures and safety nets can advance a social and economic minimum. States, supported by the international system, need to establish early warning and prevention measures for natural disasters and economic or financial crises.

Health for human security: Despite the progress in healthcare, 22 million people died of preventable diseases in 2001. HIV/AIDS will soon become the greatest health catastrophe. In their urgency, depth and impact, global infectious diseases, poverty-related threats and health deprivations arising from violence are particularly significant. All health actors should promote health services as public goods. It is essential to mobilize social action and invest in supportive social arrangements, including the access to information, to remove the root causes of ill-health, to provide early warning systems and to mitigate health impacts once a crisis occurs. Providing access to life-saving drugs is critical for those in developing countries. An equitable intellectual property rights regime needs to be developed to balance incentives for research and development with ensuring people's access to affordable life-saving drugs. The international community must also form a global network of partnerships for health, promoting, for example, a global surveillance and control system for infectious diseases.

Knowledge, skills and values - for human security: Basic education and public information that provide knowledge, life skills and respect for diversity are particularly important for human security. The Commission urges the international community to actively help the achievement of universal primary education, with a particular emphasis on girls' education. Schools should not create physical insecurities, but protect students from violence including sexual violence. Education should foster respect for diversity and promote the multiplicity of our identities by employing a balanced curriculum and method of instruction. Public media are important as they can provide information on life skills and political issues, and give people voice in public debate. Not only should education and the media provide information and skills that will improve work opportunities and family health, but they should also enable people to actively exercise their rights and fulfil their responsibility.

Based on the foregoing the Commission has arrived at policy conclusions in the following areas.

1. Protecting people in violent conflict
2. Protecting people from the proliferation of arms
3. Supporting the security of people on the move
4. Establishing human security transition funds for post-conflict situations
5. Encouraging fair trade and markets to benefit the extreme poor
6. Working to provide minimum living standards everywhere
7. According higher priority to ensuring universal access to basic health care
8. Developing an efficient and equitable global system for patent rights
9. Empowering all people with universal basic education
10. Clarifying the need for a global human identity while respecting the freedom of individuals to have diverse identities and affiliations.

Linking the many initiatives

For each of these policy conclusions joint efforts are necessary - a network of public, private, and civil society actors who can help in the clarification and development of norms, embark on integrated activities, and monitor progress and performance. Such efforts could create a horizontal, cross-border source of legitimacy that complements traditional vertical structures. This array of alliances could begin to give voice to a nascent international public opinion. Human security could serve as a catalytic concept that links many existing initiatives.

But effective and adequate resource mobilization is also required. Not only must there be greater commitment to providing additional resources but also a shift of priority assistance to people in greatest need. In this respect, the Commission recognizes the valuable contribution of the UN Trust Fund for Human Security and encourages the broadening of its donor base. It also recommends the establishment of an Advisory Board on Human Security to provide orientation to the UN Trust Fund and follow-up on the Commission's recommendations.

The Commission proposes the development of a core group made up of interested states, international organizations and civil society, around the United Nations and the Bretton Woods institutions, as a part of its critical initiative-in which a small input of resources might leverage great impact-to forge links with disparate human security actors in a strong global alliance.

We the peoples: civil society, the United Nations and global governance*
(executive summary)

Public opinion has become a key factor influencing intergovernmental
and governmental policies and actions. The involvement of a diverse
range of actors, including those from civil society and the private sector,
as well as local authorities and parliamentarians, is not only essential for
effective action on global priorities but is also a protection against further erosion of multilateralism. This presents an opportunity as well as a
challenge to the United Nations: the opportunity to harness new capacities and diverse experience to address some of the most exacting challenges the world faces today and the challenge of balancing its unique
intergovernmental characteristic with being open to work with new
actors in a profound way.

Over the years, the relationship of the United Nations to civil society
has strengthened and multiplied. The Secretary-General's personal leadership has been a major factor in this development. However, at the same
time difficulties and tensions have arisen, particularly in deliberative
processes. Governments do not always welcome sharing what has traditionally been their preserve. Many increasingly challenge the numbers
and motives of civil society organizations in the United Nations – questioning their representivity, legitimacy, integrity or accountability. Developing country Governments sometimes regard civil society organizations
as pushing a "Northern agenda" through the back door. At the same time,
many in civil society are becoming frustrated; they can speak in the
United Nations but feel they are not heard and that their participation
has little impact on outcomes.

Mindful of both the immense strengths of civil society and the stones
in the road, the Secretary-General made clear that improving United
Nations-civil society relations was an important element of his reform
agenda, set out in his 2002 report on further reforms (A/57/387 and Corr.1).
In February 2003, he established the Panel of Eminent Persons on United
Nations-Civil Society Relations, chaired by Fernando Henrique Cardoso.
The Panel agreed at the outset that its advice should be informed by the
experience of those who have sought to engage with the United Nations,
on either policy or operational matters, and whether at the country,
regional or global level. Hence it consulted extensively – through meetings, workshops, focus groups and via its web site.

Global context

The Panel was clear that, to be effective in its work, it had to start by
analysing major global changes and challenges that affect the United

---

* Report of the Panel of Eminent Persons on United Nations–Civil Society Relations,
chaired by Fernando Henrique Cardoso, UN Doc. A58/817, 11 June 2004.

Nations and multilateralism insofar as they might affect the Organization's relations with civil society and others. It is clear that the question is not How would the United Nations like to change? but Given how the world has changed, how must the United Nations evolve its civil society relations to become fully effective and remain fully relevant? Globalization, the increasing porosity of national borders, new communication technologies, the increasing power of civil society and public opinion, mounting dissatisfaction with traditional institutions of democracy, the imperative of decentralization and other factors have enormous implications for global governance:

- Concerning democracy, a clear paradox is emerging: while the substance of politics is fast globalizing (in the areas of trade, economics, environment, pandemics, terrorism, etc.), the process of politics is not; its principal institutions (elections, political parties and parliaments) remain firmly rooted at the national or local level. The weak influence of traditional democracy in matters of global governance is one reason why citizens in much of the world are urging greater democratic accountability of international organizations.
- Concerning the roles of civil society in governance, citizens increasingly act politically by participating directly, through civil society mechanisms, in policy debates that particularly interest them. This constitutes a broadening from representative to participatory democracy. Traditional democracy aggregates citizens by communities of neighbourhood (their electoral districts), but in participatory democracy citizens aggregate in communities of interest. And, thanks to modern information and communication technologies, these communities of interest can be global as readily as local.
- Concerning multilateralism, the way the multilateral agenda is shaped has changed. Previously, Governments would come together to discuss a new issue until there was a sufficient consensus for an intergovernmental resolution, which then led to action by Governments and intergovernmental organizations. Today it is increasingly likely that a civil society movement and a crescendo of public opinion will bring a new issue to global attention and that initial action on new issues will be taken through multi-constituency coalitions of Governments, civil society and others. Increasingly, multilateralism includes ongoing processes of public debate, policy dialogue and pioneering action to tackle emerging challenges.

Why strengthen United Nations–civil society engagement?
The most powerful case for reaching out beyond its constituency of central Governments and enhancing dialogue and cooperation with civil society is that doing so will make the United Nations more effective. Because of the features of global change described above and the attributes of many civil society organizations, an enhanced engagement could help the United Nations do a better job, further its global goals, become more attuned and responsive to citizens' concerns and enlist greater public support. There are trade-offs, however. The unique role of the United Nations as an intergovernmental forum is vitally important and must be protected at all costs. But today's challenges require the United Nations to

be more than just an intergovernmental forum; it must engage others too. To do so risks putting more pressure on the Organization's meeting rooms and agendas, which are becoming ever more crowded; this calls for more selective and not just increased engagement.

Paradigm shifts
The Panel consolidated its contextual analysis into four main principles – or paradigms – on which the set of reforms it proposes is based:
- Become an outward-looking organization. The changing nature of multilateralism to mean multiple constituencies entails the United Nations giving more emphasis to convening and facilitating rather than "doing" and putting the issues, not the institution, at the centre.
- Embrace a plurality of constituencies. Many actors may be relevant to an issue, and new partnerships are needed to tackle global challenges.
- Connect the local with the global. The deliberative and operational spheres of the United Nations are separated by a wide gulf, which hampers both in all areas from development to security. A closer two-way connection between them is imperative so that local operational work truly helps to realize the global goals and that global deliberations are informed by local reality. Civil society is vital for both directions. Hence the country level should be the starting point for engagement in both the operational and deliberative processes.
- Help strengthen democracy for the twenty-first century. The United Nations should accept a more explicit role in strengthening global governance and tackling the democratic deficits it is prone to, emphasizing participatory democracy and deeper accountability of institutions to the global public.

The following are the proposed reform areas, building on these principles. Civil society is now so vital to the United Nations that engaging with it well is a necessity, not an option. It must also engage with others, including the private sector, parliaments and local authorities. When, as is often the case, messages relate to all these actors, the broader term "constituencies" is used. Some of the reforms proposed are measures the Secretary-General could act upon on his own authority; other measures require intergovernmental approval.

Convening role of the United Nations: fostering multi-constituency processes

The convening power and moral authority of the United Nations enable it to bring often conflicting parties together to tackle global problems. Nowadays, non-State actors are often prime movers – as with issues of gender, climate change, debt, landmines and AIDS. The first step is often the creation of global policy networks (of Governments and others who share specific concerns) to promote global debate and/or to pilot activities to combat the problem directly. The United Nations has to date often played a weak role in such innovations. Since this mode is clearly becoming a major aspect of multilateralism, the United Nations must learn the skills and be more proactive, bringing together all constituencies relevant to global issues and galvanizing appropriate networks for effective results.

This entails innovation in global governance and tailoring forums to the task at hand. The General Assembly should include civil society organizations more regularly in its affairs, since it no longer makes sense to restrict their involvement in the intergovernmental process to the Economic and Social Council. Big global conferences can still play an important role if used sparingly to establish global norms. More modest public hearings, also involving the full range of relevant constituencies, could be more appropriate tools for reviewing progress on agreed global goals.

Investing more in partnerships

The Panel strongly affirms multi-stakeholder partnerships for tackling both operational and policy challenges. This is not a new idea; some of today's most important global advances emanate from partnerships, and their scale and breadth are growing. Although they are no panacea, the United Nations should invest much more systematically in convening and incubating them wherever the capacities of diverse actors are needed and in making them more sincere ventures. They must be viewed as "partnerships to achieve global goals" not "United Nations partnerships", decentralized to relevant country and technical units and driven by needs, not funding opportunities. To advance this goal necessitates innovations and resources at both the country and global levels.

Focusing on the country level

Priority should be placed on engagement at the country level. This could enhance the contributions of civil society organizations and others to country strategies for achieving the Millennium Development Goals and other United Nations goals, and level the playing field between civil society organizations from North and South. This would strengthen operations, tailor them to local needs and enable ground-level realities to inform the Organization's norm-setting process. Although the rhetoric already emphasizes such an approach, the reality is often quite different. United Nations Development Group agencies may involve civil society organizations in implementation but often not in strategic planning, and weak information-sharing may hamper the formation of strong partnerships. The Panel's proposals entail strengthening the capacity of resident coordinators and other United Nations staff to maximize partnership opportunities and better prioritize their relations with all constituencies. This is vital for the world's poor and for the credibility of the United Nations, which rests on demonstrating progress with the Millennium Development Goals.

Strengthening the Security Council

The Security Council has greatly benefited of late from expanded dialogue with civil society. The nature of modern conflicts makes it more important to understand their social origins and consequences. Much interaction focuses on international non-governmental organizations. Security Council members, with support from the Secretariat, should deepen this dialogue by emphasizing the involvement of participants from conflict-affected countries and including such dialogue in Security Council field missions. The United Nations could learn much by conducting commissions of inquiry after Council-mandated operations, to draw, *inter alia*, on the experience of civil society organizations.

Engaging with elected representatives

More systematic engagement of parliamentarians, national parliaments and local authorities in the United Nations would strengthen global governance, confront democratic deficits in intergovernmental affairs, buttress representational democracy and connect the United Nations better with global opinion. The Panel's proposals are designed to encourage national parliaments to give more attention to United Nations matters, to evolve more appropriate engagement for those members of Parliament who come to United Nations events and to link national parliaments more directly with the international deliberative process, particularly by experimenting with global equivalents of parliamentary select committees.

In an era when decentralization is shaping the political landscape as powerfully as globalization, it is also important for the United Nations to find deeper and more systematic ways to engage with elected representatives and authorities at the local level. They and their international networks are increasingly helping the United Nations to identify local priorities, implement solutions and build closer connections with citizens. The Secretariat should engage this constituency more, and the United Nations could promote mechanisms of decentralization and discussion of principles of local autonomy.

Tackling accreditation and access issues

Although the Panel emphasizes new forums tailored to specific needs, traditional modes of engagement – such as the accreditation of civil society organizations with defined participation rights in United Nations forums – remain important. But today this process is overly politicized, expensive and can present a barrier, especially for developing country civil society organizations, hence major reforms are proposed to emphasize technical merit. The Panel proposes joining all existing United Nations accreditation processes into a single mechanism under the authority of the General Assembly (if it is agreed to extend civil society engagement to this forum). It further proposes establishing a more thorough initial Secretariat review of applications, lessening the prominence of intergovernmental review, which tends to overpoliticize the accreditation process. Member States would retain a final say on which applicants are accredited and would also define the criteria by which applicants would be assessed. By drawing on the growing knowledge about civil society organizations that exists throughout the United Nations system (and perhaps beyond it), the Secretariat would be well-placed to advise Member States on which applicants met such criteria and which did not. The Panel suggests that by reducing the time demands of intergovernmental deliberation on applications, an existing committee of the General Assembly (perhaps the General Committee) could assume this role alongside their normal functions, discussing applications only when some Member States disagree with the proposals.

Accreditation should be seen as a cooperative agreement entailing rights and responsibilities; hence measures are also suggested that could help enhance the quality of civil society contributions, especially by encouraging self-governance and self-organizing processes within civil society networks.

Determining what the proposals mean for staff, resources and management

The Panel suggests what would be needed in terms of the skills mix, financial resources, training, management and changes to the institutional culture of the United Nations in order to achieve the reforms it proposes. It suggests in particular the creation of a new high-level position in the office of the Secretary-General to help lead and manage the change process, perhaps also assuming line management responsibility for some of the units at the front line of dialogue, partnership development and engagement with different constituencies. There should be a strong emphasis on levelling the playing field between Northern and Southern civil society, for which the Panel suggests establishing a special fund to enhance Southern civil society capacity to engage in United Nations deliberative processes, operations and partnerships.

The overall strategy would have considerable resource implications, but amounting to less than 1 per cent of the operating budget of the United Nations, most of which could be found from potential savings identified by the Panel and from donor contributions.

Providing global leadership

The United Nations should use its moral leadership to urge coordinated approaches to civil society, to encourage Governments to provide a more enabling and cooperative environment for civil society and to foster debate about reforms of global governance, including deeper roles for civil society. This should emphasize principles of constituency engagement, partnership, transparency and inclusion, with a special emphasis on those who are normally underrepresented.

Future of multilateralism

Multilateralism faces many threats and challenges; it must address new global priorities while facing the erosion of power and resources. The Panel affirms the importance of multilateralism and so is pleased to make this contribution, since civil society can help the United Nations to redress those threats. The Panel is also aware of various commissions and panels on other topics, and ends with some messages that it believes are applicable to them all.

Panels have some features in common with global conferences – albeit on a much smaller scale. They can serve a useful purpose, providing they are publicly respected. This depends on their inclusiveness, the realism and courage of their proposals and the degree to which their proposals are acted upon.

Our starting paradigms also apply to the other panels and are the foundation for the continued relevance of the United Nations: (a) multilateralism no longer concerns Governments alone but is now multifaceted, involving many constituencies; the United Nations must develop new skills to service this new way of working; (b) it must become an outward-looking or network organization, catalysing the relationships needed to get strong results and not letting the traditions of its formal processes be barriers; (c) it must strengthen global governance by advocating universality, inclusion, participation and accountability at all levels; and (d) it must engage more systematically with world public opinion to become more responsive, to help shape public attitudes and to bolster support for multilateralism.

ANNEX 9

A Fair Globalization, Creating Opportunities for All*
(synopsis)

Introduction

Our remit, the Social Dimension of Globalization, is a vast and complex one. As a Commission we were broadly representative of the diverse and contending actors and interests that exist in the real world. Co-chaired by two serving Heads of State, a woman and a man, from North and South, we came from countries in different parts of the world and at all stages of development. Our affiliations were equally diverse: government, politics, parliaments, business and multinational corporations, organized labour, academia and civil society.

Yet, through a spirit of common purpose, we arrived at the shared understandings that are before you. As a collective document it is quite different from alternative reports each one of us would have written individually. But our experience has demonstrated the value and power of dialogue as an instrument for change. Through listening patiently and respectfully to diverse views and interests we found common ground.

We were spurred on by the realization that action to build a fair and inclusive process of globalization was urgent. This could only happen in the future through forging agreements among a broad spectrum of actors on the course for action. We are convinced that our experience can and should be replicated on a larger and wider scale, expanding the space for dialogue aimed at building consensus for action.

A vision for change

Public debate on globalization is at an impasse. Opinion is frozen in the ideological certainties of entrenched positions and fragmented in a variety of special interests. The will for consensus is weak. Key international negotiations are deadlocked and international development commitments go largely unfulfilled.

The report before you offers no miraculous or simple solutions, for there are none. But it is an attempt to help break the current impasse by focusing on the concerns and aspirations of people and on the ways to better harness the potential of globalization itself.

Ours is a critical but positive message for changing the current path of globalization. We believe the benefits of globalization can be extended to more people and better shared between and within countries, with many more voices having an influence on its course. The resources and the

* Report of the World Commission on the Social Dimension of Globalization, chaired by Tarja Halonen and Benjamin William Mkapa, Geneva: ILO, 2004.

278

means are at hand. Our proposals are ambitious but feasible. We are certain that a better world is possible.

We seek a process of globalization with a strong social dimension based on universally shared values, and respect for human rights and individual dignity; one that is fair, inclusive, democratically governed and provides opportunities and tangible benefits for all countries and people.
To this end we call for:
- *A focus on people.*
  The cornerstone of a fairer globalization lies in meeting the demands of all people for: respect for their rights, cultural identity and autonomy; decent work; and the empowerment of the local communities they live in. Gender equality is essential.
- *A democratic and effective State.*
  The State must have the capability to manage integration into the global economy, and provide social and economic opportunity and security.
- *Sustainable development.*
  The quest for a fair globalization must be underpinned by the interdependent and mutually reinforcing pillars of economic development, social development and environmental protection at the local, national, regional and global levels.
- *Productive and equitable markets.*
  This requires sound institutions to promote opportunity and enterprise in a well-functioning market economy.
- *Fair rules.*
  The rules of the global economy must offer equitable opportunity and access for all countries and recognize the diversity in national capacities and developmental needs.
- *Globalization with solidarity.*
  There is a shared responsibility to assist countries and people excluded from or disadvantaged by globalization. Globalization must help to overcome inequality both within and between countries and contribute to the elimination of poverty.
- *Greater accountability to people.*
  Public and private actors at all levels with power to influence the outcomes of globalization must be democratically accountable for the policies they pursue and the actions they take. They must deliver on their commitments and use their power with respect for others.
- *Deeper partnerships.*
  Many actors are engaged in the realization of global social and economic goals – international organizations, governments and parliaments, business, labour, civil society and many others. Dialogue and partnership among them is an essential democratic instrument to create a better world.
- *An effective United Nations.*
  A stronger and more efficient multilateral system is the key instrument to create a democratic, legitimate and coherent framework for globalization.

Globalization and its impact

Globalization has set in motion a process of far-reaching change that is affecting everyone. New technology, supported by more open policies, has created a world more interconnected than ever before. This spans not only growing interdependence in economic relations – trade, investment, finance and the organization of production globally – but also social and political interaction among organizations and individuals across the world.

The potential for good is immense. The growing interconnectivity among people across the world is nurturing the realization that we are all part of a global community. This nascent sense of interdependence, commitment to shared universal values, and solidarity among peoples across the world can be channelled to build enlightened and democratic global governance in the interests of all. The global market economy has demonstrated great productive capacity. Wisely managed, it can deliver unprecedented material progress, generate more productive and better jobs for all, and contribute significantly to reducing world poverty.

But we also see how far short we still are from realizing this potential. The current process of globalization is generating unbalanced outcomes, both between and within countries. Wealth is being created, but too many countries and people are not sharing in its benefits. They also have little or no voice in shaping the process. Seen through the eyes of the vast majority of women and men, globalization has not met their simple and legitimate aspirations for decent jobs and a better future for their children. Many of them live in the limbo of the informal economy without formal rights and in a swathe of poor countries that subsist precariously on the margins of the global economy. Even in economically successful countries some workers and communities have been adversely affected by globalization. Meanwhile the revolution in global communications heightens awareness of these isparities.

A strategy for change

These global imbalances are morally unacceptable and politically unsustainable. What is required to change this is not the realization of a Utopian blueprint in one swoop. Rather it is a series of coordinated changes across a broad front, ranging from reform of parts of the global economic system to strengthening governance at the local level. All this should and can be achieved in the context of open economies and open societies. Though interests diverge, we believe that there is increasing convergence of opinion throughout the world on the need for a fair and inclusive process of globalization.

We have formulated a wide-ranging set of recommendations to realize this. Given the necessary political will, immediate action is feasible on some trade and financial issues that have been the subject of protracted multilateral negotiations and discussion in policy circles. On these issues, the required course of action is clear but the urgent need for change has not yet dawned on some major players. Here continued advocacy and a stronger public opinion is essential to carry the proposals forward. Advocacy to prepare the ground for the consideration of new issues will also be important. But on these newer issues, such as the development of a multilateral framework for the cross-border movement of people or the accountability of international organizations, the prime lever for the decision to act is broad-based dialogue among State and non-State actors. Through this, consensus and resolve can be forged on what needs to be done, how, and by whom.

The governance of globalization

We judge that the problems we have identified are not due to globalization as such but to deficiencies in its governance. Global markets have grown rapidly without the parallel development of economic and social institutions necessary for their smooth and equitable functioning. At the same time, there is concern about the unfairness of key global rules on trade and finance and their asymmetric effects on rich and poor countries.

An additional concern is the failure of current international policies to respond adequately to the challenges posed by globalization. Market opening measures and financial and economic considerations predominate over social ones. Official Development Assistance (ODA) falls far short of the minimum amounts required even for achieving the Millennium Development Goals (MDGs) and tackling growing global problems. The multilateral system responsible for designing and implementing international policies is also under-performing. It lacks policy coherence as a whole and is not sufficiently democratic, transparent and accountable.

These rules and policies are the outcome of a system of global governance largely shaped by powerful countries and powerful players. There is a serious democratic deficit at the heart of the system. Most developing countries still have very limited influence in global negotiations on rules and in determining the policies of key financial and economic institutions. Similarly, workers and the poor have little or no voice in this governance process.

Beginning at home

There is thus a wide range of issues to be addressed at the global level. But this alone will not suffice. Global governance is not a lofty, disembodied sphere. It is merely the apex of a web of governance that stretches from the local level upwards. The behaviour of nation States as global actors is the essential determinant of the quality of global governance. Their degree of commitment to multilateralism, universal values and common goals, the extent of their sensitivity to the cross-border impact of their policies, and the weight they attach to global solidarity are all vital determinants of the quality of global governance. At the same time, how they manage their internal affairs influences the extent to which people will benefit from globalization and be protected from its negative effects. In this important sense the response to globalization can be said to begin at home. This reflects the simple but crucial fact that people live locally within nations.

We therefore anchor our analysis at the national level. We do not, of course, presume to make specific recommendations for all the greatly diverse countries of the world. Rather, we set out the broad goals and principles that can guide policy to deal more effectively with the social dimension of globalization, fully recognizing that their implementation must respond to the needs and specific conditions of each country. From this perspective it is clear that national governance needs to be improved in all countries, albeit more radically in some than in others. There is wide international agreement on the essentials which we must all urgently strive for:

- good political governance based on a democratic political system, respect for human rights, the rule of law and social equity.
- an effective State that ensures high and stable economic growth, provides public goods and social protection, raises the capabilities of people through universal access to education and other social services, and promotes gender equity.
- a vibrant civil society, empowered by freedom of association and expression, that reflects and voices the full diversity of views and interests. Organizations representing public interests, the poor and other disadvantaged groups are also essential for ensuring participatory and socially just governance.
- strong representative organizations of workers and employers are essential for fruitful social dialogue.

The highest priority must be given to policies to meet the central aspiration of women and men for decent work; to raise the productivity of the informal economy and to integrate it into the economic mainstream; and to enhance the competitiveness of enterprises and economies.

Policy must focus squarely on meeting peoples' needs where they live and work. It is thus essential to nurture local communities through the devolution of power and resources and through strengthening local economic capabilities, cultural identity, and respecting the rights of indigenous and tribal peoples. Nation States should also strengthen regional and sub-regional cooperation as a major instrument for development and for a stronger voice in the governance of globalization. They should reinforce the social dimension of regional integration.

Reform at the global level

At the global level, we have more specific recommendations to make. Some key ones are highlighted below.

Global rules and policies on trade and finance must allow more space for policy autonomy in developing countries. This is essential for developing policies and institutional arrangements best suited to their level of development and specific circumstances. Existing rules that unduly restrict their policy options for accelerating agricultural growth and industrialization and for maintaining financial and economic stability need to be reviewed.

New rules must also respect this requirement. The policies of international organizations and donor countries must also shift more decisively away from external conditionality to national ownership of policies. Affirmative action provisions in favour of countries that do not have the same capabilities as those who developed earlier need to be strengthened.

Fair rules for trade and capital flows need to be complemented by fair rules for the cross-border movement of people. International migratory pressures have increased and problems such as trafficking in people and the exploitation of migrant workers have intensified. Steps have to be taken to build a multilateral framework that provides uniform and transparent rules for the cross-border movement of people and balances the interests of both migrants themselves and of countries of origin and destination. All countries stand to benefit from an orderly and managed process of international migration that can enhance global productivity and eliminate exploitative practices.

Global production systems have proliferated, generating the need for new rules on Foreign Direct Investment (FDI) and on competition. A balanced and development-friendly multilateral framework for FDI, negotiated in a generally accepted forum, will benefit all countries by promoting increased direct investment flows while limiting the problems of incentive competition which reduce the benefits from these flows. Such a framework should balance private, workers' and public interests, as well as their rights and responsibilities. Cooperation on cross-border competition policy will make global markets more transparent and competitive.

Core labour standards as defined by the ILO provide a minimum set of global rules for labour in the global economy and respect for them should be strengthened in all countries. Stronger action is required to ensure respect for core labour standards in Export Processing Zones (EPZs) and, more generally, in global production systems. All relevant international institutions should assume their part in promoting these standards and ensure that no aspect of their policies and programmes impedes implementation of these rights.

The multilateral trading system should substantially reduce unfair barriers to market access for goods in which developing countries have comparative advantage, especially textiles and garments and agricultural products. In doing so, the interests of the Least Developed Countries (LDCs) should be safeguarded through special and differential treatment to nurture their export potential.

A minimum level of social protection for individuals and families needs to be accepted and undisputed as part of the socio-economic 'floor' of the global economy, including adjustment assistance to displaced workers. Donors and financial institutions should contribute to the strengthening of social protection systems in developing countries. Greater market access is not a panacea. A more balanced strategy for sustainable global growth and full employment, including an equitable sharing among countries of the responsibility for maintaining high levels of effective demand in the global economy, is essential. Enhanced coordination of macroeconomic policies among countries to this end is a key requirement. A successful global growth strategy will ease economic tensions among countries and make market access for developing countries easier to achieve.

Decent Work for all should be made a global goal and be pursued through coherent policies within the multilateral system. This would respond to a major political demand in all countries and demonstrate the capacity of the multilateral system to find creative solutions to this critical problem.

The international financial system should be made more supportive of sustainable global growth. Cross-border financial flows have grown massively but the system is unstable, prone to crises and largely bypasses poor and capital scarce countries. Gains in the spheres of trade and FDI cannot be fully reaped unless the international financial system is reformed to achieve greater stability. In this context developing countries should be permitted to adopt a cautious and gradual approach to capital account liberalization and more socially sensitive sequencing of adjustment measures in response to crises.

A greater effort is required to mobilize more international resources to attain key global goals, particularly the MDGs. The 0.7 per cent target for ODA must be met and new sources for funding over and above this target should be actively explored and developed.

The implementation of reforms in international economic and social policy will require worldwide political support, the commitment of key global actors, and the strengthening of global institutions. The UN multilateral system constitutes the core of global governance and is uniquely equipped to spearhead the process of reform. For it to cope with the current and emerging challenges of globalization it has to enhance its effectiveness and improve the quality of its governance, especially with respect to democratic representation and decision-making, accountability to people, and policy coherence.

We call on developed countries to reconsider their decision to maintain zero nominal growth in their mandated contributions to the UN system. It is essential that the international community agree to increase financial contributions to the multilateral system and reverse the trend towards raising voluntary contributions at the expense of mandatory ones.

Heads of State and Government should ensure that the policies pursued by their countries in international fora are coherent and focus on the well-being of people.

Parliamentary oversight of the multilateral system at the global level should be progressively expanded. We propose the creation of a Parliamentary Group concerned with the coherence and consistency between global economic, social and environmental policies, which should develop an integrated oversight of major international organizations.

A critical requirement for better global governance is that all organizations, including UN agencies, should become more accountable to the public at large for the policies they pursue. National parliaments should contribute to this process by regularly reviewing decisions taken by their countries' representatives to these organizations.

Developing countries should have increased representation in the decision-making bodies of the Bretton Woods Institutions, while the working methods in the World Trade Organization (WTO) should provide for their full and effective participation in its negotiations.

Greater voice should be given to non-State actors, especially representative organizations of the poor.

The contributions of business, organized labour, civil society organizations (CSOs), and of knowledge and advocacy networks to the social dimension of globalization should be strengthened.

Responsible media can play a central role in facilitating a movement towards a fairer and more inclusive globalization. Well-informed public opinion on issues raised in this Report is essential to underpin change. Policies everywhere therefore need to emphasize the importance of diversity in information and communication flows.

Mobilizing action for change

We believe that broad-based dialogue on our recommendations, especially on issues that are not currently being negotiated on the global agenda, is the essential first step in mobilizing action for change. It is of primary importance that such dialogue begins at the national level in order to construct the foundations of the necessary consensus and political will.

At the same time the multilateral system has to play a pivotal role in carrying forward reforms at the global level. We propose a new operational tool for upgrading the quality of policy coordination between international organizations on issues in which the implementation of their mandates intersect and their policies interact. Policy Coherence Initiatives should be launched by the relevant international organizations to develop more balanced policies for achieving a fair and inclusive globalization. The objective would be to progressively develop integrated policy proposals that appropriately balance economic, social, and environmental concerns on specific issues. The first initiative should address the question of global growth, investment, and employment creation and involve relevant UN bodies, the World Bank, the International Monetary Fund (IMF), the WTO, and the ILO. Priority areas for other such initiatives include gender equality and the empowerment of women; education; health; food security; and human settlements.

A series of multi-stakeholder Policy Development Dialogues should also be organized by relevant international organizations to further consider and develop key policy proposals – such as a multilateral framework for the cross-border movement of people, a development framework for FDI, the strengthening of social protection in the global economy, and new forms of accountability of international organizations.

A Globalization Policy Forum should be organized by the UN and its specialized agencies to review on a regular and systematic basis the social impact of globalization. Participating organizations could produce a periodic 'State of Globalization Report'.

Our proposals call for a wider and more democratic participation of people and countries in the making of policies that affect them. And they also require those with the capacity and power to decide – governments, parliaments, business, labour, civil society and international organizations – to assume their common responsibility to promote a free, equitable and productive global community.

A more secure world: Our shared responsibility*

(executive summary)

In his address to the General Assembly in September 2003, United Nations Secretary-General Kofi Annan warned Member States that the United Nations had reached a fork in the road. It could rise to the challenge of meeting new threats or it could risk erosion in the face of mounting discord between States and unilateral action by them. He created the High-level Panel on Threats, Challenges and Change to generate new ideas about the kinds of policies and institutions required for the UN to be effective in the 21st century.

In its report, the High-level Panel sets out a bold, new vision of collective security for the 21st century. We live in a world of new and evolving threats, threats that could not have been anticipated when the UN was founded in 1945 – threats like nuclear terrorism, and State collapse from the witch's brew of poverty, disease and civil war.

In today's world, a threat to one is a threat to all. Globalization means that a major terrorist attack anywhere in the industrial world would have devastating consequences for the well-being of millions in the developing world. Any one of 700 million international airline passengers every year can be an unwitting carrier of a deadly infectious disease. And the erosion of State capacity anywhere in the world weakens the protection of every State against transnational threats such as terrorism and organized crime. Every State requires international cooperation to make it secure.

There are six clusters of threats with which the world must be concerned now and in the decades ahead:
- war between States;
- violence within States, including civil wars, large-scale human
- rights abuses and genocide;
- poverty, infectious disease and environmental degradation;
- nuclear, radiological, chemical and biological weapons;
- terrorism; and
- transnational organized crime.

The good news is that the United Nations and our collective security institutions have shown that they *can* work. More civil wars ended through negotiation in the past 15 years than the previous 200. In the 1960s, many believed that by now 15-25 States would possess nuclear weapons; the Nuclear Non-Proliferation Treaty has helped prevent this. The World Health Organization helped to stop the spread of SARS before it killed tens of thousands, perhaps more.

---

* Report of the High-level Panel on Threats, Challenges and Change, chaired by Anand Panyarachun, UN Doc.A/59/565, 29 November 2004.

But these accomplishments can be reversed. There is a real danger that they will be, unless we act soon to strengthen the United Nations, so that in future it responds effectively to the full range of threats that confront us.

Policies for prevention

Meeting the challenge of today's threats means getting serious about prevention; the consequences of allowing latent threats to become manifest, or of allowing existing threats to spread, are simply too severe.

Development has to be the first line of defence for a collective security system that takes prevention seriously. Combating *poverty* will not only save millions of lives but also strengthen States' capacity to combat terrorism, organized crime and proliferation. Development makes everyone more secure. There is an agreed international framework for how to achieve these goals, set out in the Millennium Declaration and the Monterrey Consensus, but implementation lags.

Biological security must be at the forefront of prevention. International response to HIV/AIDS was shockingly late and shamefully ill-resourced. It is urgent that we halt and roll back this pandemic. But we will have to do more. Our global public health system has deteriorated and is ill-equipped to protect us against existing and emerging deadly infectious diseases. The report recommends a major initiative to build public health capacity throughout the developing world, at both local and national levels. This will not only yield direct benefits by preventing and treating disease in the developing world itself, but will also provide the basis for an effective global defence against bioterrorism and overwhelming natural outbreaks of infectious disease.

Preventing *wars within States and between them* is also in the collective interest of all. If we are to do better in future, the UN will need real improvements to its capacity for preventive diplomacy and mediation. We will have to build on the successes of regional organizations in developing strong norms to protect Governments from unconstitutional overthrow, and to protect minority rights. And we will have to work collectively to find new ways of regulating the management of natural resources, competition for which often fuels conflict.

Preventing the spread and use of *nuclear, biological and chemical weapons* is essential if we are to have a more secure world. This means doing better at reducing demand for these weapons, and curbing the supply of weapons materials. It means living up to existing treaty commitments, including for negotiations towards disarmament. And it means enforcing international agreements. The report puts forward specific recommendations for the creation of incentives for States to forego the development of domestic uranium enrichment and reprocessing capacity. It urges negotiations for a new arrangement which would enable the International Atomic Energy Agency to act as a guarantor for the supply of fissile material to civilian nuclear users at market rates, and it calls on Governments to establish a voluntary time-limited moratorium on the construction of new facilities for uranium enrichment and reprocessing, matched by a guarantee of the supply of fissile materials by present suppliers.

Terrorism is a threat to all States, and to the UN as a whole. New aspects of the threat – including the rise of a global terrorist network, and the potential for terrorist use of nuclear, biological or chemical weapons – require new responses. The UN has not done all that it can. The report urges the United Nations to forge a strategy of counterterrorism that is respectful of human rights and the rule of law. Such a strategy must encompass coercive measures when necessary, and create new tools to help States combat the threat domestically. The report provides a clear definition of terrorism, arguing that it can never be justified, and calls on the General Assembly of the UN to overcome its divisions and finally conclude a comprehensive convention on terrorism.

The spread of *transnational organized crime* increases the risk of all the other threats. Terrorists use organized criminal groups to move money, men and materials around the globe. Governments and rebels sell natural resources through criminal groups to finance wars. States' capacity to establish the rule of law is weakened by corruption. Combating organized crime is essential for helping States build the capacity to exercise their sovereign responsibilities – and in combating the hideous traffic in human beings.

Response to threats

Of course, prevention sometimes fails. At times, threats will have to be met by military means.

The UN Charter provides a clear framework for the *use of force*. States have an inherent right to self-defence, enshrined in Article 51. Long-established customary international law makes it clear that States can take military action as long as the threatened attack is imminent, no other means would deflect it, and the action is proportionate. The Security Council has the authority to act preventively, but has rarely done so. The Security Council may well need to be prepared to be more proactive in the future, taking decisive action earlier. States that fear the emergence of distant threats have an obligation to bring these concerns to the Security Council.

The report endorses the emerging norm of a *responsibility to protect* civilians from large-scale violence – a responsibility that is held, first and foremost, by national authorities. When a State fails to protect its civilians, the international community then has a further responsibility to act, through humanitarian operations, monitoring missions and diplomatic pressure – and with force if necessary, though only as a last resort. And in the case of conflict or the use of force, this also implies a clear international commitment to rebuilding shattered societies.

Deploying military capacities – for *peacekeeping* as well as peace enforcement – has proved to be a valuable tool in ending wars and helping to secure States in their aftermath. But the total global supply of available peacekeepers is running dangerously low. Just to do an adequate job of keeping the peace in existing conflicts would require almost doubling the number of peacekeepers around the world. The developed States have particular responsibilities to do more to transform their armies into units suitable for deployment to peace operations. And if we are to meet the challenges ahead, more States will have to place contingents on stand-by for UN purposes, and keep air transport and other strategic lift capacities available to assist peace operations.

When wars have ended, *post-conflict peacebuilding* is vital. The UN has often devoted too little attention and too few resources to this critical challenge. Successful peacebuilding requires the deployment of peace-keepers with the right mandates and sufficient capacity to deter would-be spoilers; funds for demobilization and disarmament, built into peace-keeping budgets; a new trust fund to fill critical gaps in rehabilitation and reintegration of combatants, as well as other early reconstruction tasks; and a focus on building State institutions and capacity, especially in the rule of law sector. Doing this job successfully should be a core function of the United Nations.

A UN for the 21st century

To meet these challenges, the UN needs its existing institutions to work better. This means revitalizing the *General Assembly* and the *Economic and Social Council,* to make sure they play the role intended for them, and restoring credibility to the *Commission on Human Rights.*

It also means increasing the credibility and effectiveness of the *Security Council* by making its composition better reflect today's realities. The report provides principles for reform, and two models for how to achieve them – one involving new permanent members with no veto, the other involving new four-year, renewable seats. It argues that any reforms must be reviewed in 2020.

We also need new institutions to meet evolving challenges. The report recommends the creation of a *Peacebuilding Commission* – a new mecha-nism within the UN, drawing on the Security Council and the Economic and Social Council, donors, and national authorities. Working closely with regional organizations and the international financial institutions, such a commission could fill a crucial gap by giving the necessary atten-tion to countries emerging from conflict. Outside the UN, a forum bring-ing together the heads of the 20 largest economies, developed and devel-oping, would help the coherent management of international monetary, financial, trade and development policy.

Better collaboration with *regional organizations* is also crucial, and the report sets out a series of principles that govern a more structured part-nership between them and the UN.

The report recommends strengthening the Secretary-General's critical role in peace and security. To be more effective, the Secretary-General should be given substantially more latitude to manage the Secretariat, and be held accountable. He also needs better support for his mediation role, and new capacities to develop effective peacebuilding strategy. He currently has one Deputy Secretary-General; with a second, responsible for peace and security, he would have the capacity to ensure oversight of both the social, economic and development functions of the UN, and its many peace and security functions.

The report is the start, not the end, of a process. The year 2005 will be a crucial opportunity for Member States to discuss and build on the recommendations in the report, some of which will be considered by a summit of heads of State. But building a more secure world takes much more than a report or a summit. It will take resources commensurate with the scale of the challenges ahead; commitments that are long-term and sustained; and, most of all, it will take leadership – from within States, and between them.

In Larger Freedom: Development, Security and Human Rights for All*
(Summary)

Introduction: A Historic Opportunity in 2005

In September 2005, world leaders will come together at a summit in New York to review progress since the Millennium Declaration, adopted by all Member States in 2000. The Secretary-General's report proposes an agenda to be taken up, and acted upon, at the summit. These are policy decisions and reforms that are actionable if the necessary political will can be garnered.

Events since the Millennium Declaration demand that consensus be revitalized on key challenges and priorities and converted into collective action. The guiding light in doing so must be the needs and hopes of people everywhere. The world must advance the causes of security, development and human rights together, otherwise none will succeed. Humanity will not enjoy security without development, it will not enjoy development without security, and it will not enjoy either without respect for human rights.

In a world of inter-connected threats and opportunities, it is in each country's self-interest that all of these challenges are addressed effectively. Hence, the cause of larger freedom can only be advanced by broad, deep and sustained global cooperation among States. The world needs strong and capable States, effective partnerships with civil society and the private sector, and agile and effective regional and global intergovernmental institutions to mobilize and coordinate collective action. The United Nations must be reshaped in ways not previously imagined, and with a boldness and speed not previously shown.

I. Freedom from want

The last 25 years have seen the most dramatic reduction in extreme poverty the world has ever experienced. Yet dozens of countries have become poorer. More than a billion people still live on less than a dollar a day. Each year, 3 million people die from HIV/AIDS and 11 million children die before reaching their fifth birthday.

Today's is the first generation with the resources and technology to make the right to development a reality for everyone and to free the entire human race from want. There is a shared vision of development. The Millennium Development Goals (MDGs), which range from halving extreme poverty to putting all children into primary school and stemming the spread of infectious diseases such as HIV/AIDS, all by 2015, have become globally accepted benchmarks of broader progress, embraced by

---

* Report of the Secretary-General of the United Nations, UN Doc. A/59/2005, 21 March 2005.

donors, developing countries, civil society and major development institutions alike.

The MDGs can be met by 2015 - but only if all involved break with business as usual and dramatically accelerate and scale up action now.\

In 2005, a "global partnership for development" – one of the MDGs reaffirmed in 2002 at the International Conference on Financing for Development at Monterrey, Mexico and the World Summit on Sustainable Development in Johannesburg, South Africa – needs to be fully implemented. That partnership is grounded in mutual responsibility and accountability – developing countries must strengthen governance, combat corruption, promote private sector-led growth and maximize domestic resources to fund national development strategies, while developed countries must support these efforts through increased development assistance, a new development-oriented trade round and wider and deeper debt relief.

The following are priority areas for action in 2005:

- *National strategies:* Each developing country with extreme poverty should by 2006 adopt and begin to implement a national development strategy bold enough to meet the MDG targets for 2015. Each strategy needs to take into account seven broad "clusters" of public investments and policies: gender equality, the environment, rural development, urban development, health systems, education, and science, technology and innovation.
- *Financing for development:* Global development assistance must be more than doubled over the next few years. This does not require new pledges from donor countries, but meeting pledges already made. Each developed country that has not already done so should establish a timetable to achieve the 0.7% target of gross national income for official development assistance no later than 2015, starting with significant increases no later than 2006, and reaching 0.5% by 2009. The increase should be front-loaded through an International Finance Facility, and other innovative sources of financing should be considered for the longer term. The Global Fund to Fight HIV/AIDS, Tuberculosis and Malaria must be fully funded and the resources provided for an expanded comprehensive strategy of prevention and treatment to fight HIV/AIDS. These steps should be supplemented by immediate action to support a series of "Quick Wins" – relatively inexpensive, high-impact initiatives with the potential to generate major short-term gains and save millions of lives, such as free distribution of anti-malarial bednets.
- *Trade:* The Doha round of trade negotiations should fulfil its development promise and be completed no later than 2006. As a first step, Member States should provide duty-free and quota-free market access for all exports from the Least Developed Countries.
- *Debt relief:* Debt sustainability should be redefined as the level of debt that allows a country to achieve the MDGs and to reach 2015 without an increase in debt ratios.

New action is also needed to ensure *environmental sustainability.* Scientific advances and technological innovation must be mobilized now to develop tools for mitigating *climate change,* and a more inclusive international

framework must be developed for stabilizing greenhouse gas emissions beyond the expiry of the Kyoto Protocol in 2012, with broader participation by all major emitters and both developed and developing countries. Concrete steps are also required on *desertification and biodiversity*.
Other priorities for global action include stronger mechanisms for infectious diseasesurveillance and monitoring, a world-wide early warning system on natural disasters, support for science and technology for development, support for regional infrastructure and institutions, reform of international financial institutions, and more effective cooperation to manage migration for the benefit of all.

II. Freedom from fear

While progress on development is hampered by weak implementation, on the security side, despite a heightened sense of threat among many, the world lacks even a basic consensus - and implementation, where it occurs, is all too often contested.

The Secretary-General fully embraces a broad vision of collective security. The threats to peace and security in the 21st century include not just international war and conflict, but terrorism, weapons of mass destruction, organized crime and civil violence. They also include poverty, deadly infectious disease and environmental degradation, since these can have equally catastrophic consequences. All of these threats can cause death or lessen life chances on a large scale. All of them can undermine States as the basic unit of the international system.

Collective security today depends on accepting that the threats each region of the world perceives as most urgent are in fact equally so for all. These are not theoretical issues, but ones of deadly urgency.

The United Nations must be transformed into the effective instrument for preventing conflict that it was always meant to be, by acting on several key policy and institutional priorities:

- *Preventing catastrophic terrorism:* States should commit to a comprehensive anti-terrorism strategy based on five pillars: dissuading people from resorting to terrorism or supporting it; denying terrorists access to funds and materials; deterring States from sponsoring terrorism; developing State capacity to defeat terrorism; and defending human rights. They should conclude a comprehensive convention on terrorism, based on a clear and agreed definition. They should also complete, without delay, the convention for the suppression of acts of nuclear terrorism.

- *Nuclear, chemical and biological weapons:* Progress on both disarmament and non-proliferation are essential. On disarmament, nuclear-weapon States should further reduce their arsenals of non-strategic nuclear weapons and pursue arms control agreements that entail not just dismantlement but irreversibility, reaffirm their commitment to negative security assurances, and uphold the moratorium on nuclear test explosions. On non-proliferation, the International Atomic Energy Agency's verification authority must be strengthened through universal adoption of the Model Additional Protocol, and States should commit themselves to complete, sign and implement a fissile material cut-off treaty.

- *Reducing the prevalence and risk of war:* Currently, half the countries emerging from violent conflict revert to conflict within five years. Member States should create an inter-governmental Peacebuilding Commission, as well as a Peacebuilding Support Office within the UN Secretariat, so that the UN system can better meet the challenge of helping countries successfully complete the transition from war to peace. They should also take steps to strengthen collective capacity to employ the tools of mediation, sanctions and peacekeeping (including a "zero tolerance" policy on sexual exploitation of minors and other vulnerable people by members of peacekeeping contingents, to match the policy enacted by the Secretary-General).
- *Use of force:* The Security Council should adopt a resolution setting out the principles to be applied in decisions relating to the use of force and express its intention to be guided by them when deciding whether to authorize or mandate the use of force.

Other priorities for global action include more effective cooperation to combat organized crime, to prevent illicit trade in small arms and light weapons, and to remove the scourge of landmines which still kill and maim innocent people and hold back development in nearly half the world's countries.

III. Freedom to live in dignity

In the Millennium Declaration, Member States said they would spare no effort to promote democracy and strengthen the rule of law, as well as respect for all internationally recognized human rights and fundamental freedoms. And over the last six decades, an impressive treaty-based normative framework has been advanced.

But without implementation, these declarations ring hollow. Without action, promises are meaningless. People who face war crimes find no solace in the unimplemented words of the Geneva Conventions. Treaties prohibiting torture are cold comfort to prisoners abused by their captors, particularly if the international human rights machinery enables those responsible to hide behind friends in high places. War-weary populations despair when, even though a peace agreement has been signed, there is little progress towards government under the rule of law. Solemn commitments to strengthen democracy remain empty words to those who have never voted for their rulers, and who see no sign that things are changing.

Therefore, the normative framework that has been so impressively advanced over the last six decades must be strengthened. Even more important, concrete steps are required to reduce selective application, arbitrary enforcement and breach without consequence. The world must move from an era of legislation to implementation.

Action is called for in the following priority areas:
- *Rule of law:* The international community should embrace the "responsibility to protect", as a basis for collective action against genocide, ethnic cleansing and crimes against humanity. All treaties relating to the protection of civilians should be ratified and implemented. Steps should be taken to strengthen cooperation with the International Crim-

inal Court and other international or mixed war crimes tribunals, and to strengthen the International Court of Justice. The Secretary- General also intends to strengthen the Secretariat's capacity to assist national efforts to re-establish the rule of law in conflict and post-conflict societies.
- *Human rights:* The Office of the High Commissioner for Human Rights should be strengthened with more resources and staff, and should play a more active role in the deliberations of the Security Council and of the proposed Peacebuilding Commission. The human rights treaty bodies of the UN system should also be rendered more effective and responsive.
- *Democracy:* A Democracy Fund should be created at the UN to provide assistance to countries seeking to establish or strengthen their democracy.

IV. Strengthening the United Nations

While purposes should be firm and constant, practice and organization need to move with the times. If the UN is to be a useful instrument for its Member States, and for the world's peoples, in responding to the challenges laid out in the previous three parts, it must be fully adapted to the needs and circumstances of the 21st century.

A great deal has been achieved since 1997 in reforming the internal structures and culture of the United Nations. But many more changes are needed, both in the executive branch – the Secretariat and the wider UN system – and in the UN's intergovernmental organs:
- *General Assembly:* The General Assembly should take bold measures to streamline its agenda and speed up the deliberative process. It should concentrate on the major substantive issues of the day, and establish mechanisms to engage fully and systematically with civil society.
- *Security Council:* The Security Council should be broadly representative of the realities of power in today's world. The Secretary-General supports the principles for reform set out in the report of the High-level Panel, and urges Member States to consider the two options, Models A and B, presented in that report, or any other viable proposals in terms of size and balance that have emerged on the basis of either Model. Member States should agree to take a decision on this important issue before the Summit in September 2005.
- *Economic and Social Council:* The Economic and Social Council should be reformed so that it can effectively assess progress in the UN's development agenda, serve as a high-level development cooperation forum, and provide direction for the efforts of the various intergovernmental bodies in the economic and social area throughout the UN system.
- *Proposed Human Rights Council:* The Commission on Human Rights suffers from declining credibility and professionalism, and is in need of major reform. It should be replaced by a smaller standing Human Rights Council, as a principal organ of the United Nations or subsidiary of the General Assembly, whose members would be elected directly by the General Assembly, by a two-thirds majority of members present and voting.

- *The Secretariat:* The Secretary-General will take steps to re-align the Secretariat's structure to match the priorities outlined in the report, and will create a cabinet-style decision-making mechanism. He requests Member States to give him the authority and resources to pursue a one-time staff buy-out to refresh and re-align staff to meet current needs, to cooperate in a comprehensive review of budget and human resources rules, and to commission a comprehensive review of the Office of Internal Oversight Services to strengthen its independence and authority.

Other priorities include creating better system coherence by strengthening the role of *Resident Coordinators*, giving the *humanitarian response system* more effective stand-by arrangements, and ensuring better protection of *internally displaced people. Regional organizations,* particularly the African Union, should be given greater support. The Charter itself should also be updated to abolish the *"enemy clauses"*, the *Trusteeship Council* and the *Military Staff Committee,* all of which are outdated.

Conclusion: opportunity and challenge

It is for the world community to decide whether this moment of uncertainty presages wider conflict, deepening inequality and the erosion of the rule of law, or is used to renew institutions for peace, prosperity and human rights. Now is the time to act. The annex to the report lists specific items for consideration by Heads of State and Government. Action on them is possible. It is within reach. From pragmatic beginnings could emerge a visionary change of direction for the world.

2005 World Summit Outcome*
(achievements in brief)

Explanatory note by the authors of the present book

In the book, the authors already extensively quote from the September 2005 Summit Outcome Document. For that reason they now stick to the summary of the document, as presented by the UN itself. The full document can be consulted at <http://www.un.org/summit2005/documents.html>

The world's leaders, meeting at United Nations Headquarters in New York from 14 to 16 September, agreed to take action on a range of global challenges:

DEVELOPMENT
- Strong and unambiguous commitment by all governments, in donor and developing nations alike, to achieve the Millennium Development Goals by 2015.
- Additional $50 billion a year by 2010 for fighting poverty.
- Commitment by all developing countries to adopt national plans for achieving the Millennium Development Goals by 2006.
- Agreement to provide immediate support for quick impact initiatives to support anti-malaria efforts, education, and healthcare.
- Commitment to innovative sources of financing for development, including efforts by groups of countries to implement an International Finance Facility and other initiatives to finance development projects, in particular in the health sector.
- Agreement to consider additional measures to ensure long-term debt sustainability through increased grant-based financing, cancellation of 100 per cent of the official multilateral and bilateral debt of heavily indebted poor countries (HIPCs). Where appropriate, to consider significant debt relief or restructuring for low and middle income developing countries with unsustainable debt burdens that are not part of the HIPC initiative.
- Commitment to trade liberalization and expeditious work towards implementing the development dimensions of the Doha work programme.

TERRORISM
- Clear and unqualified condemnation – by all governments, for the first time – of terrorism "in all its forms and manifestations, committed by whomever, wherever and for whatever purposes."

---

* Fact sheet issued by the United Nations' Department on Public Information, September 2005; see <http://www.un.org/summit2005/documents.html>

- Strong political push for a comprehensive convention against terrorism within a year. Support for early entry into force of the Nuclear Terrorism Convention. All states are encouraged to join and implement it as well as the 12 other antiterrorism conventions.
- Agreement to fashion a strategy to fight terrorism in a way that makes the international community stronger and terrorists weaker.

PEACEBUILDING, PEACEKEEPING, AND PEACEMAKING
- Decision to create a Peacebuilding Commission to help countries transition from war to peace, backed by a support office and a standing fund.
- New standing police capacity for UN peacekeeping operations.
- Agreement to strengthen the Secretary-General's capacity for mediation and good offices.

RESPONSIBILITY TO PROTECT
- Clear and unambiguous acceptance by all governments of the collective international responsibility to protect populations from genocide, war crimes, ethnic cleansing and crimes against humanity. Willingness to take timely and decisive collective action for this purpose, through the Security Council, when peaceful means prove inadequate and national authorities are manifestly failing to do it.

HUMAN RIGHTS, DEMOCRACY AND RULE OF LAW
- Decisive steps to strengthen the UN human rights machinery, backing the action plan and doubling the budget of the High Commissioner.
- Agreement to establish a UN Human Rights Council during the coming year.
- Reaffirmation of democracy as a universal value, and welcome for new Democracy Fund which has already received pledges of $32 million from 13 countries.
- Commitment to eliminate pervasive gender discrimination, such as inequalities in education and ownership of property, violence against women and girls and to end impunity for such violence.
- Ratification action taken during the Summit triggered the entry into force of the Convention Against Corruption.

MANAGEMENT REFORM
- Broad strengthening of the UN's oversight capacity, including the Office of Internal Oversight Services, expanding oversight services to additional agencies, calling for developing an independent oversight advisory committee, and further developing a new ethics office.
- Update the UN by reviewing all mandates older than five years, so that obsolete ones can be dropped to make room for new priorities.
- Commitment to overhauling rules and policies on budget, finance and human resources so the Organization can better respond to current needs; and a one-time staff buy-out to ensure that the UN has the appropriate staff for today's challenges.

ENVIRONMENT
- Recognition of the serious challenge posed by climate change and a commitment to take action through the UN Framework Convention on Climate Change. Assistance will be provided to those most vulnerable, like small island developing states.
- Agreement to create a worldwide early warning system for all natural hazards.

INTERNATIONAL HEALTH
- A scaling up of responses to HIV/AIDS, TB, and malaria, through prevention, care, treatment and support, and the mobilization of additional resources from national, bilateral, multilateral and private sources.
- Commitment to fight infectious diseases, including a commitment to ensure full implementation of the new International Health Regulations, and support for the Global Outbreak Alert and Response Network of the World Health Organization.

HUMANITARIAN ASSISTANCE
- Improved Central Emergency Revolving Fund to ensure that relief arrives reliably and immediately when disasters happen.
- Recognition of the Guiding Principles on Internal Displacement as an important international framework for the protection of internally displaced persons.

UPDATING THE UN CHARTER
- A decision to revise and update the Charter by:
  - Winding up the Trusteeship Council, marking completion of UN's historic decolonisation role;
  - Deleting anachronistic references to "enemy states" in the Charter.

Index